THE MAN WHO KNEW TOO MUCH
AND OTHER STORIES

By the same Author

The Innocence of Father Brown

The Wisdom of Father Brown

Eugenics and Other Evils

The Man
Who Knew Too Much
and other Stories

By
G. K. CHESTERTON

CASSELL AND COMPANY, LTD
London, New York, Toronto and Melbourne

First published in 1922

912498

Printed in Great Britain

*To a Mob
of
Nephews and Nieces
at
Fernley, Maidenhead*

CONTENTS

THE MAN WHO KNEW TOO MUCH—

		PAGE
I.	THE FACE IN THE TARGET	1
II.	THE VANISHING PRINCE	22
III.	THE SOUL OF THE SCHOOLBOY	43
IV.	THE BOTTOMLESS WELL	57
V.	THE HOLE IN THE WALL	74
VI.	THE FAD OF THE FISHERMAN	98
VII.	THE FOOL OF THE FAMILY	118
VIII.	THE VENGEANCE OF THE STATUE	144
	THE TREES OF PRIDE	165
	THE GARDEN OF SMOKE	231
	THE FIVE OF SWORDS	255
	THE TOWER OF TREASON	283

THE MAN WHO KNEW TOO MUCH

I.—THE FACE IN THE TARGET

HAROLD MARCH, the rising reviewer and social critic, was walking vigorously across a great table-land of moors and commons, the horizon of which was fringed with the far-off woods of the famous estate of Torwood Park. He was a good-looking young man in tweeds, with very pale curly hair, and pale clear eyes. Walking in wind and sun in the very landscape of liberty, he was still young enough to remember his politics and not merely try to forget them. For his errand at Torwood Park was a political one; it was the place of appointment named by no less a person than the Chancellor of the Exchequer, Sir Howard Horne, then introducing his so-called Socialist Budget, and prepared to expound it in an interview with so promising a penman. Harold March was the sort of man who knows everything about politics; and nothing about politicians. He also knew a good deal about art, letters, philosophy and general culture; about almost everything, indeed, except the world he was living in.

Abruptly, in the middle of those sunny and windy flats, he came upon a sort of cleft, almost narrow enough to be called a crack, in the land. It was just large enough to be the water-course for a small stream which vanished at intervals under green tunnels of undergrowth, as if in a dwarfish forest. Indeed, he had an odd feeling as if he were a giant looking over the valley of the pygmies. When he dropped into the hollow, however, the impression was lost; the rocky banks, though hardly above

The Man Who Knew Too Much

the height of a cottage, hung over and had the profile of a precipice. As he began to wander down the course of the stream, in idle but romantic curiosity, and saw the water shining in short strips between the great grey boulders and bushes as soft as great green mosses, he fell into quite an opposite vein of fantasy. It was rather as if the earth had opened and swallowed him into a sort of underworld of dreams. And when he became conscious of a human figure, dark against the silver stream, sitting on a large boulder and looking rather like a large bird, it was, perhaps, with some of the premonitions proper to a man who meets the strangest friendship of his life.

The man was apparently fishing; or, at least, was fixed in a fisherman's attitude with more than a fisherman's immobility. March was able to examine the man almost as if he had been a statue, for some minutes before the statue spoke. He was a tall, fair man, cadaverous and a little lackadaisical, with heavy eyelids and a high-bridge nose. When his face was shaded with his wide white hat, his light moustache and lithe figure gave him a look of youth. But the panama lay on the moss beside him, and the spectator could see that his brow was prematurely bald; and this, combined with a certain hollowness about the eyes, had an air of headwork and even headache. But the most curious thing about him, realized after a short scrutiny, was that, though he looked like a fisherman, he was not fishing.

He was holding, instead of a rod, something that might have been the landing-net which some fishermen use, but which was much more like the ordinary toy net which children use, and which they sometimes use indifferently for shrimps or butterflies. He was dipping this into the water at intervals, gravely regarding its harvest of weed or mud, and emptying it out again.

"No, I haven't caught anything," he remarked calmly, as if answering an unspoken query. "When I do I have to throw it back again; especially the big fish. But some of the little beasts interest me when I get 'em."

"A scientific interest, I suppose?" observed March.

"Of a rather amateurish sort, I fear," answered the

The Face in the Target

strange fisherman. "But I have a sort of hobby about what they call phenomena of phosphorescence. But it would be rather awkward to go about in society crying stinking fish."

"I suppose it would," said March, with a smile.

"Rather odd to enter a drawing-room carrying a large luminous cod," continued the stranger in his listless way. "How quaint it would be if one could carry it about like a lantern, or have little sprats for candles. Some of the sea-beasts would really be very pretty—like lamp-shades; the blue sea-snail that glitters all over like starlight; and some of the red starfish really shine like red stars. But, naturally, I'm not looking for them here."

March thought of asking him what he was looking for; but feeling unequal to a technical discussion at least as deep as the deep-sea fishes, he returned to more ordinary topics.

"Delightful sort of hole this is," he said; "this little dell and river here. It's like those places Stevenson talks about, where something ought to happen."

"I know," answered the other; "I think it's because the place itself, so to speak, seems to happen and not merely to exist. Perhaps that's what old Picasso and some of the cubists are trying to express by angles and jagged lines. Look at that wall like low cliffs that juts forward just at right angles to the slope of turf sweeping up to it. That's like a silent collision. It's like a breaker and the backwash of a wave."

March looked at the low-browed crag overhanging the green slope, and nodded. He was interested in a man who turned so easily from the technicalities of science to those of art, and asked him if he admired the new angular artists.

"As I feel it, the cubists are not cubist enough," replied the stranger. "I mean, they're not thick enough. By making things mathematical, they make them thin. Take the living lines out of that landscape, simplify it to a mere right angle, and you flatten it out to a mere diagram on paper. Diagrams have their own beauty, but it is of just the other sort. They stand for the unalterable things; the calm, eternal, mathematical

The Man Who Knew Too Much

sort of truths; what somebody calls the white radiance of——."

He stopped, and before the next word came something had happened almost too quickly and completely to be realized. From behind the overhanging rock came a noise and rush like that of a railway train, and a great motor-car appeared. It topped the crest of cliff, black against the sun, like a battle chariot rushing to destruction in some wild epic. March automatically put out his hand in one futile gesture, as if to catch a falling tea-cup in a drawing-room.

For the fraction of a flash it seemed to leave the ledge of rock like a flying-ship; then the very sky seemed to turn over like a wheel, and it lay a ruin amid the tall grasses below, a line of grey smoke going up slowly from it into the silent air. A little lower the figure of a man with grey hair lay tumbled down the steep, green slope, his limbs lying all at random and his face turned away.

The eccentric fisherman dropped his net and walked swiftly towards the spot, his new acquaintance following him. As they drew near there seemed a sort of monstrous irony in the fact that the dead machine was still throbbing and thundering as busily as a factory, while the man lay so still.

He was unquestionably dead. The blood flowed in the grass from a fatal fracture at the back of the skull; but the face, which was turned to the sun, was uninjured and strangely arresting in itself. It was one of those cases of a strange face so unmistakable as to feel familiar. We feel somehow that we ought to recognize it, even though we do not. It was of the broad, square sort, with great jaws, almost like that of a highly intellectual ape; the wide mouth shut so tight as to be traced by a mere line; the nose short, with the sort of nostrils that seem to gape with an appetite for the air. The oddest thing about the face was that one of the eyebrows was cocked up at a much sharper angle than the other. March thought he had never seen a face so naturally alive as that dead one. And its ugly energy seemed all the stranger for its halo of hoary hair. Some papers lay half-fallen out of the pocket, and from among them March

The Face in the Target

extracted a card-case. He read the name on the card aloud:

"'Sir Humphrey Turnbull.' I'm sure I've heard the name somewhere."

His companion only gave a sort of little sigh, and was silent for a moment, as if ruminating. Then he merely said: "The poor fellow is quite gone," and added some scientific terms in which his auditor once more found himself out of his depth.

"As things are," continued the same curiously well-informed person, "it will be more legal for us to leave the body as it is until the police are informed. In fact, I think it will be well if nobody except the police is informed. Don't be surprised if I seem to be keeping it dark from some of our neighbours round here." Then, as if prompted to regularize his rather abrupt confidence, he said: "I've come down to see my cousin at Torwood; my name is Horne Fisher. Might be a pun on my pottering about here, mightn't it?"

"Is Sir Howard Horne your cousin?" asked March. "I'm going to Torwood Park to see him myself; only about his public work, of course, and the wonderful stand he is making for his principles. I think this Budget is the greatest thing in English history. If it fails it will be the most heroic failure in English history. Are you an admirer of your great kinsman, Mr. Fisher?"

"Rather," said Mr. Fisher. "He's the best shot I know."

Then, as if sincerely repentant of his nonchalance, he added, with a sort of enthusiasm:

"No, but really he's a *beautiful* shot."

As if fired by his own words, he took a sort of leap at the ledges of the rock above him, and scaled them with a sudden agility in startling contrast to his general lassitude. He had stood for some seconds on the headland above, with his aquiline profile under the panama hat relieved against the sky and peering over the countryside, before his companion had collected himself sufficiently to scramble up after him.

The level above was a stretch of common turf, on which the tracks of the fated car were ploughed plainly

The Man Who Knew Too Much

enough, but the brink of it was broken as with rocky teeth; broken boulders of all shapes and sizes lay near the edge; it was almost incredible that anyone could have deliberately driven into such a death-trap, especially in broad daylight.

"I can't make head or tail of it," said March. "Was he blind? Or blind drunk?"

"Neither, by the look of him," replied the other.

"Then it was suicide."

"It doesn't seem a cosy way of doing it," remarked the man called Fisher. "Besides, I don't fancy poor old Puggy would commit suicide somehow."

"Poor old who?" inquired the wondering journalist. "Did you know this unfortunate man?"

"Nobody knew him exactly," replied Fisher with some vagueness. "But one *knew* him, of course. He'd been a terror in his time, in Parliament and the courts, and so on—especially in that row about the aliens who were deported as undesirables when he wanted one of 'em hanged for murder. He was so sick about it that he retired from the bench. Since then he mostly motored about by himself; but he was coming to Torwood, too, for the week-end, and I don't see why he should deliberately break his neck almost at the very door. I believe Hoggs—I mean, my cousin Howard—was coming down especially to meet him."

"Torwood Park doesn't belong to your cousin?" inquired March.

"No; it used to belong to the Winthrops, you know," replied the other. "Now a new man's got it—a man from Montreal named Jenkins. Hoggs comes for the shooting; I told you he was a lovely shot."

This repeated eulogy on the great social statesman affected Harold March as if somebody had defined Napoleon as a distinguished player of nap. But he had another half-formed impression struggling in this flood of unfamiliar things, and he brought it to the surface before it could vanish.

"Jenkins," he repeated. "Surely you don't mean Jefferson Jenkins, the social reformer? I mean, the man who's fighting for the new cottage-estate scheme. It

The Face in the Target

would be as interesting to meet him as any Cabinet Minister in the world, if you'll excuse my saying so."

"Yes; Hoggs told him it would have to be cottages," said Fisher. "He said the breed of cattle had been improved too often, and people were beginning to laugh. And, of course, you must hang a peerage on to something, though the poor chap hasn't got it yet. Hallo, here's somebody else."

They had started walking in the tracks of the car, leaving it behind them in the hollow, still humming horribly like a huge insect that had killed a man. The tracks took them to the corner of a road, one arm of which went on in the same line towards the distant gates of the park. It was clear that the car had been driven down the long straight road, and then, instead of turning with the road to the left, had gone straight on over the turf to its doom. But it was not this discovery that had riveted Fisher's eye, but something even more solid. At the angle of the white road a dark and solitary figure was standing almost as still as a finger-post. It was that of a big man in rough shooting-clothes, bareheaded and with tousled curly hair that gave him a rather wild look. On a nearer approach this first more fantastic impression faded; in a full light the figure took on more conventional colours, as of an ordinary gentleman who happened to have come out without a hat and without very studiously brushing his hair. But the massive stature remained, and something deep and even cavernous about the setting of the eyes redeemed his animal good looks from the commonplace. But March had no time to study the man more closely, for, much to his astonishment, his guide merely observed: "Hallo, Jack!" and walked past him as if he had indeed been a signpost, and without attempting to inform him of the catastrophe beyond the rocks. It was relatively a small thing, but it was only the first in a string of singular antics on which his new and eccentric friend was leading him.

The man they had passed looked after them in rather a suspicious fashion, but Fisher continued serenely on his way along the straight road that ran past the gates of the great estate.

The Man Who Knew Too Much

"That's John Burke, the traveller," he condescended to explain. "I expect you've heard of him; shoots big game, and all that. Sorry I couldn't stop to introduce you, but I dare say you'll meet him later on."

"I know his book, of course," said March, with renewed interest. "That is certainly a fine piece of description, about their being only conscious of the closeness of the elephant when the colossal head blocked out the moon."

"Yes, young Halkett writes jolly well, I think. What? Didn't you know Halkett wrote Burke's book for him? Burke can't use anything except a gun, and you can't write with that. Oh, he's genuine enough in his way, you know; as brave as a lion—or a good deal braver."

"You seem to know all about him," observed March, with a rather bewildered laugh, "and about a good many other people."

Fisher's bald brow became abruptly corrugated, and a curious expression came into his eyes.

"I know too much," he said. "That's what's the matter with me. That's what's the matter with all of us, and the whole show; we know too much. Too much about each other, too much about ourselves. That's why I'm really interested just now about one thing that I don't know."

"And that is?" inquired the other.

"Why that poor fellow is dead."

They had walked along the straight road for nearly a mile conversing at intervals in this fashion, and March had a singular sense of the whole world being turned inside out. Mr. Horne Fisher did not especially abuse his friends and relatives in fashionable society; of some of them he spoke with affection. But they seemed to be an entirely new set of men and women who happened to have the same names as the men and women mentioned most often in the newspapers. Yet no fury of revolt could have seemed to him more utterly revolutionary than this cold familiarity. It was like daylight on the other side of stage scenery.

They reached the great lodge-gates of the park, and, to March's surprise, passed them and continued along

The Face in the Target

the interminable, white, straight road. But he was himself too early for his appointment with Sir Howard, and was not disinclined to see the end of his new friend's experiment, whatever it might be. They had long left the moorland behind them, and half the white road was grey in the great shadow of the Torwood pine forests, themselves like grey bars shuttered against the sunshine and within, amid that clear noon, manufacturing their own midnight. Soon, however, rifts began to appear in them like gleams of coloured windows; the trees thinned and fell away as the road went forward, showing the wild irregular copses in which, as Fisher said, the house party had been blazing away all day. And about two hundred yards farther on they came to the first turn of the road.

At the corner stood a sort of decayed inn with the dingy sign of The Grapes. The signboard was dark and indecipherable by now, and hung black against the sky and the grey moorland beyond, about as inviting as a gallows. March remarked that it looked like a tavern for vinegar instead of wine.

"A good phrase," said Fisher, "and so it would be if you were silly enough to drink wine in it. But the beer is very good, and so is the brandy."

March followed him into the bar-parlour with some wonder, and his dim sense of repugnance was not dismissed by the first sight of the inn-keeper, who was widely different from the genial inn-keeper of romance; a bony man, very silent behind a black moustache, but with black, restless eyes. Taciturn as he was, the investigator succeeded at last in extracting a scrap of information from him, by dint of ordering beer and talking to him persistently and minutely on the subject of motor-cars. He evidently regarded the inn-keeper as in some singular way an authority on motor-cars; as being deep in the secrets of the mechanism, management, and mismanagement of motor-cars; holding the man all the time with a glittering eye like the Ancient Mariner. Out of all this rather mysterious conversation there did emerge at last a sort of admission that one particular motor-car, of a given description, had stopped

The Man Who Knew Too Much

before the inn about an hour before, and that an elderly man had alighted, requiring some mechanical assistance. Asked if the visitor required any other assistance, the inn-keeper said shortly that the old gentleman had filled his flask and taken a packet of sandwiches. And with these words the somewhat inhospitable host had walked hastily out of the bar, and they heard him banging doors in the dark interior.

Fisher's somewhat weary eye wandered round the dusty and dreary inn-parlour and rested dreamily on a glass case containing a stuffed bird, with a gun hung on hooks above it, which seemed to be its only ornament.

"Puggy was a humorist," he observed; "at least in his own rather grim style. But it seems rather too grim a joke for a man to buy a packet of sandwiches when he is just going to commit suicide."

"If you come to that," answered March, "it isn't very usual for a man to buy a packet of sandwiches when he's just outside the door of a grand house he's going to stop at."

"No. . . . No," repeated Fisher, almost mechanically, and then suddenly cocked his eye at his interlocutor with a much livelier expression.

"By Jove, that's an idea. You're perfectly right. And that suggests a very queer idea, doesn't it?"

There was a silence, and then March started with irrational nervousness as the door of the inn was flung open and another man walked rapidly to the counter. He had struck it with a coin and called out for brandy before he saw the other two guests, who were sitting at a bare wooden table under the window. When he turned about with a rather wild stare, March had yet another unexpected emotion, for his guide hailed the man as Hoggs and introduced him as Sir Howard Horne.

He looked rather older than his boyish portraits in the illustrated papers, as is the way of politicians; his flat, fair hair was touched with grey, but his face was almost comically round, with a Roman nose which, when combined with his quick, bright eyes, raised a vague reminiscence of a parrot. He had a cap rather at the back of his head, and a gun under his arm. Harold

The Face in the Target

March had imagined many things about his meeting with the great political reformer; but he had never pictured him with a gun under his arm, drinking brandy in a public-house.

"So you're stopping at Jink's, too," said Fisher.

"Everybody seems to be at Jink's."

"Yes," replied the Chancellor of the Exchequer. "Jolly good shooting. At least, all of it that isn't Jink's shooting. I never knew a chap with such good shooting that was such a bad shot. Mind you, he's a jolly good fellow, and all that; I don't say a word against him. But he never learnt to hold a gun when he was packing pork or whatever he did. They say he shot the cockade off his own servant's hat; just like him to have cockades, of course. He shot the weathercock off his own ridiculous gilded summer-house. It's the only cock he'll ever kill, I should think. Are you coming up there now?"

Fisher said rather vaguely that he was following soon, when he had fixed something up; and the Chancellor of the Exchequer left the inn. March fancied he had been a little upset or impatient when he called for the brandy; but he had talked himself back into a satisfactory state, if the talk had not been quite what his literary visitor had expected. Fisher, a few minutes afterwards, slowly led the way out of the tavern and stood in the middle of the road, looking down it in the direction from which they had travelled. Then he walked back about two hundred yards in that direction, and stood still again.

"I should think this is about the place," he said.

"What place?" asked his companion.

"The place where the poor fellow was killed," said Fisher sadly.

"What do you mean?" demanded March. "He was smashed up on the rocks a mile and a half from here."

"No, he wasn't," replied Fisher. "He didn't fall on the rocks at all. Didn't you notice that he only fell on the slope of soft grass underneath? But I saw that he had a bullet in him already."

Then after a pause he added:

"He was alive at the inn, but he was dead long before he came to the rocks. So he was shot as he drove his

The Man Who Knew Too Much

car down this strip of straight road; and I should think somewhere about here. After that, of course, the car went straight on with nobody to stop or turn it. It's really a very cunning dodge in its way, for the body would be found far away, and most people would say, as you do, that it was an accident to a motorist. The murderer must have been a clever brute."

"But wouldn't the shot be heard at the inn or somewhere?" asked March.

"It would be heard. But it would not be noticed. That," continued the investigator, "is where he was clever again. Shooting was going on all over the place all day; very likely he timed his shot so as to drown it in a number of others. Certainly he was a first-class criminal. And he was something else as well."

"What do you mean?" asked his companion, with a creepy premonition of something coming, he knew not why.

"He was a first-class shot," said Fisher.

He had turned his back abruptly and was walking down a narrow, grassy lane, little more than a cart-track, which lay opposite the inn and marked the end of the great estate and the beginning of the open moors. March plodded after him with the same idle perseverance, and found him staring through a gap in giant weeds and thorns at the flat face of a painted paling. From behind the paling rose the great, grey columns of a row of poplars, which filled the heavens above them with dark green shadow and shook faintly in a wind which had sunk slowly into a breeze. The afternoon was already deepening into evening, and the titanic shadows of the poplars lengthened over a third of the landscape.

"Are you a first-class criminal?" asked Fisher, in a friendly tone. "I'm afraid I'm not. But I think I can manage to be a sort of fourth-rate burglar."

And before his companion could reply, he had managed to swing himself up and over the fence, March following without much bodily effort, but with considerable mental disturbance. The poplars grew so close against the fence that they had some difficulty in slipping past them, and beyond the poplars they could see only a high edge of

The Face in the Target

laurel, green and lustrous in the level sun. Something in this limitation by a series of living walls made him feel as if he were really entering a shuttered house instead of an open field. It was as if he came in by a disused door or window, and found the way blocked by furniture. When they had circumvented the laurel hedge they came out on a sort of terrace of turf, which fell by one green step to an oblong lawn like a bowling green. Beyond this was the only building in sight, a low conservatory, which seemed far away from anywhere—like a glass cottage standing on its own fields in fairyland. Fisher knew that lonely look of the outlying parts of a great house well enough. He realized that it is more of a satire on aristocracy than if it were choked with weeds and littered with ruins. For it is not neglected and yet it is deserted; at any rate, it is disused. It is regularly swept and garnished for a master who never comes.

Looking over the lawn, however, he saw one object which he had not apparently expected. It was a sort of tripod supporting a large disc like the round top of a table tipped sideways; and it was not until they had dropped on to the lawn and walked across to look at it that March realized that it was a target. It was worn and weather-stained; the gay colours of its concentric rings were faded; possibly it had been set up in those far-off Victorian days when there was a fashion of archery. March had one of his vague visions of ladies in cloudy crinolines and gentlemen in outlandish hats and whiskers revisiting that lost garden like ghosts.

Fisher, who was peering more closely at the target, startled him by an exclamation.

"Hallo," he said, "somebody has been peppering this thing with shot, after all; and quite lately too. Why, I believe old Jink's been trying to improve his bad shooting here."

"Yes, and it looks as if it still wanted improving," answered March, laughing. "Not one of those shots is anywhere near the bull's-eye; they seem just scattered about in the wildest way."

"In the wildest way," repeated Fisher, still peering intently at the target.

The Man Who Knew Too Much

He seemed merely to assent, but March fancied his eye was shining under its sleepy lid, and that he straightened his stooping figure with a strange effort.

"Excuse me a moment," he said, feeling in his pockets. "I think I've got some of my chemicals; and after that we'll go up to the house."

And he stooped again over the target, putting something with his finger over each of the shot-holes; so far as March could see merely a dull, grey smear. Then they went through the gathering twilight up the long green avenues to the great house.

Here again, however, the eccentric investigator did not enter it by the front door. He walked round the house until he found a window open, and, leaping into it, introduced his friend to what appeared to be the gun-room. Rows of the regular instruments for bringing down birds stood against the walls; but across a table in the window lay one or two weapons of a heavier and more formidable pattern.

"Hallo, those are Burke's big-game rifles," said Fisher. "I never knew he kept them here."

He lifted one of them, examined it briefly and put it down again, frowning heavily. Almost as he did so, a strange young man came hurriedly into the room. He was dark and sturdy, with a bumpy forehead and a bulldog jaw, and he spoke with a curt apology.

"I left Major Burke's guns here," he said, "and he wants them packed up. He's going away to-night."

And he carried off the two rifles without casting a glance at the stranger; through the open window they could see his short figure walking away across the glimmering garden. Fisher got out of the window again and stood looking after him.

"That's Halkett, whom I told you about," he said. "I knew he was a sort of secretary and had to do with Burke's papers; but I never knew he had anything to do with his guns. But he's just the sort of silent, sensible little devil who might be very good at anything; the sort of man you know for years before you find he's a chess champion."

He had begun to walk in the direction of the disappear-

The Face in the Target

ing secretary, and they soon came within sight of the rest of the house-party talking and laughing on the lawn. They could see the tall figure and loose mane of the lion-hunter dominating the little group.

"By the way," observed Fisher, "when we were talking about Burke and Halkett, I said that a man couldn't very well write with a gun. Well, I'm not so sure now. Did you ever hear of an artist so clever that he could draw with a gun? There's a wonderful chap loose about here."

Sir Howard hailed Fisher and his friend the journalist with almost boisterous amiability; the latter was presented to Major Burke and Mr. Halkett, and also (by way of parenthesis) to his host, Mr. Jenkins, a commonplace little man in loud tweeds, whom everybody else seemed to treat with a sort of affection, as if he were a baby.

The irrepressible Chancellor of the Exchequer was still talking about the birds he had brought down, and the birds that Jenkins their host had failed to bring down. It seemed to be a sort of sociable monomania.

"You and your big game," he ejaculated aggressively to Burke. "Why, anybody could shoot big game. You want to be a shot to shoot small game."

"Quite so," interposed Horne Fisher. "Now if only a hippopotamus could fly up in the air out of that bush, or you preserved flying elephants on the estate, why then——"

"Why even Jink might hit that sort of bird," cried Sir Howard, hilariously slapping his host on the back. "Even he might hit a haystack or a hippopotamus."

"Look here, you fellows," said Fisher. "I want you to come along with me for a minute and shoot at something else. Not a hippopotamus. Another kind of queer animal I've found on the estate. It's an animal with three legs and one eye, and it's all the colours of the rainbow."

"What the deuce are you talking about?" asked Burke.

"You come along and see," replied Fisher cheerfully.

Such people seldom reject anything nonsensical, for hey are always seeking for something new. They gravely e-armed themselves from the gun-room and trooped along t the tail of their guide; Sir Howard only pausing, in a

The Man Who Knew Too Much

sort of ecstasy, to point out the celebrated gilt summerhouse on which the gilt weathercock still stood crooked. It was dusk, turning to dark, by the time they reached the remote green by the poplars, and accepted the new and aimless game of shooting at the old mark.

The last light seemed to fade from the lawn, and the poplars against the sunset were like great, black plumes upon a purple hearse, when the futile procession finally curved round and came out in front of the target.

Sir Howard again slapped his host on the shoulder, shoving him playfully forward to take the first shot. The shoulder and arm he touched seemed unnaturally stiff and angular. Mr. Jenkins was holding his gun in an attitude more awkward than any that his satiric friends had seen or expected.

At the same instant a horrible scream seemed to come from nowhere. It was so unnatural and so unsuited to the scene, that it might have been made by some inhuman thing flying on wings above them, or eavesdropping in the dark woods beyond. But Fisher knew that it had started and stopped on the pale lips of Jefferson Jenkins of Montreal; and no one at that moment, catching sight of Jefferson Jenkins's face, would have complained that it was commonplace.

The next moment a torrent of guttural but goodhumoured oaths came from Major Burke as he and the two other men saw what was in front of them. The target stood up in the dim grass like a dark goblin grinning at them; and it was literally grinning. It had two eyes like stars, and in similar lurid points of light were picked out the two upturned and open nostrils and the two ends of the wide and tight mouth. A few white dots above each eye indicated the hoary eyebrows, and one of them ran upwards almost erect. It was a brilliant caricature done in bright, dotted lines; and March knew of whom. It shone in the shadowy grass, smeared with sea-fire, as if one of the submarine monsters had crawled into the twilight garden; but it had the head of a dead man.

"It's only luminous paint," said Burke. "Old Fisher's been having a joke with that phosphorescent stuff of his."

The Face in the Target

"Seems to be meant for old Puggy," observed Sir Howard. "Hits him off very well."

With that they all laughed, except Jenkins. When they had all done, he made a noise like the first effort of an animal to laugh. And Horne Fisher suddenly strode across to him and said: "Mr. Jenkins, I must speak to you at once in private."

It was by the little water-course in the moors, on the slope under the hanging rock, that March met his new friend Fisher, by appointment, shortly after the ugly and almost grotesque scene that had broken up the group in the garden.

"It was a monkey trick of mine," observed Fisher gloomily, "putting phosphorus on the target; but the only chance to make him jump was to give him the horrors suddenly. And when he saw the face he'd shot at shining on the target he practised on, all lit up with an infernal light, he did jump. Quite enough for my own intellectual satisfaction."

"I'm afraid I don't quite understand even now," said March, "exactly what he did, or why he did it."

"You ought to," replied Fisher, with his rather dreary smile, "for you gave me the first suggestion yourself. Oh, yes, you did, and it was a very shrewd one. You said a man wouldn't take sandwiches with him to dine at a great house. It was quite true; and the inference was that though he was going there, he didn't mean to dine there. Or, at any rate, that he might not be dining there. It occurred to me at once that he probably expected the visit to be unpleasant, or the reception doubtful, or something that would prevent his accepting hospitality. Then it struck me that Turnbull was a terror to certain shady characters in the past, and that he had come down to identify and denounce one of them. The chances at the start pointed to the host, that is Jenkins. I'm morally certain now that Jenkins was the undesirable alien Turnbull wanted to convict in another shooting affair; but you see the shooting gentleman had another shot in his locker."

"But you said he would have to be a very good shot."

The Man Who Knew Too Much

"Jenkins is a very good shot," said Fisher. "A very good shot who can pretend to be a very bad shot. Shall I tell you the second hint I hit on, after yours, to make me think it was Jenkins? It was my cousin's account of his bad shooting. He'd shot a cockade off a hat and a weathercock off a building. Now, in fact, a man must shoot very well indeed to shoot so badly as that. He must shoot very neatly to hit the cockade and not the head, or even the hat. If the shots had *really* gone at random, the chances are a thousand to one that they would not have hit such prominent and picturesque objects. They were chosen because they were prominent and picturesque objects. They make a story to go the round of society. He keeps the crooked weathercock on the summer house to perpetuate the story as a legend. And then he lay in wait with his evil eye and wicked gun, safely ambushed behind the legend of his own incompetence.

"But there is more than that. There is the summer-house itself. I mean there is the whole thing. There's all that Jenkins gets chaffed about; the gilding and the gaudy colours and all the vulgarity that's supposed to stamp him as an upstart. Now, as a matter of fact, upstarts generally don't do this. God knows there's enough of 'em in society, and one knows 'em well enough. And this is the very last thing they do. They're generally only too keen to know the right thing and do it; and they instantly put themselves body and soul into the hands of art decorators and art experts, who do the whole thing for them. There's hardly another millionaire alive who has the moral courage to have a gilt monogram on a chair, like that one in the gunroom. For that matter, there's the name as well as the monogram. Names like Tompkins and Jenkins and Jinks are funny without being vulgar; I mean they are vulgar without being common. If you prefer it, they are commonplace without being common. They are just the names to be chosen to *look* ordinary; but they're really rather extraordinary. Do you know many people called Tompkins? It's a good deal rarer than Talbot. It's pretty much the same with the comic clothes of the parvenu. Jenkins dresses like a character in *Punch*. But that's because he is a character in *Punch*.

The Face in the Target

I mean he's a fictitious character. He's a fabulous animal. He doesn't exist.

"Have you ever considered what it must be like to be a man who doesn't exist? I mean to be a man with a fictitious character, that he has to keep up at the expense not merely of his personal virtues, but of personal pleasures, and, above all, personal talents. To be a new kind of hypocrite, hiding a talent in a new kind of napkin. This man had chosen his hypocrisy very ingeniously; it was really a new one. A subtle villain has dressed up as a dashing gentleman and a worthy business man and a philanthropist and a saint; but the loud checks of a comical little cad were really rather a new disguise. But the disguise must be very irksome to a man who can really do things. This is a dexterous little cosmopolitan guttersnipe who can do scores of things; not only shoot, but draw and paint, and probably play the fiddle. Now a man like that may find the hiding of his talents useful; but he could never help wanting to use them where they were useless. If he can draw, he will draw absent-mindedly on blotting paper. I suspect this rascal has often drawn poor old Puggy's face on blotting paper. Probably he began doing it in blots as he afterwards did it in dots, or rather shots. It was the same sort of thing; he found a disused target in a deserted yard, and couldn't resist indulging in a little secret shooting, like secret drinking. You thought the shots all scattered and irregular, and so they were; but not accidental. No two distances were alike; but the different points were exactly where he wanted to put them. There's nothing needs such mathematical precision as a wild caricature. I've dabbled a little in drawing myself, and I assure you that to put one dot where you want it is a marvel with a pen close to a piece of paper. It was a miracle to do it across a garden with a gun. But a man who can work those miracles will always itch to work them—if he only does so in the dark."

After a pause March observed thoughtfully: "But he couldn't have brought him down like a bird with one of those little guns."

"No, that was why I went into the gun-room," replied

The Man Who Knew Too Much

Fisher. "He did it with one of Burke's rifles; and Burke thought he knew the sound of it. That's why he rushed out without a hat, looking so wild. He saw nothing but a car passing quickly, which he followed for a little way, and then concluded he'd made a mistake."

There was another silence, during which Fisher sat on a great stone as motionless as on their first meeting, and watched the grey and silver river eddying past under the bushes. Then March said abruptly: "Of course, he knows the truth now."

"Nobody knows the truth but you and me," answered Fisher, with a certain softening in his voice, "and I don't think you and I will ever quarrel."

"What do you mean?" asked March, in an altered accent. "What have you done about it?"

Horne Fisher continued to gaze steadily at the eddying stream. At last he said: "The police have proved it was a motor accident."

"But you know it was not," insisted March.

"I told you that I know too much," replied Fisher, with his eye on the river. "I know that, and I know a great many other things. I know the atmosphere, and the way the whole thing works. I know this fellow has succeeded in making himself something incurably commonplace and comic. I know you can't get up a prosecution of old Toole or Little Tich. If I were to tell Hoggs or Halkett that old Jink was an assassin, they would almost die of laughter before my eyes. Oh, I don't say their laughter's quite innocent, though it's genuine in its way. They want old Jink, and they couldn't do without him. I don't say I'm quite innocent. I like Hoggs; I don't want him to be down and out; and he'd be done for if Jink can't pay up for his coronet. They were devilish near the line at the last Election, I can tell you. But the only real objection to it is that it's impossible. Nobody would believe it; it's not in the picture. The crooked weathercock would always turn it into a joke."

"Don't you think this is infamous?" asked Marsh quietly.

"I think a good many things," replied the other. "If you people ever happen to blow the whole tangle of society

The Face in the Target

to hell with dynamite, I don't know that the human race will be much the worse. But don't be too hard on me merely because I know what society is. That's why I moon away my time over things like stinking fish."

There was a pause as he settled himself down again by the stream, and then he added:

"I told you before I had to throw back the big fish."

II.—THE VANISHING PRINCE

This tale begins among a tangle of tales round a name that is at once recent and legendary. The name is that of Michael O'Neill, popularly called Prince Michael; partly because he claimed descent from ancient Fenian princes, and partly because he was credited with a plan to make himself Prince President of Ireland, as the last Napoleon did of France. He was undoubtedly a gentleman of honourable pedigree and of many accomplishments; but two of his accomplishments emerged from all the rest. He had a talent for appearing when he was not wanted, and a talent for disappearing when he was wanted; especially when he was wanted by the police. It may be added that his disappearances were more dangerous than his appearances. In the latter he seldom went beyond the sensational—pasting up seditious placards, tearing down official placards, making flamboyant speeches or unfurling forbidden flags. But in order to effect the former, he would sometimes fight for his freedom with a startling energy, from which men were sometimes lucky to escape with a broken head instead of a broken neck. His most famous feats of escape, however, were due to dexterity and not to violence. On a cloudless summer morning he had come down a country road white with dust, and pausing outside a farmhouse, had told the farmer's daughter, with elegant indifference, that the local police were in pursuit of him. The girl's name was Bridget Royce, a sombre and even sullen type of beauty, and she looked at him darkly, as if in doubt, and said: "Do you want me to hide you?" Upon which he only laughed, leapt lightly over the stone wall and strode towards the farm, merely throwing over his shoulder the remark: "Thank you, I have generally been quite capable of hiding myself." In which proceeding he acted with a tragic

The Vanishing Prince

ignorance of the nature of women, and there fell on his path in that sunshine a shadow of doom.

While he disappeared through the farmhouse, the girl remained for a few moments looking up the road, and two perspiring policemen came ploughing up to the door where she stood. Though still angry, she was still silent, and a quarter of an hour later the officers had searched the house and were already inspecting the kitchen-garden and cornfield behind it. In the ugly reaction of her mood, she might have been tempted even to point out the fugitive, but for a small difficulty—that she had no more notion than the policemen had of where he could possibly have gone. The kitchen-garden was enclosed by a very low wall, and the cornfield beyond lay aslant, like a square patch on a great green hill, on which he could still have been seen even as a dot in the distance. Everything stood solid in its familiar place; the apple-tree was too small to support or hide a climber; the only shed stood open and obviously empty; there was no sound save the droning of summer flies and the occasional flutter of a bird unfamiliar enough to be surprised by the scarecrow in the field; there was scarcely a shadow save a few blue lines that fell from the thin tree; every detail was picked out by the brilliant daylight as if in a microscope. The girl described the scene later, with all the passionate realism of her race; and whether or no the policemen had a similar eye for the picturesque, they had at least an eye for the facts of the case, and were compelled to give up the chase and retire from the scene. Bridget Royce remained, as if in a trance, staring at the sunlit garden in which a man had just vanished like a fairy. She was still in a sinister mood, and the miracle took in her mind a character of unfriendliness and fear, as if the fairy were decidedly a bad fairy. The sun upon the glittering garden depressed her more than darkness, but she continued to stare at it. Then the world itself went half-witted, and she screamed. The scarecrow moved in the sunlight. It had stood with its back to her in a battered, old, black hat and a tattered garment, and with all its tatters flying, it strode away across the hill.

She did not analyse the audacious trick by which the

The Man Who Knew Too Much

man had turned to his advantage the subtle effects of the expected and the obvious; she was still under the cloud of more individual complexities, and she noticed most of all that the vanishing scarecrow did not even turn to look at the farm. And the fates that were running so adverse to his fantastic career of freedom ruled that his next adventure, though it had the same success in another quarter, should increase the danger in this quarter. Among the many similar adventures related of him in this manner, it is also said that some days afterwards another girl, named Mary Cregan, found him concealed on the farm where she worked, and if the story is true, she must also have had the shock of an uncanny experience. For when she was busy at some lonely task in the yard, she heard a voice speaking out of the well, and found that the eccentric had managed to drop himself into the bucket which was some little way below, the well being only partly full of water. In this case, however, he had to appeal to the woman to wind up the rope. And men say it was when this news was told to the other woman, that her soul walked over the border-line of treason.

Such, at least, were the stories told of them in the country-side, and there were many more: as that he had stood insolently in a splendid green dressing-gown on the steps of a great hotel, and then led the police a chase through a long suite of grand apartments, and finally through his own bedroom on to a balcony that overhung the river. The moment the pursuers stepped on to the balcony it broke under them, and they dropped pell-mell into the eddying waters, while Michael, who had thrown off his gown and dived, was able to swim away. It was said that he had carefully cut away the props so that they would not support anything so heavy as a policeman. But here again he was immediately fortunate yet ultimately unfortunate, for it is said that one of the men was drowned, leaving a family feud which made a little rift in his popularity. These stories can now be told in some detail, not because they are the most marvellous of his many adventures, but because these alone were not covered with silence by the loyalty of the peasantry. These alone found their way into official reports, and it is these which three

The Vanishing Prince

of the chief officials of the country were reading and discussing when the more remarkable part of this story begins.

Night was far advanced, and the lights shone in the cottage that served for a temporary police-station near the coast. On one side of it were the last houses of the straggling village, and on the other nothing but a waste moorland stretching away towards the sea, the line of which was broken by no landmark except a solitary tower, of the prehistoric pattern still found in Ireland, standing up as slender as a column but pointed like a pyramid. At a wooden table, in front of the window which normally looked out on this landscape, sat two men in plain clothes but with something of a military bearing, for, indeed, they were the two chiefs of the detective service of that district. The senior of the two, both in age and rank, was a sturdy man with a short white beard and frosty eyebrows, fixed in a frown which suggested rather worry than severity.

His name was Morton, and he was a Liverpool man long pickled in the Irish quarrels, and doing his duty among them in a sour fashion not altogether unsympathetic. He had spoken a few sentences to his companion Nolan, a tall, dark man with a cadaverous equine Irish face, when he seemed to remember something and touched a bell which rang in another room. The subordinate he had summoned immediately appeared with a sheaf of papers in his hand.

"Sit down, Wilson," he said. "Those are the depositions, I suppose."

"Yes," replied the third officer. "I think I've got all there is to be got out of them, so I sent the people away."

"Did Mary Cregan give evidence?" asked Morton, with a frown that looked a little heavier than usual.

"No, but her master did," answered the man called Wilson, who had flat red hair and a plain pale face, not without sharpness. "I think he's hanging round the girl himself and is out against a rival. There's always some reason of that sort when we are told the truth about anything. And you bet the other girl told right enough."

The Man Who Knew Too Much

"Well, let's hope they'll be some sort of use," remarked Nolan, in a somewhat hopeless manner, gazing out into the darkness.

"Anything is to the good," said Morton, "that lets us know anything about him."

"Do we know anything about him?" asked the melancholy Irishman.

"We know one thing about him," said Wilson, "and it's the one thing that nobody ever knew before. We know where he is."

"Are you sure?" inquired Morton, looking at him sharply.

"Quite sure," replied his assistant. "At this very minute he is in that tower over there by the shore. If you go near enough you'll see the candle burning in the window."

As he spoke the noise of a horn sounded on the road outside, and a moment after they heard the throbbing of a motor-car brought to a standstill before the door. Morton instantly sprang to his feet.

"Thank the Lord, that's the car from Dublin," he said. "I can't do anything without special authority, not if he were sitting on the top of the tower and putting out his tongue at us. But the Chief can do what he thinks best."

He hurried out to the entrance and was soon exchanging greetings with a big, handsome man in a fur coat, who brought into the dingy little station the indescribable glow of the great cities and the luxuries of the great world.

For this was Sir Walter Carey, an official of such eminence in Dublin Castle that nothing short of the case of Prince Michael would have brought him on such a journey in the middle of the night. But the case of Prince Michael, as it happened, was complicated by legalism as well as lawlessness. On the last occasion he had escaped by a forensic quibble and not, as usual, by a private escapade, and it was a question whether, at the moment, he was amenable to the law or not. It might be necessary to stretch a point; but a man like Sir Walter could probably stretch it as far as he liked.

The Vanishing Prince

Whether he intended to do so was a question to be considered. Despite the almost aggressive touch of luxury in the fur coat, it soon became apparent that Sir Walter's large leonine head was for use as well as ornament, and he considered the matter soberly and sanely enough. Five chairs were set round the plain deal table, for Sir Walter had brought with him a young relative and secretary named Horne Fisher, a rather languid young man with a light moustache and hair prematurely thinned. Sir Walter listened with grave attention, and his secretary with polite boredom, to the string of episodes by which the police had traced the flying rebel from the steps of the hotel to the solitary tower beside the sea. There, at least, he was cornered between the moors and the breakers, and the scout sent by Wilson reported him as writing under a solitary candle; perhaps composing another of his tremendous proclamations. Indeed it would have been typical of him to have chosen it as the place in which finally to turn to bay. He had some remote claim on it, as on a family castle, and those who knew him thought him capable of imitating the primitive Irish chieftain, who fell fighting against the sea.

"I saw some queer-looking people leaving as I came in," said Sir Walter Carey. "I suppose they were your witnesses. But why do they turn up here at this time of night?"

Morton smiled grimly.

"They come here by night because they would be dead men if they came here by day. They are criminals committing a crime that is more horrible here than theft or murder."

"What crime do you mean?" asked the other, with some curiosity.

"They are helping the law," said Morton.

There was a silence, and Sir Walter considered the papers before him with an abstracted eye. At last he spoke.

"Quite so; but look here, if the local feeling is as lively as that, there are a good many points to consider. I believe the new Act will enable me to collar him now if I think it best. But is it best? A serious rising here

The Man Who Knew Too Much

would do us no good in Parliament, and the Government has enemies in England as well as Ireland. It won't do if I have done what looks a little like sharp practice, and then only raised a revolution."

"It's all the other way," said the man called Wilson, rather quickly. "There won't be half so much of a revolution if you arrest him as there will if you leave him loose for three days longer. But, anyhow, there can't be anything nowadays that the proper police can't manage."

"Mr. Wilson is a Londoner," said the Irish detective, with a smile.

"Yes, I'm a Cockney all right," replied Wilson, "and I think I'm all the better for that. Especially at this job, oddly enough."

Sir Walter seemed slightly amused at the pertinacity of the third officer, and perhaps even more amused at the slight accent with which he spoke, which rendered rather needless his boast about his origin.

"Do you mean to say," he asked, "that you know more about the business here because you have come from London?"

"Sounds funny, I know, but I do believe it," answered Wilson. "I believe these affairs want fresh methods. But most of all I believe they want a fresh eye "

The superior officers laughed, and the red-haired man went on with a slight touch of temper.

"Well, look at the facts. See how the fellow got away every time, and you'll understand what I mean. Why was he able to stand in the place of the scarecrow, hidden by nothing but an old hat? Because it was a village policeman, who knew the scarecrow was there—was expecting it, and therefore took no notice of it. Now I never expect a scarecrow. I've never seen one in the street, and I stare at one when I see it in the field. It's a new thing to me, and worth noticing. And it was just the same when he hid in the well. You are ready to find a well in a place like that; you look for a well, and so you don't see it. I don't look for it, and therefore I do look at it."

"It is certainly an idea," said Sir Walter, smiling.

The Vanishing Prince

"But what about the balcony? Balconies are occasionally seen in London."

"But not rivers right under them, as if it was in Venice," replied Wilson.

"It is certainly a new idea," repeated Sir Walter, with something like respect. He had all the love of the luxurious classes for new ideas. But he also had a critical faculty, and was inclined to think, after due reflection, that it was a true idea as well.

Growing dawn had already turned the window panes from black to grey, when Sir Walter got abruptly to his feet. The others rose also, taking this for a signal that the arrest was to be undertaken. But their leader stood for a moment in deep thought, as if conscious that he had come to a parting of the ways.

Suddenly the silence was pierced by a long, wailing cry from the dark moors outside. The silence that followed it seemed more startling than the shriek itself, and it lasted until Nolan said heavily:

"'Tis the banshee. Somebody is marked for the grave."

His long, large-featured face was as pale as a moon; and it was easy to remember that he was the only Irishman in the room.

"Well, I know that banshee," said Wilson, cheerfully. "Ignorant as you think I am of these things. I talked to that banshee myself an hour ago, and I sent that banshee up to the tower and told her to sing out like that, if she could get a glimpse of our friend writing his proclamation."

"Do you mean that girl Bridget Royce?" asked Morton, drawing his frosty brows together. "Has she turned King's Evidence to that extent?"

"Yes," said Wilson. "I know very little of these local things, you tell me. But I reckon an angry woman is much the same in all countries."

Nolan, however, seemed still moody and unlike himself.

"It's an ugly noise and an ugly business altogether," he said. "If it's really the end of Prince Michael, it may well be the end of other things as well. When the spirit

The Man Who Knew Too Much

is on him he would escape by a ladder of dead men, and wade through that sea if it was made of blood."

"Is that the real reason of your pious alarms?" asked Wilson, with a slight sneer.

The Irishman's pale face blackened with a new passion.

"I have faced as many murderers in County Clare as you ever fought with in Clapham Junction, Mr. Cockney," he said.

"Hush, please," said Morton sharply. "Wilson, you have no kind of right to imply doubt of your superior's conduct. I hope you will prove yourself as courageous and trustworthy as he has always been."

The pale face of the red-haired man seemed a shade paler, but he was silent and composed, and Sir Walter went up to Nolan with marked courtesy, saying: "Shall we go outside now and get this business done?"

Dawn had lifted, leaving a wide chasm of white between a great grey cloud and the great grey moorland, beyond which the tower was outlined against the daybreak and the sea.

Something in its plain and primitive shape vaguely suggested the dawn in the first days of the earth; in some prehistoric time when even the colours were hardly created; when there was only blank daylight between cloud and clay. These dead hues were only relieved by one spot of gold: the spark of the candle alight in the window of the lonely tower, and burning on into broadening daylight. As the group of detectives, followed by a cordon of policemen, spread out into a crescent to cut off all escape, the light in the tower flashed as if it were moved for a moment, and then went out. They guessed the man inside had realized the daylight and blown out his candle.

"There are other windows, aren't there?" said Morton. "And a door, of course, somewhere round the corner—only a round tower has no corners."

"Another example of my small suggestion," observed Wilson quietly. "That queer tower was the first thing I saw when I came to these parts, and I can tell you a little more about it, or, at any rate, the outside of it. There are four windows altogether; one a little way from this

The Vanishing Prince

one, but just out of sight. Those are both on the ground floor, and so is the third on the other side, making a sort of triangle. But the fourth is just above the third, and I suppose it looks on an upper floor."

"It's only a sort of loft, reached by a ladder," said Nolan. "I've played in the place when I was a child. It's no more than an empty shell." And his face grew sadder, thinking, perhaps, of the tragedy of his country and the part that he played in it.

"The man must have got a table and chair, at any rate," said Wilson; "but no doubt he could have got those from some cottage. If I might make a suggestion, sir, I think we ought to approach all the five entrances at once, so to speak. One of us should go to the door and one to each window; Macbride here has a ladder for the upper window."

Mr. Horne Fisher, the languid secretary, turned to his distinguished relative and spoke for the first time.

"I am rather a convert to the Cockney school of psychology," he said, in an almost inaudible voice.

The others seemed to feel the same influence in different ways, for the group began to break up in the manner indicated. Morton moved towards the window immediately in front of them, where the hidden outlaw had apparently just snuffed the candle; Nolan, a little farther westward, to the next window; while Wilson, followed by Macbride with the ladder, went round to the two windows at the back. Sir Walter Carey himself, followed by his secretary, began to walk round towards the only door, to demand admittance in a more regular fashion.

"He will be armed, of course?" remarked Sir Walter casually.

"By all accounts," replied Horne Fisher, "he can do more with a candlestick than most men with a pistol. But he is pretty sure to have the pistol, too."

Even as he spoke the question was answered with a tongue of thunder. Morton had just placed himself in front of the nearest window, his broad shoulders blocking the aperture. For an instant it was lit from within as with red fire, followed by a thundering throng of echoes.

The Man Who Knew Too Much

The square shoulders seemed to alter in shape, and the sturdy figure collapsed among the tall, rank grasses at the foot of the tower. A puff of smoke floated from the window like a little cloud. The two men behind rushed to the spot and raised him; but he was dead.

Sir Walter straightened himself and called out something that was lost in another noise of firing; it was possible that the police were already avenging their comrade from the other side. Fisher had already raced round to the next window, and a new cry of astonishment from him brought his patron to the same spot. Nolan, the Irish policeman, had also fallen, sprawling all his great length in the grass, and it was red with blood. He was still alive when they reached him, but there was death on his face, and he was only able to make a final gesture telling them that all was over, and with a broken word and a heroic effort motioning them on to where his other comrades were besieging the back of the tower. Stunned by these rapid and repeated shocks, the two men could only vaguely obey the gesture, and finding their way to the other windows at the back, they found a scene equally startling, if less final and tragic. The other two officers were not dead or mortally wounded, but Macbride lay with a broken leg and his ladder on top of him, evidently thrown down from the top window of the tower; while Wilson lay on his face, quite still, as if stunned, with his red head among the grey and silver of the sea-holly. In him, however, the impotence was but momentary, for he began to move and rise as the others came round the tower.

"My God, it's like an explosion," cried Sir Walter; and, indeed, it was the only word for this unearthly energy by which one man had been able to deal death or destruction on three sides of the same small triangle at the same instant.

Wilson had already scrambled to his feet and with splendid energy flew again at the window, revolver in hand. He fired twice into the opening, and then disappeared in his own smoke; but the thud of his feet and the shock of a falling chair told them that the intrepid Londoner had managed at last to leap into the room. Then

The Vanishing Prince

followed a curious silence, and Sir Walter, walking to the window through the thinning smoke, looked into the hollow shell of the ancient tower. Except for Wilson, staring around him, there was nobody there.

The inside of the tower was a single empty room, with nothing but a plain wooden chair and a table on which were pens, ink, and paper, and the candlestick. Half way up the high wall there was a rude timber platform under the upper window: a small loft which was more like a large shelf. It was reached only by a ladder, and it seemed to be as bare as the bare walls. Wilson completed his survey of the place, and then went and stared at the things on the table. Then he silently pointed with his lean forefinger at the open page of the large notebook. The writer had suddenly stopped writing, even in the middle of a word.

"I said it was like an explosion," said Sir Walter Carey at last. "And really the man himself seems to have suddenly exploded. But he has blown himself up somehow, without touching the tower. He's burst more like a bubble than a bomb."

"He has touched more valuable things than the tower," said Wilson gloomily.

There was a long silence, and then Sir Walter said seriously: "Well, Mr. Wilson, I am not a detective. And these unhappy happenings have left you in charge of that branch of the business. We all lament the cause of this; but I should like to say that I myself have the strongest confidence in your capacity for carrying on the work. What do you think we should do next?"

Wilson seemed to rouse himself from his depression, and acknowledged the speaker's words with a warmer civility than he had hitherto shown to anybody. He called in a few of the police to assist in routing out the interior, leaving the rest to spread themselves in a search-party outside.

"I think," he said, "the first thing is to make quite sure about the inside of this place, as it was hardly physically possible for him to have got outside. I suppose poor Nolan would have brought in his banshee, and said it was supernaturally possible. But I've got no use for

The Man Who Knew Too Much

disembodied spirits when I'm dealing with facts. And the facts before me are an empty tower with a ladder, a chair, and a table."

"The spiritualists," said Sir Walter, with a smile, "would say that spirits could find a great deal of use for a table."

"I dare say they could if the spirits were on the table, in a bottle," replied Wilson, with a curl of his pale lip. "The people round here, when they're all sodden with Irish whisky, may believe in such things. I think they want a little education in this country."

Horne Fisher's heavy eyelids fluttered in a faint attempt to rise, as if he were tempted to a lazy protest against the contemptuous tone of the investigator.

"The Irish believe far too much in spirits to believe in spiritualism," he murmured. "They know too much about 'em. If you want a simple and childlike faith in any spirit that comes along, you can get it in your favourite London."

"I don't want to get it anywhere," said Wilson shortly. "I say I'm dealing with much simpler things than your simple faith; with a table and a chair and a ladder. Now what I want to say about them at the start is this. They are all three made roughly enough of plain wood. But the table and the chair are fairly new and comparatively clean. The ladder is covered with dust, and there is a cobweb under the top rung of it. That means that he borrowed the first two quite recently from some cottage, as we supposed; but the ladder has been a long time in this rotten old dustbin. Probably it was part of the original furniture; an heirloom in this magnificent palace of the Irish kings."

Again Fisher looked at him under his eyelids, but seemed too sleepy to speak; and Wilson went on with his argument.

"Now it's quite clear that something very odd has just happened in this place. The chances are ten to one, it seems to me, that it had something specially to do with this place. Probably he came here because he could only do it here; it doesn't seem very inviting otherwise. But the man knew it of old; they say it belonged

The Vanishing Prince

to his family; so that altogether, I think, everything points to something in the construction of the tower itself."

"Your reasoning seems to me excellent," said Sir Walter, who was listening attentively. "But what could it be?"

"You see now what I mean about the ladder," went on the detective. "It's the only old piece of furniture here, and the first thing that caught that Cockney eye of mine. But there is something else. That loft up there is a sort of lumber-room without any lumber. So far as I can see, it's as empty as everything else, and as things are, I don't see the use of the ladder leading to it. It seems to me, as I can't find anything unusual down here, that it may pay us to look up there."

He got briskly off the table on which he was sitting (for the only chair was allotted to Sir Walter) and ran rapidly up the ladder to the platform above. He was soon followed by the others, Mr. Fisher going last, however, with an appearance of considerable nonchalance.

At this stage, however, they were destined to disappointment; Wilson nosed in every corner like a terrier, and examined the roof almost in the posture of a fly; but half an hour afterwards they had to confess that they were still without a clue. Sir Walter's private secretary seemed more and more threatened with inappropriate slumber; and having been the last to climb up the ladder, seemed now to lack the energy even to climb down again.

"Come along, Fisher," called out Sir Walter from below, when the others had regained the floor. "We must consider whether we'll pull the whole place to pieces to see what it's made of."

"I'm coming in a minute," said the voice from the ledge above their heads; a voice somewhat suggestive of an inarticulate yawn.

"What are you waiting for?" asked Sir Walter impatiently. "Can you see anything there?"

"Well, yes, in a way," replied the voice vaguely. "In fact I see it quite plain now."

"What is it?" asked Wilson sharply, from the table on which he sat kicking his heels restlessly.

The Man Who Knew Too Much

"Well, it's a man," said Horne Fisher.

Wilson bounded off the table as if he had been kicked off it.

"What do you mean?" he cried. "How can you possibly see a man?"

"I can see him through the window," replied the secretary mildly. "I see him coming across the moor. He's making a bee-line across the open country towards this tower. He evidently means to pay us a visit. And considering who it seems to be, perhaps it would be more polite if we were all at the door to receive him." And the secretary came in a leisurely manner down the ladder.

"Who it seems to be!" repeated Wilson in astonishment.

"Well, I think it's the man you call Prince Michael," observed Mr. Fisher airily. "In fact, I'm sure it is. I've seen the police portraits of him."

There was a dead silence, and Sir Walter's usually steady brain seemed to go round like a windmill.

"But hang it all," he said at last, "even supposing his own explosion could have thrown him half a mile away, without passing through any of the windows, and left him alive enough for a country walk—even then, why the devil should he walk in this direction? The murderer does not generally revisit the scene of his crime so rapidly as all that."

"He doesn't know yet that it is the scene of his crime," answered Horne Fisher.

"What on earth do you mean? You credit him with rather singular absence of mind."

"Well, the truth is, it isn't the scene of his crime," said Fisher, and went and looked out of the window.

There was another silence, and then Sir Walter said quietly: "What sort of notion have you really got in your head, Fisher? Have you developed a new theory about how this fellow escaped out of the ring round him?"

"He never escaped at all," answered the man at the window, without turning round. "He never escaped out of the ring because he was never inside the ring. He

The Vanishing Prince

was not in this tower at all; at least, not when we were surrounding it."

He turned and leaned his back against the window; but in spite of his usual listless manner, they almost fancied that the face in shadow was a little pale.

"I began to guess something of the sort when we were some way from the tower," he said. "Did you notice that sort of flash or flicker the candle gave before it was extinguished? I was almost certain it was only the last leap the flame gives when a candle burns itself out. And then I came into this room, and I saw that."

He pointed at the table, and Sir Walter caught his breath with a sort of curse at his own blindness. For the candle in the candlestick had obviously burnt itself away to nothing, and left him, mentally at least, very completely in the dark.

"Then there is a sort of mathematical question," went on Fisher, leaning back in his limp way and looking up at the bare walls, as if tracing imaginary diagrams there. "It's not so easy for a man in the middle of a triangle to face all three sides; but it's easier for a man in the third angle to face the other two at the same moment, especially if they are at the base of an isosceles. I am sorry if it sounds like a lecture on geometry, but——"

"I'm afraid we have no time for it," said Wilson coldly. "If this man is really coming back, I must give my orders at once."

"I think I'll go on with it, though," observed Fisher, staring at the roof with an insolent serenity.

"I must ask you, Mr. Fisher, to let me conduct my inquiry on my own lines," said Wilson firmly. "I am the officer in charge now."

"Yes," remarked Horne Fisher softly, but with an accent that somehow chilled the hearer, "yes. But why?"

Sir Walter was staring, for he had never seen his rather lackadaisical young friend look like that before. Fisher was looking at Wilson with lifted lids, and the eyes under them seemed to have shed or shifted a film, as do the eyes of an eagle.

"Why are you the officer in charge now?" he asked. "Why can you conduct the inquiry on your own lines

The Man Who Knew Too Much

now? How did it come about, I wonder, that the elder officers are not here to interfere with anything you do?"

Nobody spoke, and nobody can say how soon anyone would have collected his wits to speak, when a noise came from without. It was the heavy and hollow sound of a blow upon the door of the tower, and to their shaken spirits it sounded strangely like the hammer of doom.

The wooden door of the tower moved on its rusty hinges under the hand that struck it, and Prince Michael came into the room. Nobody had the smallest doubt about his identity. His light clothes, though frayed with his adventures, were the fine and almost foppish cut, and he wore a pointed beard or imperial, perhaps as a further reminiscence of Louis Napoleon; but he was a much taller and more graceful man than his prototype. Before anyone could speak, he had silenced everyone for an instant with a slight but splendid gesture of hospitality.

"Gentlemen," he said, "this is a poor place now, but you are heartily welcome."

Wilson was the first to recover, and he took a stride towards the new-comer.

"Michael O'Neill, I arrest you in the King's name for the murder of Francis Morton and James Nolan. It is my duty to warn you——"

"No, no, Mr. Wilson," cried Fisher, suddenly, "you shall not commit a third murder."

Sir Walter Carey rose from his chair, which fell over with a crash behind him.

"What does all this mean?" he called out in an authoritative manner.

"It means," said Fisher, "that this man, Hooker Wilson, as soon as he put his head in at that window, killed his two comrades who had put their heads in at the other windows, by firing across the empty room. That is what it means. And if you want to know, count how many times he is supposed to have fired, and then count the charges left in his revolver."

Wilson, who was still sitting on the table, abruptly

The Vanishing Prince

put a hand out for the weapon that lay beside him. But the next movement was the most unexpected of all, for the Prince, standing in the doorway, passed suddenly from the dignity of a statue to the swiftness of an acrobat, and rent the revolver out of the detective's hand.

"You dog," he cried. "So you are the type of English truth, as I am of Irish tragedy; you who come to kill me, wading through the blood of your brethren. If they had fallen in a feud on the hillside, it would be called murder, and yet your sin might be forgiven you. But I, who am innocent, I was to be slain with ceremony. There would be long speeches and patient judges listening to my vain plea of innocence, noting down my despair and disregarding it. Yes, that is what I call assassination. But killing may be no murder; there is one shot left in this little gun, and I know where it should go."

Wilson turned quickly on the table, and even as he turned he twisted in agony; for Michael shot him through the body where he sat, so that he tumbled off the table like lumber.

The police rushed to lift him; Sir Walter stood speechless; and then, with a strange and weary gesture, Horne Fisher spoke.

"You are indeed a type of the Irish tragedy," he said. "You were entirely in the right, and you have put yourself in the wrong."

The Prince's face was like marble for a space; then there dawned in his eyes a light not unlike that of despair. He laughed suddenly and flung the smoking pistol on the ground.

"I am indeed in the wrong," he said. "I have committed a crime that may justly bring a curse on me and my children."

Horne Fisher did not seem entirely satisfied with this very sudden repentance; he kept his eyes on the man and only said in a low voice: "What crime do you mean?"

"I have helped English justice," replied Prince Michael. "I have avenged your King's officers; I have done the work of his hangman. For that, truly, I deserve to be hanged."

And he turned to the police with a gesture that did not

The Man Who Knew Too Much

so much surrender to them, but rather command them to arrest him.

This was the story that Horne Fisher told to Harold March, the journalist, many years after, in a little but luxurious restaurant near Piccadilly. He had invited March to dinner some time after the affair he called "The Face in the Target," and the conversation had naturally turned on that mystery and afterwards on earlier memories of Fisher's life; and the way in which he had been led to study problems as those of Prince Michael. Horne Fisher was fifteen years older; his thin hair had faded to frontal baldness, and his long thin hands dropped less with affectation and more with fatigue. And he told the story of the Irish adventure of his youth because it recorded the first occasion on which he had ever come in contact with crime, or discovered how darkly and how terribly crime can be entangled with law.

"Hooker Wilson was the first criminal I ever knew, and he was a policeman," explained Fisher, twirling his wine-glass. "And all my life has been a mixed-up business of the sort. He was a man of very real talent, and perhaps genius, and well worth studying both as a detective and a criminal. His white face and red hair were typical of him, for he was one of those who are cold and yet on fire for fame; and he could control anger but not ambition. He swallowed the snubs of his superiors in that first quarrel, though he boiled with resentment; but when he suddenly saw the two heads dark against the dawn and framed in the two windows, he could not miss the chance, not only of revenge, but of the removal of the two obstacles to his promotion. He was a dead shot, and counted on silencing both, though proof against him would have been hard in any case. But, as a matter of fact, he had a narrow escape in the case of Nolan, who lived just long enough to say 'Wilson' and point. We thought he was summoning help for his comrade, but he was really denouncing his murderer. After that it was easy to throw down the ladder above him (for a man up a ladder cannot see clearly what is below and behind) and to throw himself on the ground as another victim of the catastrophe.

The Vanishing Prince

"But there was mixed up with his murderous ambition a real belief, not only in his own talents, but in his own theories. He did believe in what he called a fresh eye, and he did want scope for fresh methods. There was something in his view; but it failed where such things commonly fail, because the fresh eye cannot see the unseen. It is true about the ladder and the scarecrow, but not about the life and the soul; and he made a bad mistake about what a man like Michael would do when he heard a woman scream. All Michael's very vanity and vainglory made him rush out at once; he would have walked into Dublin Castle for a lady's glove. Call it his pose or what you will, but he would have done it. What happened when he met her is another story, and one we may never know; but from tales I've heard since, they must have been reconciled. Wilson was wrong there, but there was something, for all that, in his notion that the new-comer sees most, and that the man on the spot may know too much to know anything. He was right about some things. He was right about me."

"About you?" asked March.

"I am the man who knows too much to know anything, or, at any rate, to do anything," said Horne Fisher. "I don't mean especially about Ireland. I mean about England. I mean about the whole way we are governed, and perhaps the only way we can be governed. You asked me just now what became of the survivors of that tragedy. Well, Wilson recovered, and we managed to persuade him to retire. But we had to pension that damnable murderer more magnificently than any hero who ever fought for England. I managed to save Michael from the worst, but we had to send that perfectly innocent man to penal servitude for a crime we know he never committed; but it was only afterwards that we could connive in a sneakish way at his escape. And Sir Walter Carey is Prime Minister of this country, which he would probably never have been if the truth had been told of such a horrible scandal in his department. It might have done for us altogether in Ireland; it would certainly have done for him. And he is my father's old friend, and has always smothered me with kindness. I am too tangled up with the whole thing, you

The Man Who Knew Too Much

see, and I was certainly never born to set it right. You look distressed, not to say shocked, and I'm not at all offended at it. Let us change the subject by all means, if you like. What do you think of this Burgundy? It's rather a discovery of mine, like the restaurant itself."

And he proceeded to talk learnedly and luxuriantly on all the wines of the world; on which subject, also, some moralists would consider that he knew too much.

III.—THE SOUL OF THE SCHOOLBOY

A LARGE map of London would be needed to display the wild and zig-zag course of one day's journey undertaken by an uncle and his nephew—or, to speak more truly, of a nephew and his uncle. For the nephew, a schoolboy on a holiday, was in theory the god in the car, or in the cab, tram, tube, and so on; while his uncle was at most a priest dancing before him and offering sacrifices. To put it more soberly, the schoolboy had something of the stolid air of a young duke doing the grand tour, while his elderly relative was reduced to the position of a courier, who nevertheless had to pay for everything like a patron. The schoolboy was officially known as Summers Minor, and in a more social manner as Stinks, the only public tribute to his career as an amateur photographer and electrician. The uncle was the Rev. Thomas Twyford, a lean and lively old gentleman with a red eager face and white hair. In a small circle of ecclesiastical archæologists, who were the only people who could even understand each other's discoveries, he occupied a recognized and respectable place. And a critic might have found even in that day's journey at least as much of the uncle's hobby as of the nephew's holiday. His original purpose had been wholly paternal and festive. But like many other intelligent people, he was not above the weakness of playing with a toy to amuse himself on the theory that it would amuse a child. His toys were crowns and mitres and crosiers and swords of state, and he had lingered over them, telling himself that the boy ought to see all the sights of London. And at the end of the day, after a tremendous tea, he rather gave the game away by winding up with a visit in which hardly any human boy could be conceived as taking an interest; an underground chamber supposed to have been a chapel, recently ex-

The Man Who Knew Too Much

cavated on the north bank of the Thames, and containing literally nothing whatever but one old silver coin. But the coin, to those who knew, was more solitary and splendid than the Koh-i-noor. It was Roman, and was said to bear the head of St. Paul, and round it raged the most vital controversies about the ancient British Church. It could hardly be denied, however, that the controversies left Summers Minor comparatively cold.

Indeed the things that interested Summers Minor and the things that did not interest him had mystified and amused his uncle for several hours. He exhibited the English schoolboy's startling ignorance and startling knowledge—knowledge of some special classification in which he can generally correct and confound his elders. He considered himself entitled at Hampton Court on a holiday to forget the very names of Cardinal Wolsey or William of Orange; but he could hardly be dragged away from some details about the arrangement of the electric bells in the neighbouring hotel. He was solidly dazed by Westminster Abbey, which is not so unnatural since that church became the lumber-room of the larger and less successful statuary of the eighteenth century. But he had a magic and minute knowledge of the Westminster omnibuses, and indeed of the whole omnibus system of London, the colours and numbers of which he knew as a herald knows heraldry. He would cry out against a momentary confusion between a light green Paddington and a dark green Bayswater vehicle as his uncle would at the identification of a Greek ikon and a Roman image.

"Do you collect omnibuses like stamps?" asked his uncle. "They must need a rather large album. Or do you keep them in your locker?"

"I keep them in my head," replied the nephew, with legitimate firmness.

"It does you credit, I admit," replied the clergyman. "I suppose it were vain to ask for what purpose you have learnt that out of a thousand things. There hardly seems to be a career in it, unless you could be permanently on the pavement to advise old ladies getting into the wrong 'bus. Well, we must get out of this one, for this is our

The Soul of the Schoolboy

place. I want to show you what they call St. Paul's Penny."

"Is it like St. Paul's Cathedral?" asked the youth with resignation, as they alighted.

At the entrance their eyes were arrested by a singular figure evidently hovering there with a similar anxiety to enter. It was that of a dark thin man in a long black robe rather like a cassock, but the black cap on his head was of too strange a shape to be a biretta. It suggested rather some archaic headdress of Persia or Babylon. He had a curious black beard appearing only at the corners of his chin, and his large eyes were oddly set in his face like the flat decorative eyes painted in old Egyptian profiles. Before they had gathered more than a general impression of him, he had dived into the doorway that was their own destination.

Nothing could be seen above ground of the sunken sanctuary except a strong wooden hut of the sort recently run up for many military and official purposes, the wooden floor of which was indeed a mere platform over the excavated cavity below. A soldier stood as a sentry outside, and a superior soldier, an Anglo-Indian officer of distinction, sat writing at the desk inside. Indeed, the sightseers soon found that this particular sight was surrounded with the most extraordinary precautions. I have compared the silver coin to the Koh-i-noor, and in one sense it was even conventionally comparable; since by an historical accident it was at one time almost counted among the Crown jewels, or at least the Crown relics, until one of the royal princes publicly restored it to the shrine to which it was supposed to belong. Other causes combined to concentrate official vigilance upon it. There had been a scare about spies carrying explosives in small objects; and one of those experimental orders that pass like waves over bureaucracy had decreed, first that all visitors should change their clothes for a sort of official sackcloth, and then (when this method caused some murmurs) that they should at least turn out their pockets. Colonel Morris, the officer in charge, was a short, active man, with a grim and leathery face but a lively and humorous eye, a contradiction borne out by his conduct,

The Man Who Knew Too Much

for he at once derided the safeguards and yet insisted on them.

"I don't care a button myself for Paul's Penny or such things," he admitted in answer to some antiquarian openings from the clergyman, who was slightly acquainted with him, "but I wear the King's coat, you know, and it's a serious thing when the King's uncle leaves a thing here with his own hands under my charge. But as for saints and relics and things, I fear I'm a bit of a Voltairean—what you would call a sceptic."

"I'm not sure it's even sceptical to believe in the Royal Family and not in the Holy Family," replied Mr. Twyford. "But, of course, I can easily empty my pockets to show I don't carry a bomb."

The little heap of the parson's possessions, which he left on the table, consisted chiefly of papers, over and above a pipe and a tobacco pouch and some Roman and Saxon coins. The rest were catalogues of old books, and pamphlets like one entitled "The Use of Sarum," one glance at which was sufficient both for the colonel and the schoolboy. They could not see the use of Sarum at all. The contents of the boy's pockets naturally made a larger heap, and included marbles, a ball of string, an electric torch, a magnet, a small catapult, and, of course, a large pocket-knife, almost to be described as a small tool-box; a complex apparatus on which he seemed disposed to linger, pointing out that it included a pair of nippers, a tool for punching holes in wood, and above all an instrument for taking stones out of a horse's hoof. The comparative absence of any horse he appeared to regard as irrelevant, as if it were a mere appendage easily supplied. But when the turn came of the gentleman in the black gown, he did not turn out his pockets, but merely spread out his hands.

"I have no possessions," he said.

"I'm afraid I must ask you to empty your pockets and make sure," observed the colonel gruffly.

"I have no pockets," said the stranger.

Mr. Twyford was looking at the long black gown with a learned eye.

"Are you a monk?" he asked in a puzzled fashion.

The Soul of the Schoolboy

"I am a magus," replied the stranger. "You have heard of the Magi, perhaps? I am a magician."

"Oh I say!" exclaimed Summers Minor with prominent eyes.

"But I was once a monk," went on the other. "I am what you would call an escaped monk. Yes, I have escaped into eternity. But the monks held one truth at least, that the highest life should be without possessions. I have no pocket money and no pockets, and all the stars are my trinkets."

"They are out of reach, anyhow," observed Colonel Morris, in a tone that suggested that it was well for them. "I've known a good many magicians myself in India, mango-plant and all. But the Indian ones are all frauds, I'll swear. In fact I had a good deal of fun showing them up. More fun than I have over this dreary job, anyhow. But here comes Mr. Symon, who will show you over the old cellar downstairs."

Mr. Symon, the official guardian and guide, was a young man, prematurely grey, with a grave mouth which contrasted curiously with a very small dark moustache with waxed points that seemed somehow separate from it, as if a black fly had settled on his face. He spoke with the accent of Oxford and the permanent official, but in as dead a fashion as the most indifferent hired guide. They descended a dark, stone staircase, at the foot of which Symon pressed a button and a door opened on a dark room, or rather a room which had an instant before been dark. For almost as the heavy iron door swung open an almost blinding blaze of electric lights filled the whole interior. The fitful enthusiasm of Stinks at once caught fire, and he eagerly asked if the lights and the door worked together.

"Yes, it's all one system," replied Symon. "It was all fitted up for the day His Royal Highness deposited the thing here. You see, it's locked up behind a glass case exactly as he left it."

A glance showed that the arrangements for guarding the treasure were indeed as strong as they were simple. A single pane of glass cut off one corner of the room in an iron framework let into the rock walls and the wooden

The Man Who Knew Too Much

roof above; there was now no possibility of reopening the case without elaborate labour, except by breaking the glass, which would probably arouse the night watchman, who was always within a few feet of it, even if he had fallen asleep. A close examination would have showed many more ingenious safeguards; but the eye of the Reverend Thomas Twyford at least was already riveted on what interested him much more, the dull silver disc which shone in the white light against a plain background of black velvet.

"St. Paul's Penny, said to commemorate the visit of St Paul to Britain, was probably preserved in this chapel until the eighth century," Symon was saying in his clear but colourless voice. "In the ninth century it is supposed to have been carried away by the barbarians, and it reappears, after the conversion of the northern Goths, in the possession of the royal family of Gothland. His Royal Highness the Duke of Gothland retained it always in his own private custody, and when he decided to exhibit it to the public, placed it here with his own hand. It was immediately sealed up in such a manner——"

Unluckily at this point Summers Minor, whose attention had somewhat strayed from the religious wars of the ninth century, caught sight of a short length of wire appearing in a broken patch in the wall. He precipitated himself at it, calling out: "I say, does that connect——?"

It was evident that it did connect. For no sooner had the boy given it a twitch than the whole room went black as if they had all been struck blind, and an instant afterwards they heard the dull crash of the closing door.

"Well, you've done it now," said Symon in his tranquil fashion. Then after a pause he added: "I suppose they'll miss us sooner or later, and no doubt they can get it open; but it may take some little time."

There was a silence, and then the unconquerable Stinks observed:

"Rotten that I had to leave my electric torch."

"I think," said his uncle with restraint, "that we are sufficiently convinced of your interest in electricity."

The Soul of the Schoolboy

Then after a pause he remarked more amiably: "I suppose if I regretted any of my own *impedimenta*, it would be the pipe. Though, as a matter of fact, it's not much fun smoking in the dark. Everything seems different in the dark."

"Everything is different in the dark," said a third voice, that of the man who called himself a magician. It was a very musical voice, and rather in contrast with his sinister and swarthy visage which was now invisible. "Perhaps you don't know how terrible a truth that is. All you see are pictures made by the sun, faces and furniture and flowers and trees. The things themselves may be quite strange to you. Something else may be standing now where you saw a table or a chair. The face of your friend may be quite different in the dark."

A short indescribable noise broke the stillness. Twyford started for a second, and then said sharply: "Really, I don't think it's a suitable occasion for trying to frighten a child."

"Who's a child?" cried the indignant Summers, with a voice that had a crow but also something of a crack in it. "And who's a funk either? Not me."

"I will be silent then," said the other voice. "But silence also makes and unmakes."

The required silence remained unbroken for a long time, until at last the clergyman said to Symon in a low voice: "I suppose it's all right about air?"

"Oh, yes," replied the other aloud; "there's a fireplace and a chimney in the office just by the door."

A bound and the noise of a falling chair told them that the irrepressible rising generation had once more thrown itself across the room. They heard the ejaculation: "A chimney! Why, I'll be——" and the rest was lost in muffled but exultant cries.

The uncle called repeatedly and vainly, groped his way at last to the opening, and peering up it caught a glimpse of a disc of daylight, which seemed to suggest that the fugitive had vanished in safety. Making his way back to the group by the glass case, he fell over the fallen chair, and took a moment to collect himself again. He had opened his mouth to speak to Symon, when he stopped,

The Man Who Knew Too Much

and suddenly found himself blinking in the full shock of the white light. And looking over the other man's shoulder, he saw that the door was standing open.

"So they've got at us at last," he observed to Symon.

The man in the black robe was leaning against the wall some yards away with a smile carved on his face.

"Here comes Colonel Morris," went on Twyford, still speaking to Symon. "One of us will have to tell him how the light went out. Will you?"

But Symon still said nothing. He was standing as still as a statue, and looking steadily at the black velvet behind the glass screen. He was looking at the black velvet because there was nothing else to look at. St. Paul's Penny was gone.

Colonel Morris entered the room with two new visitors, presumably two new sight-seers delayed by the accident. The foremost was a tall, fair, rather languid-looking man with a bald brow and a high-bridged nose; his companion was a younger man with light curly hair and frank and even innocent eyes. Symon scarcely seemed to hear the new-comers; it seemed almost as if he had not realized that the return of the light revealed his brooding attitude. Then he started in a guilty fashion, and when he saw the elder of the two strangers his pale face seemed to turn a shade paler.

"Why, it's Horne Fisher," and then after a pause he said in a low voice: "I'm in a devil of a hole, Fisher."

"There does seem a bit of a mystery to be cleared up," observed the gentleman so addressed.

"It will never be cleared up," said the pale Symon. "If anybody could clear it up, you could. But nobody could."

"I rather think I could," said another voice from outside the group, and they turned in surprise to realize that the man in the black robe had spoken again.

"You!" said the colonel sharply. "And how do you propose to play the detective?"

"I do not propose to play the detective," answered the other in a clear voice like a bell. "I propose to play the magician—one of the magicians you show up in India, Colonel."

The Soul of the Schoolboy

No one spoke for a moment, and then Horne Fisher surprised everybody by saying: "Well, let's go upstairs, and this gentleman can have a try."

He stopped Symon who had an automatic finger on the button, saying: "No, leave all the lights on; it's a sort of safeguard."

"The thing can't be taken away now," said Symon bitterly.

"It can be put back," replied Fisher.

Twyford had already run upstairs for news of his vanishing nephew, and he received news of him in a way that at once puzzled and reassured him. On the floor above lay one of those large paper darts, which boys throw at each other when the schoolmaster is out of the room. It had evidently been thrown in at the window, and on being unfolded displayed a scrawl of bad handwriting, which ran, "DEAR UNCLE, I am all right. Meet you at the hotel later on," and then the signature.

Insensibly comforted by this, the clergyman found his thoughts reverting voluntarily to his favourite relic, which came a good second in his sympathies to his favourite nephew. And before he knew where he was he found himself encircled by the group discussing its loss and more or less carried away on the current of their excitement. But an undercurrent of query continued to run in his mind as to what had really happened to the boy, and what was the boy's exact definition of being all right.

Meanwhile Horne Fisher had considerably puzzled everybody with his new tone and attitude. He had talked to the colonel about the military and mechanical arrangements, and displayed a remarkable knowledge both of the details of discipline and the technicalities of electricity. He had talked to the clergyman, and shown an equally surprising knowledge of the religious and historical interests involved in the relic. He had talked to the man who called himself a magician, and not only surprised but scandalized the company by an equally sympathetic familiarity with the most fantastic forms of Oriental occultism and psychic experiment. And in this last and least respectable line of inquiry he was evidently prepared to go farthest; he openly encouraged the magician, and

The Man Who Knew Too Much

was plainly prepared to follow the wildest ways of investigation in which that magus might lead him.

"How would you begin now?" he inquired, with an anxious politeness that reduced the colonel to a congestion of rage.

"It is all a question of a force, of establishing communications for a force," replied that adept affably, ignoring some military mutterings about the police force. "It is what you in the West used to call animal magnetism; but it is much more than that. I had better not say how much more. As to setting about it, the usual method is to throw some susceptible person into a trance, which serves as a sort of bridge or cord of communication, by which the force beyond can give him, as it were, an electric shock and awaken his higher senses. It opens the sleeping eye of the mind."

"I'm susceptible," said Fisher, either with simplicity or with a baffling irony. "Why not open my mind's eye for me? My friend Harold March here will tell you I sometimes see things even in the dark."

"Nobody sees anything except in the dark," said the magician.

Heavy clouds of sunset were closing round the wooden hut, enormous clouds of which only the corners could be seen in the little window like purple horns and tails, almost as if some huge monsters were prowling round the place. But the purple was already deepening to dark grey; it would soon be night.

"Do not light the lamp," said the magus with quiet authority, arresting a movement in that direction. "I told you before that things only happen in the dark."

How such a topsy-turvy scene ever came to be tolerated in the colonel's office, of all places, was afterwards a puzzle in the memory of many, including the colonel. They recalled it like a sort of nightmare, like something they could not control. Perhaps there was really a magnetism about the man mesmerized. Anyhow, the man was being mesmerized. For Horne Fisher had collapsed into a chair, with his long limbs loose and sprawling and his eyes staring at vacancy; and the other man was mesmerizing him, making sweeping movements with his

The Soul of the Schoolboy

darkly draped arms as if with black wings. The colonel lit a cigar. He had passed the point of explosion, and he dimly realized that eccentric aristocrats are allowed their fling. He comforted himself with the knowledge that he had already sent for the police, who would break up any such masquerade.

"Yes, I see pockets," the man in the trance was saying. "I see many pockets, but they are all empty. No, I see one pocket that is not empty."

There was a faint stir in the stillness, and the magician said: "Can you see what is in the pocket?"

"Yes," answered the other, "there are two bright things. I think they are two bits of steel. One of the pieces of steel is bent or crooked."

"Have they been used in the removal of the relic from downstairs?"

"Yes."

There was another pause, and the inquirer added: "Do you see anything of the relic itself?"

"I see something shining on the floor, like the shadow or the ghost of it. It is over there in the corner beyond the desk."

There was a movement of men turning and then a sudden stillness as of their stiffening. For over in the corner on the wooden floor there was really a round spot of pale light. It was the only light in the room. The cigar had gone out.

"It points the way," came the voice of the oracle. "The spirits are pointing the way to penitence, and urging the thief to restitution; I can see nothing more." His voice trailed off into a silence. It was broken by the ring of metal on the floor and the sound of something spinning and falling like a tossed halfpenny.

"Light the lamp," cried Fisher in a loud and even jovial voice, leaping to his feet with far less languor than usual. "I must be going now, but I should like to see it before I go. Why, I came on purpose to see it."

The lamp was lit, and he did see it, for St. Paul's Penny was lying on the floor at his feet.

"Oh, as for that," explained Fisher, when he was

The Man Who Knew Too Much

entertaining March and Twyford at lunch about a month later, "I merely wanted to play with the magician at his own game."

"I thought you meant to catch him in his own trap," said Twyford. "I can't make head or tail of anything yet, but to my mind he was always the suspect. I don't think he was necessarily a thief in the vulgar sense. The police always seem to think that silver is stolen for the sake of silver; but a thing like that might well be stolen out of some religious mania. A runaway monk turned mystic might well want it for some mystical purpose."

"No," replied Fisher. "The runaway monk is not a thief. At any rate, he is not the thief. And he's not altogether a liar either. He said one true thing at least."

"And what was that?" inquired March.

"He said it was all magnetism. As a matter of fact, it was done by means of a magnet."

Then, seeing they still looked puzzled, he added: "It was that toy magnet belonging to your nephew, Mr. Twyford."

"But I don't understand," objected March. "If it was done with the schoolboy's magnet, I suppose it was done by the schoolboy."

"Well," replied Fisher reflectively, "it rather depends which schoolboy."

"What on earth do you mean?"

"The soul of a schoolboy is a curious thing," Fisher continued in a meditative manner. "It can survive a great many things besides climbing out of a chimney. A man can grow grey in great campaigns and still have the soul of a schoolboy. A man can return with a great reputation from India and be put in charge of a great public treasure and still have the soul of a schoolboy, waiting to be awakened by an accident. And it is ten times more so when to the schoolboy you add the sceptic, who is generally a sort of stunted schoolboy. You said just now that things might be done by religious mania. Have you ever heard of irreligious mania? I assure you it exists very violently, especially in men who like showing up magicians in India."

The Soul of the Schoolboy

"Do you really mean," Twyford said, "that Colonel Morris took the relic?"

"He was the only person who could use the magnet," replied Fisher. "In fact your obliging nephew left him a number of things he could use. He had a ball of string and an instrument for making a hole in the wooden floor—I made a little play with that hole in the floor in my trance, by the way: with the lights left on below it shone like a new shilling."

Twyford suddenly bounded on his chair.

"But in that case," he cried in a new and altered voice —"why, then, of course—you said a piece of steel——"

"I said there were two pieces of steel," said Fisher. "The bent piece of steel was the boy's magnet. The other was the penny."

"But that is silver," answered the archæologist.

"Oh," replied Fisher soothingly, "I dare say it was painted with silver a little."

There was a heavy silence, but at last Harold March said: "But where is the real relic?"

"Where it has been for five years," replied Horne Fisher. "In the possession of a mad millionaire named Vandam, in Nebraska."

Harold March frowned at the tablecloth; then after an interval he said: "I think I understand your notion of how the thing was actually done; according to that Morris just made a hole and fished it up with a magnet at the end of a string. Such a monkey trick looks like mere madness; but I suppose he was mad, partly with the boredom of watching over what he felt was a fraud, though he couldn't prove it. Then came a chance to prove it, to himself at least, and he had what he called 'fun' with it. Yes, I think I see a lot of details now. But it's just the whole thing that knocks me. How did it all come to be like that?"

Fisher was looking at him with level lids and an immovable manner.

"Every precaution was taken," he said. "The Duke carried the relic on his own person and locked it up in the case with his own hands."

March was silent, but Twyford stammered: "I don't

The Man Who Knew Too Much

understand you. You give me the creeps. Why don't you speak plainer?"

"Oh, very well," replied Fisher with a sigh. "The plain truth is, of course, that it's a bad business. Everybody knows it's a bad business who knows anything about it. But it's always happening, and in one way one can hardly blame them. They get stuck on to a foreign princess that's as stiff as a Dutch doll, and they have their fling. In this case it was a pretty big fling.

"If it were some decent morganatic affair I wouldn't say, but he must have been a fool to throw away thousands on a woman like that. At the end it was sheer blackmail; but it's something that the old ass didn't get it out of the taxpayers. He could only get it out of the Yank, and there you are."

"Well, I'm glad my nephew had nothing to do with it," said the Rev. Thomas Twyford. "And if the great world is like that, I hope he will never have anything to do with it."

"Nobody knows better than I," said Horne Fisher, "that one can have far too much to do with it."

For Summers Minor had indeed nothing to do with it; and it is part of his higher significance that he has really nothing to do with the story, or with any such stories. The boy went like a bullet through the tangle of this tale of crooked politics and crazy mockery and came out on the other side, pursuing his own unspoilt purposes. From the top of the chimney he climbed he had caught sight of a new omnibus, whose colour and name he had never known, as a naturalist might see a new bird or a botanist a new flower. And he had been sufficiently enraptured in rushing after it, and riding away upon that fairy ship.

IV.—THE BOTTOMLESS WELL

ON an oasis, or green island in the red and yellow seas of sand that stretch beyond Europe towards the sunrise, there can be found a rather fantastic contrast which is none the less typical of such a place, since international treaties have made it an outpost of the British occupation. The site is famous among archæologists for something that is hardly a monument but merely a hole in the ground. But it is a round shaft like that of a well, and probably a part of some great irrigation works of remote and disputed date; perhaps more ancient than anything in that ancient land. There is a green fringe of palm and prickly pear round the black mouth of the well; but nothing of the upper masonry remains except two bulky and battered stones standing like the pillars of a gateway of nowhere; in which some of the more transcendental archæologists, in certain moods at moonrise or sunset, think they can trace the faint lines of figures or features of more than Babylonian monstrosity; while the more rationalistic archæologists, in the more rational hours of daylight, see nothing but two shapeless rocks. It may have been noticed, however, that all Englishmen are not archæologists. Many of those assembled in such a place for official and military purposes have hobbies other than archæology. And it is a solemn fact that the English in this eastern exile have contrived to make a small golf links out of the green scrub and sand; with a comfortable club-house at one end of it and this primeval monument at the other. They did not actually use this archaic abyss as a bunker; because it was by tradition unfathomable, and even for practical purposes unfathomed. Any sporting projectile sent into it might be counted most literally as a lost ball. But they often sauntered round it in their interludes of talking and smoking cigarettes, and

The Man Who Knew Too Much

one of them had just come down from the club house to find another gazing somewhat moodily into the well.

The two Englishmen both wore light clothes and white pith helmets and pugarees, but there for the most part their resemblance ended. And they both almost simultaneously said the same word; but they said it on two totally different notes of the voice.

"Have you heard the news?" asked the man from the club. "Splendid."

"Splendid," replied the man by the well. But the first man pronounced the word as a young man might say it about a woman; and the second as an old man might say it about the weather; not without sincerity but certainly without fervour.

And in this the tone of the two men was sufficiently typical of them. The first, who was a certain Captain Boyle, was of a bold and boyish type, dark and with a sort of native heat in his face that did not belong to the atmosphere of the East, but rather to the ardours and ambitions of the West. The other was an older man and certainly an older resident; a civilian official named Horne Fisher; and his drooping eyelids and drooping light moustaches expressed all the paradox of the Englishman in the East. He was much too hot to be anything but cool.

Neither of them thought it necessary to mention what it was that was splendid. That would indeed have been superfluous conversation about something that everybody knew. The striking victory over a menacing combination of Turks and Arabs in the north, won by troops under the command of Lord Hastings, the veteran of so many striking victories, was already spread by the newspapers all over the Empire, let alone to this small garrison so near to the battlefield.

"Now no other nation in the world could have done a thing like that," cried Captain Boyle emphatically.

Horne Fisher was still looking silently into the well; a moment later he answered:

"We certainly have the art of unmaking mistakes. That's where the poor old Prussians went wrong. They

The Bottomless Well

could only make mistakes and stick to them. There is really a certain talent in unmaking mistakes."

"What do you mean?" asked Boyle. "What mistake?"

"Well, everybody knows it looked like biting off more than we could chew," replied Horne Fisher. It was a peculiarity of Mr. Fisher that he always said that everybody knew things that about one person in two million was ever allowed to hear of. "And it was certainly jolly lucky that Travers turned up so well in the nick of time. Odd how often the right thing's been done for us by the second in command, even when a great man was first in command. Like Colborne at Waterloo."

"It ought to add a whole province to the Empire," observed the other.

"Well, I suppose the Zimmerns would have insisted on it as far as the canal," observed Fisher thoughtfully, "though everybody knows adding provinces doesn't always pay much nowadays."

Captain Boyle frowned in a slightly puzzled fashion. Being cloudily conscious of never having heard of the Zimmerns in his life, he could only remark stolidly:

"Well, one can't be a Little Englander."

Horne Fisher smiled; and he had a pleasant smile.

"Every man out here is a Little Englander," he said. "He wishes he were back in Little England."

"I don't know what you're talking about, I'm afraid," said the younger man rather suspiciously. "One would think you didn't really admire Hastings or—or anything."

"I admire him no end," replied Fisher. "He's by far the best man for this post; he understands the Moslems and can do anything with them. That's why I'm all against pushing Travers against him, merely because of this last affair."

"I really don't understand what you're driving at," said the other frankly.

"Perhaps it isn't worth understanding," answered Fisher lightly, "and, anyhow, we needn't talk politics. Do you know the Arab legend about that well?"

"I'm afraid I don't know much about Arab legends," said Boyle rather stiffly.

The Man Who Knew Too Much

"That's rather a mistake," replied Fisher, "especially from your point of view. Lord Hastings himself is an Arab legend. That is perhaps the very greatest thing he really is. If his reputation went, it would weaken us all over Asia and Africa. Well, the story about that hole in the ground, that goes down nobody knows where, has always fascinated me rather. It's Mahomedan in form now; but I shouldn't wonder if the tale is a long way older than Mahomet. It's all about somebody they call the Sultan Aladin; not our friend of the lamp, of course, but rather like him in having to do with genii or giants or something of that sort. They say he commanded the giants to build him a sort of pagoda rising higher and higher above all the stars. The Utmost for the Highest, as the people said when they built the Tower of Babel. But the builders of the Tower of Babel were quite modest and domestic people, like mice, compared with old Aladin. They only wanted a tower that would reach heaven, a mere trifle. He wanted a tower that would *pass* heaven, and rise above it, and go on rising for ever and ever. And Allah cast him down to earth with a thunderbolt, which sank into the earth, boring a hole deeper and deeper, till it made a well that was without a bottom as the tower was to have been without a top. And down that inverted tower of darkness the soul of the proud Sultan is falling for ever and ever."

"What a queer chap you are," said Boyle, "you talk as if a fellow could believe those fables."

"Perhaps I believe the moral and not the fable," answered Fisher, "but here comes Lady Hastings. You know her, I think?"

The club house on the golf links was used, of course, for many other purposes besides that of golf. It was the only social centre of the garrison besides the strictly military headquarters; it had a billiard-room and a bar, and even an excellent reference library for those officers who were so perverse as to take their profession seriously. Among these was the great general himself, whose head of silver and face of bronze, like that of a brazen eagle, were often to be found bent over the charts and folios of the library. The great Lord Hastings believed in

The Bottomless Well

science and study, as in other severe ideals of life; and had given much paternal advice on the point to young Boyle, whose appearances in that place of research were rather more intermittent. It was from one of these snatches of study that the young man had just come out through the glass doors of the library on to the golf links. But above all the club was so appointed as to serve the social conveniences of ladies at least as much as gentlemen; and Lady Hastings was able to play the queen in such a society almost as much as in her own ballroom. She was eminently calculated, and, as some said, eminently inclined to play such a part. She was much younger than her husband; an attractive and sometimes dangerously attractive lady; and Mr. Horne Fisher looked after her, a little sardonically, as she swept away with the young soldier. Then his rather dreary eye strayed to the green and prickly growths round the well; growths of that curious cactus formation in which one thick leaf grows directly out of the other without stalk or twig. It gave his fanciful mind a sinister feeling of a blind growth without shape or purpose. A flower or shrub in the West grows to the blossom which is its crown, and is content. But this was as if hands could grow out of hands or legs grow out of legs in a nightmare. "Always adding a province to the Empire," he said with a smile; and then added more sadly: "But I doubt if I was right after all."

A strong but genial voice broke in on his meditations; and he looked up and smiled, seeing the face of an old friend. The voice was indeed rather more genial than the face, which was at the first glance decidedly grim. It was a typically legal face, with angular jaws and heavy grizzled eyebrows; and it belonged to an eminently legal character, though he was now attached in a semi-military capacity to the police of that wild district. Cuthbert Grayne was perhaps more of a criminologist than either a lawyer or a policeman; but in his more barbarous surroundings he had proved successful in turning himself into a practical combination of all three. The discovery of a whole series of strange Oriental crimes stood to his credit; but as few people were acquainted with, or

The Man Who Knew Too Much

attracted to, such a hobby or branch of knowledge, his intellectual life was somewhat solitary. Among the few exceptions was Horne Fisher, who had a curious capacity for talking to almost anybody about almost anything.

"Studying botany, or is it archæology?" inquired Grayne. "I shall never come to the end of your interests, Fisher. I should say that what you don't know isn't worth knowing."

"You are wrong," replied Fisher with a very unusual abruptness and even bitterness. "It's what I do know that isn't worth knowing. All the seamy side of things; all the secret reasons and rotten motives and bribery and blackmail they call politics. I needn't be so proud of having been down all these sewers that I should brag about it to the little boys in the street."

"What do you mean? What's the matter with you?" asked his friend. "I never knew you taken like this before."

"I'm ashamed of myself," replied Fisher. "I've just been throwing cold water on the enthusiasms of a boy."

"Even that explanation is hardly exhaustive," observed the criminal expert.

"Damned newspaper nonsense the enthusiasms were, of course," continued Fisher, "but I ought to know that at that age illusions can be ideals. And they're better than the reality, anyhow. But there is one very ugly responsibility about jolting a young man out of the rut of the most rotten ideal."

"And what may that be?"

"It's very apt to set him off with the same energy in a much worse direction," answered Fisher. "A pretty endless sort of direction—a bottomless pit, as deep as the Bottomless Well."

Fisher did not see his friend until a fortnight later, when he found himself in the garden at the back of the club house on the opposite side from the links—a garden heavily coloured and scented with semi-tropical plants in the glow of a desert sunset. Two other men were with him, the third being the now celebrated second in command, familiar to everybody as Tom Travers, a lean, dark man who looked older than his years, with a furrow in his

The Bottomless Well

brow and something morose about the very shape of his black moustache. They had just been served with black coffee by the Arab now officiating as the temporary servant of the club, though he was a figure already familiar, and even famous, as the old servant of the General. He went by the name of Said, and was notable among other Semites for that unnatural length of his yellow face and height of his narrow forehead which is sometimes seen among them, and gave an irrational impression of something sinister, in spite of his agreeable smile.

"I never feel as if I could quite trust that fellow," said Grayne, when the man had gone away. "It's very unjust, I take it, for he was certainly devoted to Hastings, and saved his life, they say. But Arabs are often like that—loyal to one man. I can't help feeling he might cut anybody else's throat, and even do it treacherously."

"Well," said Travers, with a rather sour smile, "so long as he leaves Hastings alone the world won't mind much."

There was a rather embarrassing silence, full of memories of the great battle, and then Horne Fisher said quietly:

"The newspapers aren't the world, Tom. Don't you worry about them. Everybody in your world knows the truth well enough."

"I think we'd better not talk about the General just now," remarked Grayne, "for he's just coming out of the club."

"He's not coming here," said Fisher "He's only seeing his wife to the car."

As he spoke, indeed, the lady came out on the steps of the club, followed by her husband, who then went swiftly in front of her to open the garden gate. As he did so she turned back and spoke for a moment to a solitary man still sitting in a cane chair in the shadow of the doorway, the only man left in the deserted club, save for the three that lingered in the garden. Fisher peered for a moment into the shadow and saw that it was Captain Boyle.

The next moment, rather to their surprise, the General

The Man Who Knew Too Much

reappeared, and remounting the steps, spoke a word or two to Boyle in his turn. Then he signalled to Said, who hurried up with two cups of coffee, and the two men re-entered the club, each carrying his cup in his hand. The next moment a gleam of white light in the growing darkness showed that the electric lamps had been turned on in the library beyond.

"Coffee and scientific researches," said Travers grimly. "All the luxuries of learning and theoretical research. Well, I must be going, for I have my work to do as well."

And he got up rather stiffly, saluted his companions and strode away into the dusk.

"I only hope Boyle *is* sticking to scientific researches," said Horne Fisher. "I'm not very comfortable about him myself. But let's talk about something else."

They talked about something else longer than they probably imagined, until the tropical night had come and a splendid moon painted the whole scene with silver; but before it was bright enough to see by, Fisher had already noted that the lights in the library had been abruptly extinguished. He waited for the two men to come out by the garden entrance, but nobody came.

"They must have gone for a stroll on the links," he said.

"Very possibly," replied Grayne. "It's going to be a beautiful night."

A moment or two after he had spoken they heard a voice hailing them out of the shadow of the club-house, and were astonished to perceive Travers hurrying towards them, calling out as he came:

"I shall want your help, you fellows," he cried. "There's something pretty bad out on the links."

They found themselves plunging through the club smoking-room and the library beyond in complete darkness, mental as well as material. But Horne Fisher, in spite of his affectation of indifference, was a person of a curious and almost transcendental sensibility to atmospheres, and he already felt the presence of something more than an accident. He collided with a piece of furniture in the library and almost shuddered with the shock;

The Bottomless Well

for the thing moved as he could never have fancied a piece of furniture moving. It seemed to move like a living thing, yielding and yet striking back. The next moment Grayne had turned on the lights; and he saw he had only stumbled against one of the revolving bookstands that had swung round and struck him; but his own involuntary recoil had revealed to him his own subconsciousness of something mysterious and monstrous. There were several of these revolving bookcases here and there about the library; on one of them stood the two cups of coffee, and on another a large open book. It was Budge's book on Egyptian hieroglyphics, with coloured plates of strange birds and gods; and even as he rushed past, he was conscious of something odd about the fact that this, and not any work of military science, should be open in that place at that moment. He was even conscious of the gap in the well-lined bookshelf from which it had been taken; and it seemed almost to gape at him in an ugly fashion, like a gap in the teeth of some sinister face.

A run brought them in a few minutes to the other side of the ground in front of the Bottomless Well; and a few yards from it, in a moonlight almost as broad as daylight, they saw what they had come to see.

The great Lord Hastings lay prone on his face, in a posture in which there was a touch of something strange and stiff, with one elbow erect above his body, the arm being doubled, and his big bony hand clutching the rank and ragged grass. A few feet away was Boyle, almost as motionless, but supported on his hands and knees, and staring at the body. It might have been no more than shock and accident; but there was something ungainly and unnatural about the quadrupedal posture and the gaping face. It was as if his reason had fled him. Behind there was nothing but the clear blue southern sky and the beginning of the desert, except for the two great broken stones in front of the well. And it was in such a light and atmosphere that men could fancy they traced in them enormous and evil faces, looking down.

Horne Fisher stooped and touched the strong hand that was still clutching the grass; and it was as cold as

The Man Who Knew Too Much

a stone. He knelt by the body and was busy for a moment applying other tests; then he rose again and said with a sort of confident despair: "Lord Hastings is dead."

There was a stony silence; and then Travers remarked gruffly: "This is your department, Grayne; I will leave you to question Captain Boyle. I can make no sense of what he says."

Boyle had pulled himself together and risen to his feet, but his face still wore an awful expression, making it like a new mask or the face of another man.

"I was looking at the well," he said, "and when I turned he had fallen down."

Grayne's face was very dark.

"As you say, this is my affair," he said. "I must first ask you to help me carry him to the library, and let me examine things thoroughly."

When they had deposited the body in the library, Grayne turned to Fisher, and said in a voice that had recovered its fullness and confidence: "I am going to lock myself in and make a thorough examination first. I look to you to keep in touch with the others, and make a preliminary examination of Boyle. I will talk to him later. And just telephone to headquarters for a policeman; and let him come here at once, and stand by till I want him."

Without more words, the great criminal investigator went into the lighted library, shutting the door behind him; and Fisher, without replying, turned and began to talk quietly to Travers.

"It is curious," he said, "that the thing should happen just in front of that place."

"It would certainly be very curious," replied Travers, "if the place played any part in it."

"I think," replied Fisher, "that the part it didn't play is more curious still."

And with these apparently meaningless words he turned to the shaken Boyle, and, taking his arm, began to walk him up and down in the moonlight, talking in low tones.

Dawn had begun to break abrupt and white when

The Bottomless Well

Cuthbert Grayne turned out the lights in the library and came out on to the links. Fisher was lounging about alone in his listless fashion; but the police messenger for whom he had sent was standing at attention in the background.

"I sent Boyle off with Travers," observed Fisher carelessly, "he'll look after him; and he'd better have some sleep, anyhow."

"Did you get anything out of him?" asked Grayne. "Did he tell you what he and Hastings were doing?"

"Yes," answered Fisher, "he gave me a pretty clear account after all. He said that after Lady Hastings went off in the car, the General asked him to take coffee with him in the library, and look up a point about local antiquities. He himself was beginning to look for Budge's book in one of the revolving bookstands, when the General found it in one of the book-shelves on the wall. After looking at some of the plates they went out, it would seem rather abruptly, on to the links and walked towards the old well; and while Boyle was looking into it, he heard a thud behind him and turned round to find the General lying as we found him. He himself dropped on his knees to examine the body, and then was paralysed with a sort of terror and could not come nearer to it or touch it. But I think very little of that; people caught in a shock of surprise are sometimes found in the queerest postures."

Grayne wore a grim smile of attention, and said after a short silence:

"Well, he hasn't told you many lies. It's really a creditably clear and consistent account of what happened, with everything of importance left out."

"Have you discovered anything in there?" asked Fisher.

"I have discovered everything," answered Grayne.

Fisher maintained a somewhat gloomy silence, as the other resumed his explanation in quiet and assured tones.

"You were quite right, Fisher, when you said that young fellow was in danger of going down dark ways towards the pit Whether or no, as you fancied, the jolt

The Man Who Knew Too Much

you gave to his view of the General had anything to do with it, he has not been treating the General well for some time. It's an unpleasant business, and I don't want to dwell on it, but it's pretty plain that his wife was not treating him well either. I don't know how far it went, but it went as far as concealment anyhow; for when Lady Hastings spoke to Boyle, it was to tell him she had hidden a note in the Budge book in the library. The General overheard, or came somehow to know, and he went straight to the book and found it. He confronted Boyle with it, and they had a scene, of course. And Boyle was confronted with something else; he was confronted with an awful alternative; in which the life of one old man meant ruin, and his death meant triumph and even happiness."

"Well," observed Fisher at last. "I don't blame him for not telling you the woman's part of the story. But how do you know about the letter?"

"I found it on the General's body," answered Grayne, "but I found worse things than that. The body had stiffened in the way rather peculiar to poisons of a certain Asiatic sort. Then I examined the coffee cups, and I knew enough chemistry to find poison in the dregs of one of them. Now the General went straight to the bookcase, leaving his cup of coffee on the book-stand in the middle of the room. While his back was turned and Boyle was pretending to examine the book-stand, he was left alone with the coffee cups. The poison takes about ten minutes to act; and ten minutes' walk would bring them to the Bottomless Well."

"Yes," remarked Horne Fisher, "and what about the Bottomless Well?"

"What has the Bottomless Well got to do with it?" asked his friend.

"It has nothing to do with it," replied Fisher. "That is what I find utterly confounding and incredible."

"And why should that particular hole in the ground have anything to do with it?"

"It is a particular hole in your case," said Fisher. "But I won't insist on that just now. By the way, there is another thing I ought to tell you. I said I sent Boyle

The Bottomless Well

away in charge of Travers. It would be just as true to say I sent Travers in charge of Boyle."

"You don't mean to say you suspect Tom Travers?" cried the other.

"He was a deal bitterer against the General than Boyle ever was," observed Horne Fisher, with a curious indifference.

"Man, you're not saying what you mean," cried Grayne. "I tell you I found the poison in one of the coffee cups."

"There was always Said, of course," added Fisher, "either for hatred or for hire. We agreed he was capable of almost anything."

"And we agreed he was incapable of hurting his master," retorted Grayne.

"Well, well," said Fisher amiably, "I dare say you are right, but I should just like to have a look at the library and the coffee cups."

He passed inside, while Grayne turned to the policeman in attendance and handed him a scribbled note to be telegraphed from headquarters. The man saluted and hurried off; and Grayne, following his friend into the library, found him beside the book-stand in the middle of the room, on which were the empty cups.

"This is where Boyle looked for Budge, or pretended to look for him, according to your account," he said.

As Fisher spoke he bent down in a half crouching attitude, to look at the volumes in the low revolving shelf; for the whole book-stand was not much higher than an ordinary table. The next moment he sprang up as if he had been stung.

"Oh, my God!" he cried.

Very few people, if any, had ever seen Mr. Horne Fisher behave as he behaved just then. He flashed a glance at the door, saw that the open window was nearer, went out of it with a flying leap as if over a hurdle, and went racing across the turf in the track of the disappearing policeman. Grayne, who stood staring after him, soon saw his tall, loose figure returning, restored to all its normal limpness and air of leisure. He was fanning

The Man Who Knew Too Much

himself slowly with a piece of paper: the telegram he had so violently intercepted.

"Lucky I stopped that," he observed. "We must keep this affair as quiet as death. Hastings must die of apoplexy or heart disease."

"What on earth is the trouble?" demanded the other investigator.

"The trouble is," said Fisher, "that in a few days we should have a very agreeable alternative: of hanging an innocent man or knocking the British Empire to hell."

"Do you mean to say," asked Grayne, "that this infernal crime is not to be punished?"

Fisher looked at him steadily.

"It is already punished," he said.

After a moment's pause he went on.

"You reconstructed the crime with admirable skill, old chap, and nearly all you said was true. Two men with two coffee cups did go into the library and did put their cups on the book-stand and did go together to the well, and one of them was a murderer and had put poison in the other's cup. But it was not done while Boyle was looking at the revolving bookcase. He did look at it, though, searching for the Budge book with the note in it; but I fancy that Hastings had already moved it to the shelves on the wall. It was part of that grim game that he should find it first.

"Now how does a man search a revolving bookcase? He does not generally hop all round it in a squatting attitude, like a frog. He simply gives it a touch and makes it revolve."

He was frowning at the floor as he spoke, and there was a light under his heavy lids that was not often seen there. The mysticism that was buried deep under all the cynicism of his experience was awake and moving in the depths. His voice took unexpected turns and inflexions, almost as if two men were speaking.

"That was what Boyle did; he barely touched the thing, and it went round as easily as the world goes round. Yes, very much as the world goes round; for the hand that turned it was not his. God, who turns the

The Bottomless Well

wheel of all the stars, touched that wheel and brought it full circle, that his dreadful justice might return."

"I am beginning," said Grayne slowly, "to have some hazy and horrible idea of what you mean."

"It is very simple," said Fisher. "When Boyle straightened himself from his stooping posture, something had happened which he had not noticed, which his enemy had not noticed, which nobody had noticed. The two coffee cups had exactly changed places."

The rocky face of Grayne seemed to have sustained a shock in silence; not a line of it altered, but his voice when it came was unexpectedly weakened.

"I see what you mean," he said, "and, as you say, the less said about it the better. It was not the lover who tried to get rid of the husband, but—the other thing. And a tale like that about a man like that would ruin us here. Had you any guess of this at the start?"

"The Bottomless Well, as I told you," answered Fisher quietly, "that was what stumped me from the start. Not because it had anything to do with it. Because it had nothing to do with it."

He paused a moment, as if choosing an approach, and then went on: "When a murderer knows his enemy will be dead in ten minutes, and takes him to the edge of an unfathomable pit, he means to throw his body into it. What else should he do? A born fool would have the sense to do it; and Boyle is not a born fool. Well, why did not Boyle do it? The more I thought of it the more I suspected there was some mistake in the murder, so to speak. Somebody had taken somebody there to throw him in; and yet he was not thrown in. I had already an ugly unformed idea of some substitution or reversal of parts; then I stooped to turn the bookstand myself, by accident, and I instantly knew everything; for I saw the two cups revolve once more, like moons in the sky."

After a pause Cuthbert Grayne said: "And what are we to say to the newspapers?"

"My friend Harold March is coming along from Cairo to-day," said Fisher. "He is a very brilliant and successful journalist. But for all that he's a thoroughly honourable man; so you must not tell him the truth."

The Man Who Knew Too Much

Half an hour later Fisher was again walking to and fro in front of the club house with Captain Boyle, the latter by this time with a very buffeted and bewildered air; perhaps a sadder and a wiser man.

"What about me, then?" he was saying. "Am I cleared? Aren't I going to be cleared?"

"I believe and hope," answered Fisher, "that you are not going to be suspected. But you are certainly not going to be cleared. There must be no suspicion against him, and therefore no suspicion against you. Any suspicion against him, let alone such a story against him, would knock us endways from Malta to Mandalay. He was a hero as well as a holy terror among the Moslems. Indeed, you might almost call him a Moslem hero in the English service. Of course he got on with them partly because of his own little dose of Eastern blood; he got it from his mother, the dancer from Damascus; everybody knows that."

"Oh," repeated Boyle mechanically, staring at him with round eyes. "Everybody knows that."

"I dare say there was a touch of it in his jealousy and ferocious vengeance," went on Fisher. "But for all that the crime would ruin us among the Arabs, all the more because it was something like a crime against hospitality. It's been hateful for you, and it's pretty horrid for me. But there are some things that damned well can't be done, and while I'm alive that's one of them."

"What do you mean?" asked Boyle, glancing at him curiously. "Why should you, of all people, be so passionate about it?"

Horne Fisher looked at the young man with a baffling expression.

"I suppose," he said, "it's because I'm a Little Englander."

"I can never make out what you mean by that sort of thing," answered Boyle doubtfully.

"Do you think Englind is so little as all that," said Fisher, with a warmth in his cold voice; "that it can't hold a man across a few thousand miles? You lectured me with a lot of ideal patriotism, my young friend; but it's practical patriotism now for you and me, and with no lies

The Bottomless Well

to help it. You talked as if everything went right with us, all over the world, in a triumphant crescendo culminating in Hastings. I tell you everything has gone wrong with us here, except Hastings. His was the one name we had left to conjure with; and that mustn't go as well; no, by God! It's bad enough that a gang of infernal Jews should plant us here, where there's no earthly English interest to serve, and all hell beating up against us, simply because Nosey Zimmern has lent money to half the Cabinet. It's bad enough that an old pawnbroker from Bagdad should make us fight his battles; we can't fight with our right hand cut off. Our one score was Hastings and his victory; which was really somebody else's victory. Tom Travers has to suffer, and so have you."

Then, after a moment's silence, he pointed towards the Bottomless Well and said in a quieter tone:

"I told you," he said, "that I didn't believe in the philosophy of the Tower of Aladdin. I don't believe in the Empire growing until it reaches the sky; I don't believe in the Union Jack going up and up eternally like the Tower. But if you think I am going to let the Union Jack go down and down eternally like the Bottomless Well, down into the blackness of the Bottomless Pit, down in defeat and derision amid the jeers of the very Jews who have sucked us dry—no, I won't, and that's flat; not if the Chancellor were blackmailed by twenty millionaires with their gutter rags, not if the Prime Minister married twenty Yankee Jewesses, not if Woodville and Carstairs had shares in twenty swindling mines. If the thing is really tottering, God help it, it mustn't be we who tip it over."

Boyle was regarding him with a bewilderment that was almost fear, and had even a touch of distaste.

"Somehow," he said, "there seems to be something rather horrid about the things you know."

"There is," replied Horne Fisher. "I am not at all pleased with my small stock of knowledge and reflection. But as it is partly responsible for your not being hanged, I don't know that you need complain of it."

And as if a little ashamed of his first boast, he turned and strolled away towards the Bottomless Well.

V.—THE HOLE IN THE WALL

Two men, the one an architect and the other an archæologist, met on the steps of the great house at Prior's Park; and their host, Lord Bulmer, in his breezy way, thought it natural to introduce them. It must be confessed that he was hazy as well as breezy, and had no very clear connexion in his mind, beyond the sense that an architect and an archæologist begin with the same series of letters. The world must remain in a reverent doubt as to whether he would, on the same principles, have presented a diplomatist to a dipsomaniac or a ratiocinator to a rat-catcher. He was a big, fair, bull-necked young man abounding in outward gestures, unconsciously flapping his gloves and flourishing his stick.

"You two ought to have something to talk about," he said cheerfully. "Old buildings and all that sort of thing; this is rather an old building, by the way, though I say it who shouldn't. I must ask you to excuse me a moment; I've got to go and see about the cards for this Christmas romp my sister's arranging. We hope to see you all there, of course. Juliet wants it to be a fancy-dress affair; abbots and crusaders and all that. My ancestors, I suppose, after all."

"I trust the abbot was not an ancestor," said the archæological gentleman with a smile.

"Only a sort of great-uncle, I imagine," answered the other, laughing. Then his rather rambling eye rolled round the ordered landscape in front of the house; an artificial sheet of water ornamented with an antiquated nymph in the centre and surrounded by a park of tall trees now grey and black and frosty, for it was in the depth of a severe winter.

"It's getting jolly cold," his lordship continued. "My sister hopes we shall have some skating as well as dancing."

The Hole in the Wall

"If the crusaders come in full armour," said the other, "you must be careful not to drown your ancestors."

"Oh, there's no fear of that," answered Bulmer; "this precious lake of ours is not two feet deep anywhere."

And with one of his flourishing gestures he stuck his stick into the water to demonstrate its shallowness. They could see the short end bent in the water; so that he seemed for a moment to lean his large weight on a breaking staff.

"The worst you can expect is to see an abbot sit down rather suddenly," he added, turning away. "Well, au revoir; I'll let you know about it later."

The archæologist and the architect were left on the great stone steps smiling at each other; but whatever their common interests, they presented a considerable personal contrast; and the fanciful might even have found some contradiction in each considered individually. The former, a Mr. James Haddow, came from a drowsy den in the Inns of Court, full of leather and parchment; for the law was his profession and history only his hobby; he was indeed, among other things, the solicitor and agent of the Prior's Park estate. But he himself was far from drowsy and seemed remarkably wide-awake, with shrewd and prominent blue eyes and red hair brushed as neatly as his very neat costume. The latter, whose name was Leonard Crane, came straight from a crude and almost cockney office of builders and house-agents in the neighbouring suburb, sunning itself at the end of a new row of jerry-built houses with plans in very bright colours and notices in very large letters. But a serious observer, at a second glance, might have seen in his eyes something of that shining sleep that is called vision; and his yellow hair, while not affectedly long, was unaffectedly tidy. It was a manifest if melancholy truth that the architect was an artist. But the artistic temperament was far from explaining him; there was something else about him that was not definable but which some even felt to be dangerous. Despite his dreaminess he would sometimes surprise his friends with arts and even sport apart from his ordinary life, like memories of some previous existence. On this occasion, never-

The Man Who Knew Too Much

theless, he hastened to disclaim any authority on the other man's hobby.

"I mustn't appear on false pretences," he said with a smile. "I hardly even know what an archæologist is; except that a rather rusty remnant of Greek suggests that he is a man who studies old things."

"Yes," replied Haddow grimly. "An archæologist is a man who studies old things and finds they are new."

Crane looked at him steadily for a moment and then smiled again.

"Dare one suggest," he said, "that some of the things we have been talking about are among the old things that turn out not to be old?"

His companion also was silent for a moment; and the smile on his rugged face was fainter as he replied quietly:

"The wall round the park is really old. The one gate in it is Gothic, and I cannot find any trace of destruction or restoration. But the house and the estate generally—well, the romantic ideas read into these things are often rather recent romances, things almost like fashionable novels. For instance, the very name of this place, Prior's Park, makes everybody think of it as a moonlit mediæval abbey; I dare say the spiritualists by this time have discovered the ghost of a monk there. But according to the only authoritative study of the matter I can find, the place was simply called Prior's as any rural place is called Podger's. It was the house of a Mr. Prior; a farmhouse probably, that stood here at some time or other and was a local landmark. Oh, there are a great many examples of the same thing, here and everywhere else. This suburb of ours used to be a village; and because some of the people slurred the name and pronounced it Holliwell, many a minor poet indulged in fancies about a Holy Well, with spells and fairies and all the rest of it, filling the suburban drawing-rooms with the Celtic twilight. Whereas anyone acquainted with the facts knows that 'Hollinwall' simply means 'the hole in the wall' and probably referred to some quite trivial accident. That's what I mean when I say that we don't so much find old things as we find new ones."

Crane seemed to have grown somewhat inattentive

The Hole in the Wall

to the little lecture on antiquities and novelties; and the cause of his restlessness was soon apparent and indeed approaching. Lord Bulmer's sister, Juliet Bray, was coming slowly across the lawn, accompanied by one gentleman and followed by two others. The young architect was in the illogical condition of mind in which he preferred three to one.

The man walking with the lady was no other than the eminent Prince Borodino, who was at least as famous as a distinguished diplomatist ought to be, in the interests of what is called secret diplomacy. He had been paying a round of visits at various English country houses; and exactly what he was doing for diplomacy at Prior's Park was as much a secret as any diplomatist could desire. The obvious thing to say of his appearance was that he would have been extremely handsome if he had not been entirely bald. But indeed that would itself be a rather bald way of putting it. Fantastic as it sounds, it would fit the case better to say that people would have been surprised to see hair growing on him; as surprised as if they had found hair growing on the bust of a Roman Emperor. His tall figure was buttoned up in a rather tight-waisted fashion that rather accentuated his potential bulk, and he wore a red flower in his button-hole. Of the two men walking behind one also was bald, but in a more partial and also a more premature fashion; for his dropping moustache was still yellow, and if his eyes were somewhat heavy it was with languor and not with age. His name was Horne Fisher; and he talked so easily and idly about everything, that nobody had ever discovered his favourite subject. His companion was a more striking and even more sinister figure; and he had the added importance of being Lord Bulmer's oldest and most intimate friend. He was generally known with a severe simplicity as Mr Brain; but it was understood that he had been a judge and police official in India; and that he had enemies, who had represented his measures against crime as themselves almost criminal. He was a brown skeleton of a man with dark, deep sunken eyes and a black moustache that hid the meaning of his mouth. Though he had the look of one wasted by some

The Man Who Knew Too Much

tropical disease, his movements were much more alert than those of his lounging companion.

"It's all settled," announced the lady with great animation when they came within hailing distance. "You've all got to put on masquerade things and very likely skates as well; though the Prince says they don't go with it; but we don't care about that. It's freezing already, and we don't often get such a chance in England."

"Even in India we don't exactly skate all the year round," observed Mr. Brain.

"And even Italy is not primarily associated with ice," said the Italian.

"Italy is primarily associated with ices," remarked Mr. Horne Fisher, "I mean with ice-cream men. Most people in this country imagine that Italy is entirely populated with ice-cream men and organ grinders. There certainly are a lot of them; perhaps they're an invading army in disguise."

"How do you know they are not the secret emissaries of our diplomacy?" asked the Prince with a slightly scornful smile. "An army of organ-grinders might pick up hints, and their monkeys might pick up all sorts of things."

"The organs are organized, in fact," said the flippant Mr. Fisher. "Well, I've known it pretty cold before now in Italy and even in India, up on the Himalayan slopes. The ice on our own little round pond will be quite cosy by comparison."

Juliet Bray was an attractive lady with dark hair and eyebrows and dancing eyes; and there was a geniality and even generosity in her rather imperious ways. In most matters she could command her brother; though that nobleman, like many other men of vague ideas, was not without a touch of the bully when he was at bay. She could certainly command her guests; even to the extent of decking out the most respectable and reluctant of them with her mediæval masquerade. And it really seemed as if she could command the elements also, like a witch. For the weather steadily hardened and sharpened; that night the ice of the lake, glimmering

The Hole in the Wall

in the moonlight, was like a marble floor; and they had begun to dance and skate on it before it was dark.

Prior's Park, or more properly the surrounding district of Hollinwall, was a country-seat that had become a suburb; having once had only a dependent village at its doors, it now found outside all its doors the signals of the expansion of London. Mr. Haddow, who was engaged in historical researches both in the library and the locality, could find little assistance in the latter. He had already gathered from the documents that Prior's Park had originally been something like Prior's Farm, named after some local figure; but the new social conditions were all against his tracing the story by its traditions. Had any of the real rustics remained, he would probably have found some lingering legend of Mr. Prior, however remote he might be. But the new nomadic population of clerks and artisans, constantly shifting their homes from one suburb to another, or their children from one school to another, could have no corporate continuity. They had all that forgetfulness of history that goes everywhere with the extension of education.

Nevertheless when he came out of the library next morning, and saw the wintry trees standing round the frozen pond like a black forest, he felt he might well have been far in the depths of the country. The old wall running round the park kept that enclosure itself still entirely rural and romantic; and one could easily imagine that the depths of that dark forest faded away indefinitely into distant vales and hills. The grey and black and silver of the wintry wood were all the more severe or sombre as a contrast to the coloured carnival groups that already stood on and around the frozen pool. For the house-party had already flung themselves impatiently into fancy-dress; and the lawyer, with his neat black suit and red hair, was the only modern figure left among them.

"Aren't you going to dress up?" asked Juliet indignantly, shaking at him a horned and towering blue head-dress of the fourteenth century which framed her face very becomingly, fantastic as it was. "Everybody here has to be in the Middle Ages. Even Mr. Brain has put on a sort of brown dressing-gown and says he's a monk;

The Man Who Knew Too Much

and Mr. Fisher got hold of some old potato-sacks in the kitchen and sewed them together; he's supposed to be a monk too. As to the Prince, he's perfectly glorious, in great crimson robes, as a cardinal. He looks as if he could poison everybody. You simply must be something."

"I will be something later in the day," he replied; "at present I am nothing but an antiquary and an attorney. I have to see your brother presently, about some legal business and also some local investigations he asked me to make. I must look a little like a steward when I give an account of my stewardship."

"Oh, but my brother has dressed up," cried the girl, "very much so. No end, if I may say so. Why, he's bearing down on you now in all his glory."

The noble lord was indeed marching towards them in a magnificent sixteenth-century costume of purple and gold, with a gold-hilted sword and a plumed cap, and manners to match. Indeed, there was something more than his usual expansiveness of bodily action in his appearance at that moment. It almost seemed, so to speak, that the plumes on his hat had gone to his head. He flapped his great gold-lined cloak like the wings of a fairy king in a pantomime; he even drew his sword with a flourish and waved it about as he did his walking-stick. In the light of after events there seemed to be something monstrous and ominous about that exuberance; something of the spirit that is called *fey*. At the time it merely crossed a few people's minds that he might possibly be drunk.

As he strode towards his sister, the first figure he passed was that of Leonard Crane, clad in Lincoln green with the horn and baldrick and sword appropriate to Robin Hood; for he was standing nearest to the lady, where indeed he might have been found during a disproportionate part of the time. He had displayed one of his buried talents in the matter of skating, and now that the skating was over seemed disposed to prolong the partnership. The boisterous Bulmer playfully made a pass at him with his drawn sword, going forward with the lunge in the proper fencing fashion, and making a

The Hole in the Wall

somewhat too familiar Shakespearean quotation about a rodent and a Venetian coin.

Probably in Crane also there was a subdued excitement just then; anyhow, in one flash he had drawn his own sword and parried; and then suddenly, to the surprise of everyone, Bulmer's weapon seemed to spring out of his hand into the air and rolled away on the ringing ice.

"Well, I never," said the lady, as if with justifiable indignation, "you never told me you could fence too."

Bulmer put up his sword with an air rather bewildered than annoyed, which increased the impression of something irresponsible in his mood at the moment; then he turned rather abruptly to his lawyer, saying: "We can settle up about the estate after dinner; I've missed nearly all the skating as it is; and I doubt if the ice will hold till to-morrow night. I think I shall get up early and have a spin by myself."

"You won't be disturbed with my company," said Horne Fisher in his weary fashion. "If I have to begin the day with ice, in the American fashion, I prefer it in smaller quantities. But no early hours for me in December. The early bird catches the cold."

"Oh, I shan't die of catching a cold," answered Bulmer, and laughed.

A considerable group of the skating party had consisted of the guests staying at the house; and the rest had tailed off in twos and threes some time before most of the guests began to retire for the night. Neighbours always invited to Prior's Park on such occasions went back to their own houses in motors or on foot; the legal and archæological gentleman had returned to the Inns of Court by a late train, to get a paper called for during his consultation with his client; and most of the other guests were drifting and lingering at various stages on their way up to bed. Horne Fisher, as if to deprive himself of any excuse for his refusal of early rising, had been the first to retire to his room; but, sleepy as he looked, he could not sleep. He had picked up from a table the book of antiquarian topography, in which Haddow had found his first hints about the origin of the local name; and being a man with a quiet and quaint

The Man Who Knew Too Much

capacity for being interested in anything, he began to read it steadily, making notes now and then of details on which his previous reading left him with a certain doubt about his present conclusions. His room was the one nearest to the lake in the centre of the woods, and was therefore the quietest; and none of the last echoes of the evening's festivity could reach him. He had followed carefully the argument which established the derivation from Mr. Prior's farm and the hole in the wall, and disposed of any fashionable fancy about monks and magic wells, when he began to be conscious of a noise audible in the frozen silence of the night. It was not a particularly loud noise; but it seemed to consist of a series of thuds or heavy blows, such as might be struck on a wooden door by a man seeking to enter. They were followed by something like a faint creak or crack, as if the obstacle had either been opened or had given way. He opened his own bedroom door and listened; but as he heard talk and laughter all over the lower floors, he had no reason to fear that a summons would be neglected or the house left without protection. He went to his open window, looking out over the frozen pond and the moonlit statue in the middle of their circle of darkling woods, and listened again. But silence had returned to that silent place; and after straining his ears for a considerable time he could hear nothing but the solitary hoot of a distant departing train. Then he reminded himself how many nameless noises can be heard by the wakeful during the most ordinary night; and, shrugging his shoulders, went wearily to bed.

He awoke suddenly and sat up in bed with his ears filled, as with thunder, with the throbbing echoes of a rending cry. He remained rigid for a moment, and then sprang out of bed, throwing on the loose gown of sacking he had worn all day. He went first to the window, which was open but covered with a thick curtain, so that his room was still completely dark; but when he tossed the curtain aside and put his head out, he saw that a grey and silver daybreak had already appeared behind the black woods that surrounded the little lake. And that

The Hole in the Wall

was all he did see. Though the sound had certainly come in through the open window from this direction, the whole scene was still and empty under the morning light as under the moonlight. Then the long, rather lackadaisical hand he had laid on a window-sill gripped it tighter as if to master a tremor, and his peering blue eyes grew bleak with fear. It may seem that his emotion was exaggerated and needless, considering the effort of common sense by which he had conquered his nervousness about the noise on the previous night. But that had been a very different sort of noise. It might have been made by half a hundred things, from the chopping of wood to the breaking of bottles. There was only one thing in nature from which could come the sound that echoed through that dark house at daybreak. It was the awful articulate voice of man; and it was something worse, for he knew what man.

He knew also that it had been a shout for help. It seemed to him that he had heard the very word; but the word, short as it was, had been swallowed up, as if the man had been stifled or snatched away even as he spoke. Only the mocking reverberations of it remained even in his memory; but he had no doubt of the original voice. He had no doubt that the great bull's voice of Francis Bray, Baron Bulmer, had been heard for the last time between the darkness and the lifting dawn.

How long he stood there he never knew; but he was startled into life by the first living thing that he saw stirring in that half-frozen landscape. Along the path beside the lake, and immediately under his window, a figure was walking slowly and softly but with great composure; a stately figure in robes of a splendid scarlet; it was the Italian Prince, still in his Cardinal's costume. Most of the company had indeed lived in their costumes for the last day or two, and Fisher himself had assumed his frock of sacking as a convenient dressing-gown; but there seemed nevertheless something unusually finished and formal, in the way of an early bird, about this magnificent red cockatoo. It was as if the early bird had been up all night.

"What is the matter?" he called sharply, leaning out

The Man Who Knew Too Much

of the window; and the Italian turned up his great yellow face like a mask of brass.

"We had better discuss it downstairs," said Prince Borodino.

Fisher ran downstairs, and encountered the great red-robed figure entering the doorway and blocking the entrance with his bulk.

"Did you hear that cry?" demanded Fisher.

"I heard a noise and I came out," answered the diplomatist, and his face was too dark in the shadow for its expression to be read.

"It was Bulmer's voice," insisted Fisher. "I'll swear it was Bulmer's voice."

"Did you know him well?" asked the other.

The question seemed irrelevant though it was not illogical; and Fisher could only answer in a random fashion that he only knew Lord Bulmer slightly.

"Nobody seems to have known him well," continued the Italian in level tones. "Nobody except that man Brain. Brain is rather older than Bulmer, but I fancy they shared a good many secrets."

Fisher moved abruptly, as if waking from a momentary trance, and said in a new and more vigorous voice: "But look here, hadn't we better get outside and see if anything has happened."

"The ice seems to be thawing," said the other, almost with indifference.

When they emerged from the house, dark stains and stars in the grey field of ice did indeed indicate that the frost was breaking up, as their host had prophesied the day before; and the very memory of yesterday brought back the mystery of to-day.

"He knew there would be a thaw," observed the Prince. "He went out skating quite early on purpose. Did he call out because he landed in the water, do you think?"

Fisher looked puzzled.

"Bulmer was the last man to bellow like that because he got his boots wet. And that's all he could do here; the water would hardly come up to the calf of a man of his size. You can see the flat weeds on the floor of

The Hole in the Wall

the lake as if it were through a thin pane of glass. No, if Bulmer had only broken the ice he wouldn't have said much at the moment, though possibly a good deal afterwards. We should have found him stamping and damning up and down this path, and calling for clean boots."

"Let us hope we shall find him as happily employed," remarked the diplomatist. "In that case the voice must have come out of the wood."

"I'll swear it didn't come out of the house," said Fisher; and the two disappeared together into the twilight of wintry trees.

The plantation stood dark against the fiery colours of sunrise; a black fringe having that feathery appearance which makes trees when they are bare the very reverse of rugged. Hours and hours afterwards, when the same dense but delicate margin was dark against the cool greenish colours opposite the sunset, the search thus begun at sunrise had not come to an end. By successive stages, and to slowly gathering groups of the company, it became apparent that the most extraordinary of all gaps had appeared in the party; the guests could find no trace of their host anywhere. The servants reported that his bed had been slept in and his skates and his fancy costume were gone, as if he had risen early for the purpose he had himself avowed. But from the top of the house to the bottom, from the walls round the park to the pond in the centre, there was no trace of Lord Bulmer, dead or alive. Horne Fisher realized that a chilling premonition had already prevented him from expecting to find the man alive. But his bald brow was wrinkled over an entirely new and unnatural problem in not finding the man at all.

He considered the possibility of Bulmer having gone off on his own accord, for some reason; but after fully weighing it he finally dismissed it. It was inconsistent with the unmistakable voice heard at daybreak, and with many other practical obstacles. There was only one gateway in the ancient and lofty wall round the small park; the lodge-keeper kept it locked till late in the morning, and the lodge-keeper had seen no one pass. Fisher was fairly sure that he had before him a mathematical

The Man Who Knew Too Much

problem in an enclosed space. His instinct had been from the first so attuned to the tragedy that it would have been almost a relief to him to find the corpse. He would have been grieved, but not horrified, to come on the nobleman's body dangling from one of his own trees as from a gibbet, or floating in his own pool like a pallid weed. What horrified him was to find nothing.

He soon became conscious that he was not alone even in his most individual and isolated experiments. He often found a figure following him like his shadow, in silent and almost secret clearings in the plantation or outlying nooks and corners of the old wall. The dark-moustached mouth was as mute as the deep eyes were mobile, darting incessantly hither and thither, but it was clear that Brain of the Indian police had taken up the trail like an old hunter after a tiger. Seeing that he was the only personal friend of the vanished man, this seemed natural enough; and Fisher resolved to deal frankly with him.

"This silence is rather a social strain," he said. "May I break the ice by talking about the weather; which, by the way, has already broken the ice? I know that breaking the ice might be a rather melancholy metaphor in this case."

"I don't think so," replied Brain shortly. "I don't fancy the ice had much to do with it. I don't see how it could."

"What would you propose doing?" asked Fisher.

"Well, we've sent for the authorities, of course, but I hope to find something out before they come," replied the Anglo-Indian. "I can't say I have much hope from police methods in this country. Too much red tape: Habeas Corpus and that sort of thing. What we want is to see that nobody bolts; the nearest we could get to it would be to collect the company and count them, so to speak. Nobody's left lately, except that lawyer who was poking about for antiquities."

"Oh, he's out of it; he left last night," answered the other. "Eight hours after Bulmer's chauffeur saw his lawyer off by the train, I heard Bulmer's own voice as plain as I hear yours now."

"I suppose you don't believe in spirits?" said the

The Hole in the Wall

man from India. After a pause he added: "There's somebody else I should like to find, before we go after a fellow with an alibi in the Inner Temple. What's become of that fellow in green; the architect dressed up as a forester? I haven't seen him about."

Mr. Brain managed to secure his assembly of all the distracted company before the arrival of the police. But when he first began to comment once more on the young architect's delay in putting in an appearance, he found himself in the presence of a minor mystery, and a psychological development of an entirely unexpected kind.

Juliet Bray had confronted the catastrophe of her brother's disappearance with a sombre stoicism in which there was perhaps more paralysis than pain; but when the other question came to the surface she was both agitated and angry.

"We don't want to jump to any conclusions about anybody," Brain was saying in his staccato style, "but we should like to know a little more about Mr. Crane. Nobody seems to know much about him or where he comes from. And it seems a sort of coincidence that yesterday he actually crossed swords with poor Bulmer, and could have stuck him too, since he showed himself the better swordsman. Of course, that may be an accident, and couldn't possibly be called a case against anybody; but then we haven't the means to make a real case against anybody. Till the police come we are only a pack of very amateur sleuth-hounds."

"And I think you're a pack of snobs," said Juliet. "Because Mr. Crane is a genius who's made his own way, you try to suggest he's a murderer without daring to say so. Because he wore a toy sword, and happened to know how to use it, you want us to believe he used it like a blood-thirsty maniac for no reason in the world. And because he could have hit my brother and didn't, you deduce that he did. That's the sort of way you argue. And as for his having disappeared, you're wrong in that as you are in everything else, for here he comes."

And, indeed, the green figure of the fictitious Robin Hood slowly detached itself from the grey background of the trees and came towards them as she spoke.

The Man Who Knew Too Much

He approached the group slowly, but with composure; but he was decidedly pale, and the eyes of Brain and Fisher had already taken in one detail of the green-clad figure more clearly than all the rest. The horn still swung from his baldrick, but the sword was gone.

Rather to the surprise of the company, Brain did not follow up the question thus suggested, but, while retaining an air of leading the inquiry, had also an appearance of changing the subject.

"Now we're all assembled," he observed quietly, "there is a question I want to ask to begin with. Did anybody here actually see Lord Bulmer this morning?"

Leonard Crane turned his pale face round the circle of faces till he came to Juliet's; then he compressed his lips a little and said: "Yes, I saw him."

"Was he alive and well?" asked Brain quickly. "How was he dressed?"

"He appeared exceedingly well," replied Crane, with a curious intonation. "He was dressed as he was yesterday, in that purple costume copied from the portrait of his ancestor in the sixteenth century. He had his skates in his hand."

"And his sword at his side, I suppose," added the questioner. "Where is your own sword, Mr. Crane?"

"I threw it away."

In the singular silence that ensued the train of thought in many minds became involuntarily a series of coloured pictures. They had grown used to their fanciful garments looking more gay and gorgeous against the dark grey and streaky silver of the frost, so that the moving figures glowed like stained-glass saints walking. The effect had been more fitting because so many of them had idly parodied pontifical or monastic dress. But the most arresting attitude that remained in their memories had been anything but merely monastic: that of the moment when the figure in bright green and the other in vivid violet had for a moment made a silver cross of their crossing swords. Even when it was a jest it had been something of a drama; and it was a strange and sinister thought that, in the grey daybreak, the same figures in the same posture might have been repeated as a tragedy,

The Hole in the Wall

"Did you quarrel with him?" asked Brain suddenly.

"Yes," replied the immovable man in green. "Or he quarrelled with me."

"Why did he quarrel with you?" asked the investigator; and Leonard Crane made no reply.

Horne Fisher, curiously enough, had only given half his attention to this crucial cross-examination. His heavy-lidded eyes had languidly followed the figure of Prince Borodino, who at this stage had strolled away towards the fringe of the wood and, after a pause as of meditation, had disappeared into the darkness of the trees.

He was recalled from his irrelevance by the voice of Juliet Bray, which rang out with an altogether new note of decision:

"If that is the difficulty, it had best be cleared up. I am engaged to Mr. Crane; and when we told my brother, he did not approve of it, that is all."

Neither Brain nor Fisher exhibited any surprise, but the former added quietly:

"Except, I suppose, that he and your brother went off into the wood to discuss it—where Mr. Crane mislaid his sword, not to mention his companion."

"And may I ask," inquired Crane, with a certain flicker of mockery passing over his pallid features, "what I am supposed to have done with either of them? Let us adopt the cheerful thesis that I am a murderer. It has yet to be shown that I am a magician. If I ran your unfortunate friend through the body, what did I do with the body? Did I have it carried away by seven flying dragons, or was it merely a trifling matter of turning it into a milk-white hind?"

"It is no occasion for sneering," said the Anglo-Indian judge with abrupt authority. "It doesn't make it look better for you that you can joke about the loss."

Fisher's dreamy and even dreary eye was still on the edge of the wood behind, and he became conscious of masses of dark red, like a stormy sunset cloud, glowing through the grey network of the thin trees; and the Prince, in his cardinal's robes, re-emerged on to the pathway. Brain had had half a notion that the Prince might have gone to look for the lost rapier, but when he re-

The Man Who Knew Too Much

appeared he was carrying in his hand, not a sword, but an axe.

The incongruity between the masquerade and the mystery had created a curious psychological atmosphere. At first they had all felt horribly ashamed at being caught in the foolish disguises of a festival by an event that had only too much the character of a funeral. Many of them would have already gone back and dressed in clothes that were more funereal, or at least more formal. But somehow at the moment this seemed like a second masquerade, more artificial and frivolous than the first. And as they reconciled themselves to their ridiculous trappings a curious sensation had come over some of them, notably over the more sensitive, like Crane and Fisher and Juliet, but in some degree over everybody except the practical Mr. Brain. It was almost as if they were the ghosts of their own ancestors haunting that dark wood and dismal lake, and playing some old part that they only half remembered. The movements of those coloured figures seemed to mean something that had been settled long before, like a silent heraldry. Acts, attitudes, external objects, were accepted as an allegory even without the key; and they knew when a crisis had come, when they did not know what it was. And somehow they knew subconsciously that the whole tale had taken a new and terrible turn when they saw the Prince stand in the gap of the gaunt trees, in his robes of angry crimson and with his lowering face of bronze, bearing in his hand a new shape of death. They could not have named a reason; but the two swords seemed indeed to have become toy swords, and the whole tale of them broken and tossed away like a toy. Borodino looked like the old-world headsman, clad in terrible red, and carrying the axe for the execution of the criminal. And the criminal was not Crane.

Mr. Brain, of the Indian police, was glaring at the new object, and it was a moment or two before he spoke, harshly and almost hoarsely.

"What are you doing with that?" he asked. "Seems to be a woodman's chopper."

"A natural association of ideas," observed Horne

The Hole in the Wall

Fisher. "If you meet a cat in a wood, you think it's a wild cat, though it may have just strolled from the drawing-room sofa. As a matter of fact, I happen to know that is not the woodman's chopper. It's the kitchen chopper, or meat axe or something like that, that somebody has thrown away in the wood. I saw it in the kitchen myself when I was getting the potato sacks with which I reconstructed a mediæval hermit."

"All the same, it is not without interest," remarked the Prince, holding out the instrument to Fisher, who took it and examined it carefully. "A butcher's cleaver that has done butcher's work."

"It was certainly the instrument of the crime," assented Fisher in a low voice.

Brain was staring at the dull blue gleam of the axe-head with fierce and fascinated eyes.

"I don't understand you," he said; "there is no—there are no marks on it."

"It has shed no blood," answered Fisher, "but for all that it has committed a crime. This is as near as the criminal came to the crime when he committed it."

"What do you mean?"

"He was not there when he did it," explained Fisher. "It's a poor sort of murderer who can't murder people when he isn't there."

"You seem to be talking merely for the sake of mystification," said Brain. "If you have any practical advice to give, you might as well make it intelligible."

"The only practical advice I can suggest," said Fisher thoughtfully, "is a little research into local topography and nomenclature. They say there used to be a Mr. Prior, who had a farm in this neighbourhood. I think some details about the domestic life of the late Mr. Prior would throw a light on this terrible business."

"And you have nothing more immediate than your topography to offer," said Brain, with a sneer, "to help me to avenge my friend."

"Well," said Fisher, "I should find out the truth about the Hole in the Wall."

That night, at the close of a stormy twilight and under a strong west wind that followed the breaking of the

The Man Who Knew Too Much

frost, Leonard Crane was wending his way in a wild rotatory walk round and round the high continuous wall that enclosed the little wood. He was driven by a desperate idea of solving for himself the riddle that had clouded his reputation and already even threatened his liberty. The police authorities, now in charge of the inquiry, had not arrested him; but he knew well enough that if he tried to move far afield he would be instantly arrested. Horne Fisher's fragmentary hints, though he had refused to expand them as yet, had stirred the artistic temperament of the architect to a sort of wild analysis, and he was resolved to read the hieroglyph upside down and every way until it made sense. If it was something connected with a hole in the wall, he would find the hole in the wall; but as a matter of fact he was unable to find the faintest crack in the wall. His professional knowledge told him that the masonry was all of one workmanship and one date; and except for the regular entrance, which threw no light on the mystery, he found nothing suggesting any sort of hiding-place or means of escape. Walking a narrow path between the windy wall and the wild eastward bend and sweep of the grey and feathery trees, seeing shifting gleams of a lost sunset winking almost like lightning as the clouds of tempest scudded across the sky and mingling with the first faint blue light from a slowly strengthened moon behind him, he began to feel his head going round as his heels were going round and round the blind recurrent barrier. He had thoughts on the border of thought, fancies about a fourth dimension which was itself a hole to hide anything, of seeing everything from a new angle out of a new window in the senses, or of some mystical light and transparency, like the new rays of chemistry, in which he could see Bulmer's body, horrible and glaring, floating in a lurid halo over the woods and the wall. He was haunted also with the hint, which somehow seemed to be equally horrifying, that it all had something to do with Mr. Prior. There seemed even to be something creepy in the fact that he was always respectfully referred to as Mr. Prior, and that it was in the domestic life of the dead farmer that he had been bidden to seek the seed of these dreadful

The Hole in the Wall

things. As a matter of fact, he had found that no local inquiries had revealed anything at all about the Prior family. He dimly imagined Mr. Prior in an old top-hat, perhaps with a chin-beard or whiskers. But he had no face.

The moonlight had broadened and brightened, the wind had driven off the clouds and itself died fitfully away, when he came round again to the artificial lake in front of the house. For some reason it looked a very artificial lake; indeed, the whole scene was like a classical landscape with a touch of Watteau; the Palladian façade of the house pale in the moon, and the same silver touching the very pagan and naked marble nymph in the middle of the pond. Rather to his surprise he found another figure there beside the statue, sitting almost equally motionless; and the same silver pencil traced the wrinkled brow and patient face of Horne Fisher, still dressed as a hermit, and apparently practising something of the solitude of a hermit. Nevertheless he looked up at Leonard Crane and smiled, almost as if he had expected him.

"Look here," said Crane, planting himself in front of him. "Can you tell me anything about this business?"

"I shall soon have to tell everybody everything about it," replied Fisher, "but I've no objection to telling you something first. But, to begin with, will you tell me something? What really happened when you met Bulmer this morning? You did throw away your sword, but you didn't kill him."

"I didn't kill him because I threw away my sword," said the other. "I did it on purpose, or I'm not sure what might have happened."

After a pause he went on quietly:

"The late Lord Bulmer was a very breezy gentleman, extremely breezy. He was very genial with his inferiors, and would have his lawyer and his architect staying in his house for all sorts of holidays and amusements. But there was another side to him, which they found out when they tried to be his equals. When I told him that his sister and I were engaged, something happened which I simply can't and won't describe. It seemed to me like some monstrous upheaval of madness. But I suppose the

93

The Man Who Knew Too Much

truth is painfully simple. There is such a thing as the coarseness of a gentleman. And it is the most horrible thing in humanity."

"I know," said Fisher. "The Renascence nobles of the Tudor time were like that."

"It is odd that you should say that," Crane went on, " for while we were talking there came on me a curious feeling that we were repeating some scene of the past, and that I was really some outlaw, found in the woods like Robin Hood, and that he had really stepped, in all his plumes and purple, out of the picture-frame of the ancestral portrait. Anyhow, he was the man in possession, and he neither feared God nor regarded man. I defied him, of course, and walked away. I might really have killed him if I had not walked away."

"Yes," said Fisher, nodding, "his ancestor was in possession and he was in possession; and this is the end of the story. It all fits in."

"Fits in with what?" cried his companion, with sudden impatience; "I can't make head or tail of it. You tell me to look for the secret in the hole in the wall, but I can't find any hole in the wall."

"There isn't any," said Fisher. "That's the secret."

After reflecting a moment, he added:

"Unless you call it a hole in the wall of the world Look here, I'll tell you, if you like, but I'm afraid it involves an introduction. You've got to understand one of the tricks of the modern mind, a tendency that most people obey without noticing it.

"In the village or suburb outside there's an inn with the sign of St. George and the Dragon. Now suppose I went about telling everybody that this was only a corruption of King George and the Dragoon. Scores of people would believe it, without any inquiry, from a vague feeling that it's probable because it's prosaic. It turns something romantic and legendary into something recent and ordinary. And that somehow makes it sound rational, though it is unsupported by reason. Of course, some people would have the sense to remember having seen St. George in old Italian pictures and French romances; but a good many wouldn't think about it at all. They would

The Hole in the Wall

just swallow the scepticism because it was scepticism. Modern intelligence won't accept anything on authority. But it will accept anything without authority. That's exactly what has happened here.

"When some critic or other chose to say that Prior's Park was not a priory, but was named after some quite modern man named Prior, nobody really tested the theory at all. It never occurred to anybody repeating the story to ask if there *was* any Mr. Prior, if anybody had ever seen him or heard of him. As a matter of fact, it was a priory, and shared the fate of most priories; that is, the Tudor gentleman with the plumes simply stole it by brute force and turned it into his own private house; he did worse things, as you shall hear. But the point here is that this is how the trick works; and the trick works in the same way in the other part of the tale. The name of this district is printed Holinwall in all the best maps produced by the scholars, and they allude lightly, not without a smile, to the fact that it was pronounced Holiwell by the most ignorant and old-fashioned of the poor. But it is spelt wrong and pronounced right."

"Do you mean to say," asked Crane quickly, "that there really was a well?"

"There is a well," said Fisher, "and the truth lies at the bottom of it."

As he spoke he stretched out his hand and pointed towards a sheet of water in front of him.

"The well is under that water somewhere," he said, "and this is not the first tragedy connected with it. The founder of this house did something which his fellow-ruffians very seldom did, something that had to be hushed up even in the anarchy of the pillage of the monasteries. The well was connected with the miracles of some saint, and the last prior that guarded it was something like a saint himself; certainly he was something very like a martyr. He defied the new owner and dared him to pollute the place, till the noble, in a fury, stabbed him and flung his body into the well; whither after four hundred years it has been followed by an heir of the usurper, clad in the same purple and walking the world with the same pride."

The Man Who Knew Too Much

"But how did it happen," demanded Crane, "that for the first time Bulmer fell in at that particular spot?"

"Because the ice was only loosened at that particular spot by the only man who knew it," answered Horne Fisher. "It was cracked deliberately with the kitchen chopper at that special place, and I myself heard the hammering and did not understand it. The place had been covered with an artificial lake, if only because the whole truth had to be covered with an artificial legend. But don't you see that it is exactly what those pagan nobles would have done, to desecrate it with a sort of heathen goddess, as the Roman Emperor built a temple to Venus on the Holy Sepulchre? But the truth could still be traced out by any scholarly man determined to trace it. And this man was determined to trace it."

"What man?" asked the other, with a shadow of the answer in his mind.

"The only man who has an alibi," replied Fisher. "James Haddow, the antiquarian lawyer, left the night before the fatality, but he left that black star of death on the ice. He left abruptly, having previously proposed to stay; probably, I think, after an ugly scene with Bulmer at their legal interview. As you know yourself, Bulmer could make a man feel pretty murderous; and I rather fancy the lawyer had himself irregularities to confess, and was in danger of exposure by his client. But it's my reading of human nature that a man will cheat in his trade but not in his hobby. Haddow may have been a dishonest lawyer, but he couldn't help being an honest antiquary. When he got on the track of the truth about the Holy Well, he had to follow it up; he was not to be bamboozled with newspaper anecdotes about Mr. Prior and a hole in the wall; he found out everything, even to the exact location of the well, and he was rewarded, if being a successful assassin can be regarded as a reward."

"And how did you get on the track of all this hidden history?" asked the young architect.

A cloud came across the brow of Horne Fisher.

"I knew only too much about it already," he said, "and, after all, it's shameful for me to be speaking lightly of poor Bulmer, who has paid his penalty, when the rest

The Hole in the Wall

of us haven't. I dare say every cigar I smoke and every liqueur I drink comes directly or indirectly from the harrying of the holy places and the persecution of the poor. After all, it needs very little poking about in the past to find that hole in the wall; that great breach in the defences of English history. It lies just under the surface of a thin sheet of sham information and instruction, just as the black and bloodstained well lies just under the floor of shallow water and flat weeds. Oh, the ice is thin, but it bears; it is strong enough to support us when we dress up as monks and dance on it in mockery of the dear quaint old Middle Ages. They told me I must put on fancy dress; so I did put on fancy dress, according to my own taste and fancy. You see I do know a little about our national and imperial history, our prosperity and our progress, our commerce and our colonies, our centuries of success or splendour. So I did put on an antiquated sort of costume, when I was asked to do so. I put on the only costume I think fit for a man who has inherited the position of a gentleman and yet has not entirely lost the feelings of one."

In answer to a look of inquiry he rose with a sweeping and downward gesture.

"Sackcloth," he said, "and I would wear the ashes as well, if they would stay on my bald head when I put them there."

VI.—THE FAD OF THE FISHERMAN

A THING can sometimes be too extraordinary to be remembered. If it is clean out of the course of things, and has apparently no causes and no consequences, subsequent events do not recall it; and it remains only a subconscious thing, to be stirred by some accident long after. It drifts apart like a forgotten dream; and it was in the hour of many dreams, at daybreak and very soon after the end of dark, that such a strange sight was given to a man sculling a boat down a river in the West Country. The man was awake; indeed, he considered himself rather wide awake, being a rising political journalist named Harold March, on his way to interview various political celebrities in their country seats. But the thing he saw was so inconsequent that it might have been imaginary. It simply slipped past his mind and was lost in later and utterly different events; nor did he even recover the memory, till he had long afterwards discovered the meaning.

Pale mists of morning lay on the fields and the rushes along one margin of the river; along the other side ran a wall of dark red brick almost overhanging the water. He had shipped his oars and was drifting for a moment with the stream, when he turned his head and saw that the monotony of the long brick wall was broken by a bridge; rather an elegant, eighteenth century sort of bridge, with little columns of white stone turning grey. There had been floods and the river still stood very high, with dwarfish trees waist deep in it, and rather a narrow arc of white dawn gleamed under the curve of the bridge.

As his own boat went under the dark archway he saw another boat coming towards him, rowed by a man as solitary as himself. His posture prevented much being seen of him; but as he neared the bridge he stood up in the boat and turned round. He was already so close

The Fad of the Fisherman

to the dark entry, however, that his whole figure was black against the morning light; and March could see nothing of his face except the ends of two long whiskers or moustaches that gave something sinister to the silhouette, like horns in the wrong place. Even these details March would never have noticed but for what happened in the same instant. As the man came under the low bridge he made a leap at it and hung, with his legs dangling, letting the boat float away from under him. March had a momentary vision of two black kicking legs; then of one black kicking leg, and then of nothing except the eddying stream and the long perspective of the wall. But whenever he thought of it again, long afterwards when he understood the story in which it figured, it was always fixed in that one fantastic shape; as if those wild legs were a grotesque graven ornament of the bridge itself, in the manner of a gargoyle. At the moment he merely passed staring down the stream. He could see no flying figure on the bridge, so it must have already fled; but he was half conscious of some faint significance in the fact that among the trees round the bridge-head opposite the wall he saw a lamp-post, and, beside the lamp-post, the broad blue back of an unconscious policeman.

Even before reaching the shrine of his political pilgrimage he had many other things to think of besides the odd incident of the bridge; for the management of a boat by a solitary man was not always easy even on such a solitary stream. And, indeed, it was only by an unforeseen accident that he was solitary. The boat had been purchased and the whole expedition planned in conjunction with a friend, who had at the last moment been forced to alter all his arrangements. Harold March was to have travelled with his friend Horne Fisher on that inland voyage to Willowood Place, where the Prime Minister was a guest at the moment. More and more people were hearing of Harold March; for his striking political articles were opening to him the doors of larger and larger salons; but he had never met the Prime Minister yet. Scarcely anybody among the general public had ever heard of Horne Fisher; but he had known the

The Man Who Knew Too Much

Prime Minister all his life. For these reasons, had the two taken the projected journey together, March might have been slightly disposed to hasten it and Fisher vaguely content to lengthen it out. For Fisher was one of those people who are born knowing the Prime Minister. The knowledge seemed to have no very exhilarant effect; and in his case bore some resemblance to being born tired. Horne Fisher was a tall, pale, fair man, with a bald brow and a listless manner; and it was seldom that he expressed irritation in any warmer form than that of weariness. But he was distinctly annoyed to receive, just as he was doing a little light packing of fishing tackle and cigars for the journey, a telegram from Willowood asking him to come down at once by train, as the Prime Minister had to leave that night. Fisher knew that his friend the journalist could not possibly start till the next day; and he liked his friend the journalist, and had looked forward to a few days on the river. He did not particularly like or dislike the Prime Minister; but he intensely disliked the alternative of a few hours in the train. Nevertheless, he accepted Prime Ministers as he accepted railway trains; as part of a system which he at least was not the revolutionist sent on earth to destroy. So he telephoned to March asking him, with many apologetic curses and faint damns, to take the boat down the river as arranged, that they might meet at Willowood by the time appointed. Then he went outside and hailed a taxicab to take him to the railway station. There he paused at the bookstall to add to his light luggage a number of cheap murder stories, which he read with great pleasure, and without any premonition that he was about to walk into as strange a story in real life.

A little before sunset he arrived with his light suitcase in his hand before the gate of the long riverside gardens of Willowood Place, one of the smaller seats of Sir Isaac Hook, the master of much shipping and many newspapers. He entered by the gate giving on the road, at the opposite side to the river; but there was a mixed quality in all that watery landscape which perpetually reminded a traveller that the river was near. White

The Fad of the Fisherman

gleams of water would shine suddenly like swords or spears in the green thickets; and even in the garden itself, divided into courts and curtained with hedges and high garden trees, there hung everywhere in the air the music of water. The first of the green courts which he entered appeared to be a somewhat neglected croquet lawn, in which was a solitary young man playing croquet against himself. Yet he was not an enthusiast for the game, thus snatching a moment's practice; and his sallow but well-featured face looked rather sullen than otherwise. He was only one of those young men who cannot support the burden of consciousness unless they are doing something, and whose conceptions of doing something are limited to a game of some kind. He was dark and well dressed in a light holiday fashion, and Fisher recognized him at once as a young man named James Bullen, called for some unknown reason Bunker. He was the nephew of Sir Isaac. But, what was much more important at the moment, he was also the private secretary of the Prime Minister.

"Hallo, Bunker," observed Horne Fisher. "You're the sort of man I wanted to see. Has your chief come down yet?"

"He's only staying for dinner," replied Bullen, with his eye on the yellow ball. "He's got a great speech to-morrow at Birmingham, and he's going straight through to-night. He's motoring himself there; driving the car, I mean. It's the one thing he's really proud of."

"You mean you're staying here with your uncle, like a good boy?" replied Fisher. "But what will he do at Birmingham without the epigrams whispered to him by his brilliant secretary?"

"Don't you start ragging me," said the young man called Bunker. "I'm only too glad not to go trailing after him. He doesn't know a thing about maps or money or hotels or anything, and I have to dance about like a courier. As for my uncle, as I'm supposed to come into the estate it's only decent to be here sometimes."

"Very proper," replied the other. "Well, I shall see

The Man Who Knew Too Much

you later on"; and crossing the lawn he passed out through a gap in the hedge.

He was walking across the lawn towards the landing-stage on the river, and still felt all around him, under the dome of golden evening, an old-world savour and reverberation in that river-haunted garden. The next square of turf which he crossed seemed at first sight quite deserted, till he saw that in the twilight of trees in one corner of it a hammock, and in the hammock a man, reading a newspaper and swinging one leg over the edge of the net. Him also he hailed by name, and the man slipped to the ground and strolled forward. It seemed fated that he should feel something of the past in the accidents of that place; for the figure might well have been an Early Victorian ghost revisiting the ghosts of the croquet hoop and mallets. It was the figure of an elderly man with long whiskers that looked almost fantastic; and a quaint and careful cut of collar and cravat. Having been a fashionable dandy forty years ago he had managed to preserve the dandyism while ignoring the fashions. A white top hat lay beside the *Morning Post* in the hammock behind him. This was the Duke of Westmoreland, the relic of a family really some centuries old —and the antiquity was not heraldry but history. Nobody knew better than Fisher how rare such noblemen are in fact, and how numerous in fiction. But whether the duke owed the general respect he enjoyed to the genuineness of his pedigree or to the fact that he owned a vast amount of very valuable property, was a point about which Mr. Fisher's opinion might have been more interesting to discover.

"You were looking so comfortable," said Fisher, "that I thought you must be one of the servants. I'm looking for somebody to take this bag of mine I haven't brought a man down, as I came away in a hurry."

"Nor have I, for that matter," replied the duke with some pride. "I never do If there's one animal alive I loathe it's a valet. I learnt to dress myself at an early age, and was supposed to do it decently. I may be in my second childhood, but I've not got so far as being dressed like a child."

The Fad of the Fisherman

"The Prime Minister hasn't brought a valet, he's brought a secretary instead," observed Fisher. "Devilish inferior job. Didn't I hear that Harker was staying down here?"

"He's over there on the landing-stage," replied the duke indifferently, and resumed the study of the *Morning Post*.

Fisher made his way beyond the last green wall of the garden on to a sort of towing-path looking on the river and a wooded island opposite. There indeed he saw a lean dark figure with a stoop almost like that of a vulture; a posture well known in the law courts as that of Sir John Harker, the Attorney-General. His face was lined with headwork, for alone among the three idlers in the garden he was a man who had made his own way; and round his bald brow and hollow temples clung dull red hair quite flat like plates of copper.

"I haven't seen my host yet," said Horne Fisher in a slightly more serious tone than he had used to the others. "But I suppose I shall meet him at dinner."

"You can see him now, but you can't meet him," answered Harker.

He nodded his head towards one end of the island opposite, and looking steadily in the same direction the other guest could see the dome of a bald head and the top of a fishing-rod, both equally motionless, rising out of the tall undergrowth against the background of the stream beyond. The fisherman seemed to be seated against the stump of a tree and facing towards the other bank, so that his face could not be seen, but the shape of his head was unmistakable.

"He doesn't like to be disturbed when he's fishing," continued Harker. "It's a sort of fad of his to eat nothing but fish; and he's very proud of catching his own. Of course he's all for simplicity, like so many of these millionaires. He likes to come in saying he's worked for his daily food like a labourer."

"Does he explain how he blows all the glass and stuffs all the upholstery?" asked Fisher, "and makes all the silver forks, and grows all the grapes and peaches,

The Man Who Knew Too Much

and designs all the patterns on the carpets? I've always heard he was a busy man."

"I don't think he mentioned it," answered the lawyer. "What is the meaning of this social satire?"

"Well, I am a trifle tired," said Fisher, "of the Simple Life and the Strenuous Life as lived by our little set. We're all really dependent in nearly everything, and we all make a fuss about being independent in something. The Prime Minister prides himself on doing without a chauffeur, but he can't do without a factotum and jack-of-all-trades; and poor old Bunker has to play the part of a universal genius, which God knows he was never meant for. The duke prides himself on doing without a valet; but for all that, he must give a lot of people an infernal lot of trouble to collect such extraordinary old clothes as he wears. He must have them looked up in the British Museum or excavated out of the tombs. That white hat alone must require a sort of expedition fitted out to find it, like the North Pole. And here we have old Hook pretending to produce his own fish when he couldn't produce his own fish-knives or fish-forks to eat it with. He may be simple about simple things like food, but you bet he's luxurious about luxurious things, especially little things. I don't include you; you've worked too hard to enjoy playing at work."

"I sometimes think," said Harker, "that you conceal a horrid secret of being useful sometimes. Haven't you come down here to see Number One before he goes on to Birmingham?"

Horne Fisher answered in a lower voice: "Yes; and I hope to be lucky enough to catch him before dinner. He's got to see Sir Isaac about something just afterwards."

"Hallo," exclaimed Harker, "Sir Isaac's finished his fishing. I know he prides himself on getting up at sunrise and going in at sunset."

The old man on the island had indeed risen to his feet, facing round and showing a bush of grey beard with rather small sunken features but fierce eyebrows and keen choleric eyes.

Carefully carrying his fishing tackle he was already

The Fad of the Fisherman

making his way back to the mainland across a bridge of flat stepping-stones a little way down the shallow stream; then he veered round, coming towards his guests and civilly saluting them. There were several fish in his basket, and he was in a good temper.

"Yes," he said, acknowledging Fisher's polite expression of surprise, "I get up before anybody else in the house, I think. The early bird catches the worm."

"Unfortunately," said Harker, "it is the early fish that catches the worm."

"But the early man catches the fish," replied the old man gruffly.

"But from what I hear, Sir Isaac, you are the late man, too," interposed Fisher. "You must do with very little sleep."

"I never had much time for sleeping," answered Hook, "and I shall have to be the late man to-night anyhow. The Prime Minister wants to have a talk, he tells me. And all things considered I think we'd better be dressing for dinner."

Dinner passed off that evening without a word of politics and little enough but ceremonial trifles. The Prime Minister, Lord Merivale, who was a long slim man with curly grey hair, was gravely complimentary to his host about his success as a fisherman, and the skill and patience he displayed; the conversation flowed like the shallow stream through the stepping-stones.

"It wants patience to wait for fish, no doubt," said Sir Isaac, "and skill to play them, but I'm generally pretty lucky with them."

"Does a big fish ever break the line and get away?" inquired the politician with respectful interest.

"Not the sort of line I use," answered Hook with satisfaction. "I rather specialize in tackle, as a matter of fact. If he were strong enough to do that, he'd be strong enough to pull me into the river."

"A great loss to the community," said the Prime Minister bowing.

Fisher had listened to all these futilities with inward impatience, waiting for his own opportunity, and when

The Man Who Knew Too Much

their host rose he sprang to his feet with an alertness he rarely showed. He managed to catch Lord Merivale before Sir Isaac bore him off for the final interview. He had only a few words to say, but he wanted to get them said.

He said in a low voice as he opened the door for the Premier: "I have seen Montmirail; he says that unless we protest immediately on behalf of Denmark, Sweden will certainly seize the ports."

Lord Merivale nodded.

"I'm just going to hear what Hook has to say about it," he said.

"I imagine," said Fisher with a faint smile, "that there is very little doubt what he will say about it."

Merivale did not answer but lounged gracefully towards the library, whither his host had already preceded him. The rest drifted towards the billiard-room; Fisher merely remarking to the lawyer: "They won't be long. We know they're practically in agreement."

"Hook entirely supports the Prime Minister," assented Harker

"Or the Prime Minister entirely supports Hook," said Horne Fisher; and began idly to knock the balls about on the billiard-table.

Horne Fisher came down next morning in a late and leisurely fashion, as was his reprehensible habit; he had evidently no appetite for catching worms. But the other guests seemed to have felt a similar indifference, and they helped themselves to breakfast from the sideboard at intervals during the hours verging upon lunch. So that it was not many hours later when the first sensation of that strange day came upon them. It came in the form of a young man with light hair and a candid expression who came sculling down the river and disembarked at the landing-stage. It was in fact no other than Mr. Harold March, the journalistic friend of Mr. Fisher, whose journey had begun far away up the river in the earliest hours of that day. He arrived late in the afternoon, having stopped for tea in a large riverside town, and he had a pink evening paper sticking out of his pocket. He fell on the riverside garden like a quiet

The Fad of the Fisherman

and well-behaved thunderbolt; but he was a thunderbolt without knowing it.

The first exchange of salutations and introductions was commonplace enough, and consisted indeed of the inevitable repetition of excuses for the eccentric seclusion of the host. He had gone fishing again, of course, and must not be disturbed till the appointed hour, though he sat within a stone's throw of where they stood.

"You see it's his only hobby," observed Harker apologetically, "and after all it's his own house; and he's very hospitable in other ways."

"I'm rather afraid," said Fisher in a lower voice, "that it's becoming more of a mania than a hobby. I know how it is when a man of that age begins to collect things, if it's only collecting those rotten little river fish. You remember Talbot's uncle with his toothpicks, and poor old Buzzy and the waste of cigar ashes. Hook has done a lot of big things in his time—the great deal in the Swedish timber trade and the Peace Conference at Chicago—but I doubt whether he cares now for any of those big things as he cares for those little fish."

"Oh, come, come," protested the Attorney-General. "You'll make Mr. March think he has come to call on a lunatic. Believe me, Hook only does it for fun like any other sport; only he's of the kind that takes his fun sadly. But I bet if there were big news about timber or shipping he would drop his fun and his fish all right."

"Well, I wonder," said Horne Fisher, looking sleepily at the island in the river.

"By the way, is there any news of anything?" asked Harker of Harold March. "I see you've got an evening paper; one of those enterprising evening papers that come out in the morning."

"The beginning of Lord Merivale's Birmingham speech," replied March, handing him the paper. "It's only a paragraph, but it seems to me rather good."

Harker took the paper, flapped and refolded it, and looked at the stop-press news. It was, as March had said, only a paragraph. But it was a paragraph that had a peculiar effect on Sir John Harker. His lowering brows lifted with a flicker and his eyes blinked, and for

The Man Who Knew Too Much

a moment his leathery jaw was loosened. He looked in some odd fashion like a very old man. Then, hardening his voice and handing the paper to Fisher without a tremor, he simply said:

"Well, here's a chance for the bet. You've got your big news to disturb the old man's fishing."

Horne Fisher was looking at the paper, and over his more languid and less expressive features a change also seemed to pass. Even that little paragraph had two or three large headlines, and his eye encountered "Sensational Warning to Sweden," and "We Shall Protest."

"What the devil," he said, and his words softened first to a whisper and then a whistle.

"We must tell old Hook at once or he'll never forgive us," said Harker. "He'll probably want to see Number One instantly, though it may be too late now. I'm going across to him at once; I bet I'll make him forget his fish, anyhow." And turning his back he made his way hurriedly along the riverside to the causeway of flat stones.

March was staring at Fisher in amazement at the effect his pink paper had produced.

"What does it all mean?" he cried. "I always supposed we should protest in defence of the Danish ports, for their sakes and our own. What is all this botheration about Sir Isaac and the rest of you? Do you think it bad news?"

"Bad news!" repeated Fisher, with a sort of soft emphasis beyond expression.

"Is it as bad as all that?" asked his friend at last.

"As bad as all that," repeated Fisher. "Why, of course, it's as good as it can be. It's great news. It's glorious news. That's where the devil of it comes in, to knock us all silly. It's admirable. It's inestimable. It is also quite incredible."

He gazed again at the grey and green colours of the island and the river, and his rather dreary eye travelled slowly round to the hedges and the lawns.

"I felt this garden was a sort of dream," he said, "and I suppose I must be dreaming. But there is grass growing and water moving, and something impossible has happened."

The Fad of the Fisherman

Even as he spoke the dark figure with a stoop like a vulture appeared in the gap of the hedge just above him.

"You have won your bet," said Harker in a harsh and almost croaking voice. "The old fool cares for nothing but fishing. He cursed me and told me he would talk no politics."

"I thought it might be so," said Fisher modestly. "What are you going to do next?"

"I shall use the old idiot's telephone, anyhow," replied the lawyer. "I must find out exactly what has happened. I've got to speak for the Government myself to-morrow." And he hurried away towards the house.

In the silence that followed, a very bewildering silence so far as March was concerned, they saw the quaint figure of the Duke of Westmoreland, with his white hat and whiskers, approaching them across the garden. Fisher instantly stepped towards him with the pink paper in his hand, and with a few words pointed out the apocalyptic paragraph. The duke, who had been walking slowly, stood quite still, and for some seconds he looked like a tailor's dummy standing and staring outside some antiquated shop. Then March heard his voice, and it was high and almost hysterical.

"But he must see it, he must be made to understand. It cannot have been put to him properly." Then, with a certain recovery of fullness and even pomposity in the voice: "I shall go and tell him myself."

Among the queer incidents of that afternoon March always remembered something almost comical about the clear picture of the old gentleman in his wonderful white hat carefully stepping from stone to stone across the river, like a figure crossing the traffic in Piccadilly. Then he disappeared behind the trees of the island, and March and Fisher turned to meet the Attorney-General, who was coming out of the house with a visage of grim assurance.

"Everybody is saying," he said, "that the Prime Minister has made the greatest speech of his life. Peroration and loud and prolonged cheers. Corrupt financiers and heroic peasants. We will not desert Denmark again."

Fisher nodded and turned away towards the towing-

The Man Who Knew Too Much

path, where he saw the duke returning with a rather dazed expression. In answer to questions he said in a husky and confidential voice:

"I really think our poor friend cannot be himself. He refused to listen; he—ah—suggested that I might frighten the fish."

A keen ear might have detected a murmur from Mr. Fisher on the subject of a white hat, but Sir John Harker struck in more decisively.

"Fisher was quite right. I didn't believe it myself; but it's quite clear that the old fellow is fixed on this fishing notion by now. If the house caught fire behind him he would hardly move till sunset."

Fisher had continued his stroll towards the higher embanked ground of the towing-path, and he now swept a long and searching gaze, not towards the island but towards the distant wooded heights that were the walls of the valley. An evening sky as clear as that of the previous day was settling down all over the dim landscape, but towards the west it was now red rather than gold; there was scarcely any sound but the monotonous music of the river. Then came the sound of a half stifled exclamation from Horne Fisher, and Harold March looked up at him in wonder.

"You spoke of bad news," said Fisher. "Well, there is really bad news now. I am afraid this is a bad business."

"What bad news do you mean?" asked his friend, conscious of something strange and sinister in his tone.

"The sun has set," answered Fisher.

He went on with the air of one conscious of having said something fatal: "We must get somebody to go across whom he will really listen to. He may be mad, but there's method in his madness. There nearly always is method in madness. It's what drives men mad, being methodical. And he never goes on sitting there after sunset, with the whole place getting dark. Where's his nephew? I believe he's really fond of his nephew."

"Look," cried March abruptly, "why, he's been across already. There he is coming back."

And looking up the river once more they saw, dark

The Fad of the Fisherman

against the sunset reflections, the figure of James Bullen stepping hastily and rather clumsily from stone to stone. Once he slipped on a stone with a slight splash. When he rejoined the group on the bank his olive face was unnaturally pale.

The other four men had already gathered on the same spot and almost simultaneously were calling out to him: "What does he say now?"

"Nothing. He says—nothing."

Fisher looked at the young man steadily for a moment; then he started from his immobility and, making a motion to March to follow him, himself strode down to the river crossing. In a few moments they were on the little beaten track that ran round the wooded island, to the other side of it where the fisherman sat. Then they stood and looked at him without a word.

Sir Isaac Hook was still sitting propped up against the stump of the tree, and that for the best of reasons. A length of his own infallible fishing-line was twisted and tightened twice round his throat, and then twice round the wooden prop behind him. The leading investigator ran forward and touched the fisherman's hand; and it was as cold as a fish.

"The sun has set," said Horne Fisher in the same terrible tone, "and he will never see it rise again."

Ten minutes afterwards the five men shaken by such a shock were again together in the garden, looking at each other with white but watchful faces. The lawyer seemed the most alert of the group; he was articulate if somewhat abrupt.

"We must leave the body as it is and telephone for the police," he said. "I think my own authority will stretch to examining the servants and the poor fellow's papers, to see if there is anything that concerns them. Of course none of you gentlemen must leave this place."

Perhaps there was something in his rapid and rigorous legality that suggested the closing of a net or trap. Anyhow young Bullen suddenly broke down; or perhaps blew up, for his voice was like an explosion in the silent garden.

The Man Who Knew Too Much

"I never touched him," he cried. "I swear I had nothing to do with it!"

"Who said you had?" demanded Harker, with a hard eye. "Why do you cry out before you're hurt?"

"Because you all look at me like that," cried the young man angrily. "Do you think I don't know you're always talking about my damned debts and expectations?"

Rather to March's surprise, Fisher had drawn away from this first collision, leading the duke with him to another part of the garden. When he was out of earshot of the others he said with a curious simplicity of manner:

"Westmoreland, I am going straight to the point."

"Well?" said the other, staring at him stolidly.

"You had a motive for killing him," said Fisher.

The duke continued to stare, but he seemed unable to speak.

"I hope you had a motive for killing him," continued Fisher mildly. "You see, it's rather a curious situation. If you had a motive for murdering, you probably didn't murder. But if you hadn't any motive, why, then perhaps you did."

"What on earth are you talking about?" demanded the duke violently.

"It's quite simple," said Fisher. "When you went across he was either alive or dead. If he was alive, it might be you who killed him, or why should you have held your tongue about his death? But if he was dead, and you had a reason for killing him, you might have held your tongue for fear of being accused."

Then after a silence he added abstractedly:

"Cyprus is a beautiful place, I believe. Romantic scenery and romantic people. Very intoxicating for a young man."

The duke suddenly clenched his hands and said thickly: "Well, I had a motive."

"Then you're all right," said Fisher, holding out his hand with an air of huge relief. "I was pretty sure you wouldn't really do it; you had a fright when you saw it done, as was only natural. Like a bad dream come true, wasn't it?"

The Fad of the Fisherman

While this curious conversation was passing Harker had gone into the house, disregarding the demonstrations of the sulky nephew, and came back presently with a new air of animation and a sheaf of papers in his hand.

"I've telephoned for the police," he said, stopping to speak to Fisher, "but I think I've done most of their work for them. I believe I've found out the truth. There's a paper here——"

He stopped, for Fisher was looking at him with a singular expression, and it was Fisher who spoke next:

"Are there any papers that are not there, I wonder. I mean that are not there now."

After a pause he added: "Let us have the cards on the table. When you went through his papers in such a hurry, Harker, weren't you looking for something to—to make sure it shouldn't be found?"

Harker did not turn a red hair on his hard head, but he looked at the other out of the corners of his eyes.

"And I suppose," went on Fisher smoothly, "that is why you too told us lies about having found Hook alive. You knew there was something to show that you might have killed him, and you didn't dare tell us he was killed. But believe me, it's much better to be honest now."

Harker's haggard face suddenly lit up as if with infernal flames.

"Honest!" he cried, "it's not so damned fine of you fellows to be honest! You're all born with silver spoons in your mouths, and then you swagger about with everlasting virtue because you haven't got other people's spoons in your pockets. But I was born in a Pimlico lodging-house and I had to make my spoon, and there'd be plenty to say I only spoilt a horn or an honest man. And if a struggling man staggers a bit over the line in his youth in the lower parts of the law, which are pretty dingy, anyhow, there's always some old vampire to hang on to him all his life for it."

"Guatemalan Golcondas, wasn't it?" said Fisher sympathetically.

Harker suddenly shuddered. Then he said:

"I believe you must know everything, like God Almighty."

The Man Who Knew Too Much

"I know too much," said Horne Fisher, "and all the wrong things."

The other three men were drawing nearer to them, but before they came too near Harker said in a voice that had recovered all its firmness:

"Yes, I did destroy a paper, but I really did find a paper, too, and I believe that it clears us all."

"Very well," said Fisher in a louder and more cheerful tone, "let us all have the benefit of it."

"On the very top of Sir Isaac's papers," explained Harker, "there was a threatening letter from a man named Hugo. It threatens to kill our unfortunate friend very much in the way that he was actually killed. It is a wild letter, full of taunts—you can see it for yourselves—but it makes a particular point of poor Hook's habit of fishing from the island. Above all the man professes to be writing from a boat. And since we alone went across to him "—and he smiled in a rather ugly fashion—"the crime must have been committed by a man passing in a boat."

"Why, dear me," cried the duke, with something almost amounting to animation. "Why, I remember the man called Hugo quite well. He was a sort of body-servant and bodyguard of Sir Isaac; you see, Sir Isaac was in some fear of assault. He was—he was not very popular with several people. Hugo was discharged after some row or other; but I remember him well. He was a great big Hungarian fellow with great moustaches that stood out on each side of his face——"

A door opened in the darkness of Harold March's memory, or rather oblivion, and showed a shining landscape like that of a lost dream. It was rather a waterscape than a landscape, a thing of flooded meadows and low trees and the dark archway of a bridge. And for one instant he saw again the man with moustaches like dark horns leap up on to the bridge and disappear.

"Good heavens," he cried, "why, I met the murderer this morning."

Horne Fisher and Harold March had their day on the river after all, for the little group broke up when the police arrived. They declared that the coincidence of March's evidence had cleared the whole company and

The Fad of the Fisherman

clinched the case against the flying Hugo. Whether that Hungarian fugitive would ever be caught appeared to Horne Fisher to be highly doubtful; nor can it be pretended that he displayed any very demoniac detective energy in the matter, as he leaned back in the boat cushions smoking and watching the swaying reeds slide past.

"It was a very good notion to hop up on to the bridge," he said. "An empty boat means very little; he hasn't been seen to land on either bank, and he's walked off the bridge without walking on to it, so to speak. He's got twenty-fours hours start, his moustaches will disappear, and then he will disappear. I think there is every hope of his escape."

"Hope?" repeated March, and stopped sculling for an instant.

"Yes, hope," repeated the other. "To begin with, I'm not going to be exactly consumed with Corsican revenge because somebody has killed Hook. Perhaps you may guess by this time what Hook was. A damned blood-sucking blackmailer was that simple, strenuous, self-made captain of industry. He had secrets against nearly everybody; one against poor old Westmoreland about an early marriage in Cyprus that might have put the duchess in a queer position, and one against Harker about some flutter with his client's money when he was a young lawyer. That's why they went to pieces when they found him murdered, of course. They felt as if they'd done it in a dream. But I admit I have another reason for not wanting our Hungarian friend actually hanged for the murder "

"And what is that?" asked his friend

"Only that he didn't commit the murder," answered Fisher.

Harold March laid down the oars and let the boat drift for a moment.

"Do you know, I was half expecting something like that," he said. "It was quite irrational, but it was hanging about in the atmosphere like thunder in the air."

"On the contrary, it's finding Hugo guilty that's irrational," replied Fisher. "Don't you see that they're

The Man Who Knew Too Much

condemning him for the very reason for which they acquit everybody else? Harker and Westmoreland were silent because they found him murdered, and knew there were papers that made them look like the murderers. Well, so did Hugo find him murdered, and so did Hugo know there was a paper that would make him look like the murderer. He had written it himself the day before."

"But in that case," said March, frowning, "at what sort of unearthly hour in the morning was the murder really committed? It was barely daylight when I met him at the bridge, and that's some way above the island."

"The answer is very simple," replied Fisher. "The crime was not committed in the morning. The crime was not committed on the island."

March stared at the shining water without replying, but Fisher resumed like one who had been asked a question.

"Every intelligent murder involves taking advantage of some one uncommon feature in a common situation. The feature here was the fancy of old Hook for being the first man up every morning, his fixed routine as an angler, and his annoyance at being disturbed. The murderer strangled him in his own house after dinner on the night before, carried his corpse, with all his fishing tackle, across the stream in the dead of night, tied him to the tree, and left him there under the stars. It was a dead man who sat fishing there all day. Then the murderer went back to the house, or rather to the garage, and went off in his motor-car. The murderer drove his own motor-car."

Fisher glanced at his friend's face and went on: "You look horrified, and the thing is horrible. But other things are horrible, too. If some obscure man had been hag-ridden by a blackmailer, and had his family life ruined, you wouldn't think the murder of his persecutor the most inexcusable of murders. Is it any worse when a whole great nation is set free as well as a family?

"By this warning to Sweden we shall probably prevent war and not precipitate it, and save many thousand lives rather more valuable than the life of that viper. Oh, I'm not talking sophistry or seriously justifying the thing,

The Fad of the Fisherman

but the slavery that held him and his country was a thousand times less justifiable. If I'd really been sharp I should have guessed it from his smooth, deadly smiling at dinner that night. Do you remember I told you of that silly talk about how old Isaac could always play his fish? In a pretty hellish sense he was a fisher of men."

Harold March took the oars and began to row again.

"I remember," he said, "and about how a big fish might break the line and get away."

VII.—THE FOOL OF THE FAMILY

HAROLD MARCH and the few who cultivated the friendship of Horne Fisher, especially if they saw something of him in his own social setting, were conscious of a certain solitude in his very sociability. They seemed to be always meeting his relations and never meeting his family. Perhaps it would be truer to say that they saw much of his family and nothing of his home. His cousins and connections ramified like a labyrinth all over the governing class of Great Britain, and he seemed to be on good, or at least on good-humoured, terms with most of them. For Horne Fisher was remarkable for a curious impersonal information and interest touching all sorts of topics, so that one could sometimes fancy that his culture, like his colourless fair moustache and pale drooping features, had the neutral nature of a chameleon. Anyhow, he could always get on with Viceroys and Cabinet Ministers and all the great men responsible for great departments, and talk to each of them on his own subject, on the branch of study with which he was most seriously concerned. Thus he could converse with the Minister for War about silkworms, with the Minister of Education about detective stories, with the Minister of Labour about Limoges enamel, and with the Minister of Missions and Moral Progress (if that be his correct title) about the pantomime boys of the last four decades. And as the first was his first cousin, the second his second cousin, the third his brother-in-law, and the fourth his uncle by marriage, this conversational versatility certainly served in one sense to create a happy family. But March never seemed to get a glimpse of that domestic interior to which men of the middle classes are accustomed in their friendships and which is, indeed, the foundation of friendship and love and everything else in any sane and stable society. He

The Fool of the Family

wondered whether Horne Fisher was both an orphan and an only child.

It was, therefore, with something like a start that he found that Fisher had a brother, much more prosperous and powerful than himself, though hardly, March thought, so entertaining. Sir Henry Harland Fisher, with half the alphabet after his name, was something at the Foreign Office far more tremendous than the Foreign Secretary. Apparently it ran in the family, after all, for it seemed there was another brother, Ashton Fisher, in India, rather more tremendous than the Viceroy. Sir Henry Fisher was a heavier but handsomer edition of his brother, with a brow equally bald but much more smooth. He was very courteous, but a shade patronizing, not only to March, but even, as March fancied, to Horne Fisher as well. The latter gentleman, who had many intuitions about the half-formed thoughts of others, glanced at the topic himself as they came away from the great house in Berkeley Square.

"Why, don't you know," he observed quietly, "that I am the fool of the family?"

"It must be a clever family," said Harold March, with a smile.

"Very gracefully expressed," replied Fisher. "That is the best of having a literary training. Well, perhaps it is an exaggeration to say I am the fool of the family. It's enough to say I am the failure of the family."

"It seems queer to me that you should fail especially," remarked the journalist. "As they say in the examinations, what did you fail in?"

"Politics," replied his friend. "I stood for Parliament when I was quite a young man, and got in by an enormous majority, with loud cheers and chairing round the town. Since then, of course, I've been rather under a cloud."

"I'm afraid I don't quite understand the ' of course,' " answered March, laughing.

"That part of it isn't worth understanding," said Fisher, "but as a matter of fact, old chap, the other part of it was rather odd and interesting. Quite a detective story in its way, as well as the first lesson I had in what

The Man Who Knew Too Much

modern politics are made of. If you like, I'll tell you all about it." And the following, recast in a less allusive and conversational manner, is the story that he told.

Nobody privileged of late years to meet Sir Henry Harland Fisher could believe that he had ever been called Harry. But, indeed, he had been boyish enough when he was a boy, and that serenity that shone on him through life, and which now took the form of gravity, had once taken the form of gaiety. His friends would have said that he was all the more ripe in his maturity for having been young in his youth. His enemies would have said that he was still light-minded but no longer light-hearted. But in any case the whole of the story Horne Fisher had to tell arose out of the accident which had made young Harry Fisher private secretary to Lord Saltoun. Hence his later connexion with the Foreign Office, which had, indeed, come to him as a sort of legacy from his lordship when that great man was the power behind the throne. This is not the place to say much about Saltoun, little as was known of him and much as there was worth knowing. England has had at least three or four such secret statesmen. An aristocratic polity produces every now and then an aristocrat who is also an accident, a man of intellectual independence and insight, a Napoleon born in the purple. His vast work was mostly invisible, and very little could be got out of him in private life except a crusty and rather cynical sense of humour. But it was certainly the accident of his presence at a family dinner of the Fishers, and the unexpected opinion he expressed, which turned what might have been a dinner-table joke into a sort of small sensational novel.

Save for Lord Saltoun it was a family party of Fishers, for the only other distinguished stranger had just departed after the dinner, leaving the rest to their coffee and cigars. This had been a figure of some interest: a young Cambridge man named Eric Hughes, who was the rising hope of the party of Reform to which the Fisher family, along with their friend Saltoun, had long been at least formally attached. The personality of Hughes was substantially summed up in the fact that he talked eloquently and earnestly through the whole of dinner, but left immediately

The Fool of the Family

after to be in time for an appointment. All his actions had something at once ambitious and conscientious; he drank no wine, but was slightly intoxicated with words. And his face and phrases were on the front page of all the newspapers just then, because he was contesting the safe seat of Sir Francis Verner in the great by-election in the west. Everybody was talking about the powerful speech against squirearchy which he had just delivered; even in the Fisher circle everybody talked about it, except Horne Fisher himself, who sat in a corner lowering over the fire. In his early manhood the manner which afterwards became languid had rather the air of being sullen; he drifted about and dipped into odd books on odd subjects; in contrast with his political family, his future seemed featureless and undetermined.

"We jolly well have to thank him for putting some new life into the old party," Ashton Fisher was saying. "This campaign against the old squires just hits the degree of democracy there is in this country. This act for extending County Council control is practically his bill, so you may say he's in the Government even before he's in the House."

"One's easier than the other," said Harry carelessly. "I bet the squire's a bigger pot than the County Council in that county. Verner is pretty well rooted; all these rural places are what you call reactionary. Damning aristocrats won't alter it."

"He damns them rather well," observed Ashton. "We never had a better meeting than the one in Barkington, which generally goes Constitutional. And when he said, 'Sir Francis may boast of blue blood, let us show we have red blood,' and went on to talk about manhood and liberty, the room simply rose at him."

"Speaks very well," said Lord Saltoun gruffly, making his only contribution to the conversation so far.

Then the almost equally silent Horne Fisher suddenly spoke, without taking his brooding eyes off the fire.

"What I can't understand," he said, "is why nobody is ever slanged for the real reason."

"Hallo," remarked Harry humorously. "You beginning to take notice?"

The Man Who Knew Too Much

"Well, take Verner," continued Horne Fisher. "If we want to attack Verner, why not attack him? Why compliment him on being a romantic reactionary aristocrat? Who is Verner? Where does he come from? His name sounds old, but I never heard of it before, as the man said of the Crucifixion. Why talk about his blue blood? His blood may be gamboge yellow with green spots for all anybody knows. All we know is that the old squire, Hawker, somehow ran through his money (and his second wife's, I suppose, for she was rich enough) and sold the estate to a man named Verner. What did he make his money in? Oil? Army contracts?"

"I don't know," said Saltoun, looking at him thoughtfully.

"First thing I ever knew you didn't know," cried the exuberant Harry.

"And there's more besides," went on Horne Fisher, who seemed to have suddenly found his tongue. "If we want country people to vote for us, why don't we get somebody with some notion about the country? We don't talk to people in Threadneedle Street about nothing but turnips and pigstyes. Why do we talk to people in Somerset about nothing but slums and Socialism? Why don't we give the squire's land to the squire's tenants, instead of dragging in the county council?"

"Three acres and a cow," cried Harry, emitting what the Parliamentary reports call an ironical cheer.

"Yes," replied his brother stubbornly. "Don't you think agricultural labourers would rather have three acres and a cow than three acres of printed forms and a committee? Why doesn't somebody start a yeoman party in politics, appealing to the old traditions of the small landowner. And why don't they attack men like Verner for what they are; which is something about as old and traditional as an American oil trust?"

"You'd better lead the yeoman party yourself," laughed Harry. "Don't you think it would be a joke, Lord Saltoun? To see my brother and his merry men, with their bows and bills, marching down to Somerset all in Lincoln green instead of Lincoln and Bennet hats?"

"No," answered old Saltoun, "I don't think it would

The Fool of the Family

be a joke. I think it would be an exceedingly serious and sensible idea."

"Well, I'm jiggered," cried Harry Fisher, staring at him. "I said just now it was the first fact you didn't know, and I should say this is the first joke you didn't see."

"I've seen a good many things in my time," said the old man in his rather sour fashion. "I've told a good many lies in my time too, and perhaps I've got rather sick of them. But there are lies and lies for all that. Gentlemen used to lie just as schoolboys lie, because they hung together and partly to help each other out. But I'm damned if I can see why we should lie for those cosmopolitan cads who only help themselves. They're not backing us up any more, they're simply crowding us out. If a man like your brother likes to go into Parliament as a yeoman or a gentleman or a Jacobite or an Ancient Briton, I should say it would be a jolly good thing."

In the rather startled silence that followed Horne Fisher sprang to his feet, and all his dreary manner dropped off him.

"I'm ready to do it to-morrow," he cried. "I suppose none of you fellows would back me up?"

Then Harry Fisher showed the finer side of his impetuosity. He made a sudden movement as if to shake hands.

"You're a sport," he said, "and I'll back you up if nobody else will. But we can all back you up, can't we? I see what Lord Saltoun means, and of course he's right. He's always right."

"So I will go down to Somerset," said Horne Fisher.

"Yes, it is on the way to Westminster," said Lord Saltoun with a smile.

And so it happened that Horne Fisher arrived some days later at the little station of a rather remote market-town in the west, accompanied by a light suit-case and a lively brother. It must not be supposed, however, that the brother's cheerful tone consisted entirely of chaff. He supported the new candidate with hope as well as hilarity; and at the back of his boisterous partnership

The Man Who Knew Too Much

there was an increasing sympathy and encouragement. Harry Fisher had always had an affection for his more quiet and eccentric brother, and was now coming more and more to have a respect for him. As the campaign proceeded the respect increased to ardent admiration. For Harry was still young; and could feel the sort of enthusiasm for his captain in electioneering that a schoolboy can feel for his captain in cricket.

Nor was the admiration undeserved. As the new three-cornered contest developed, it became apparent to others besides his devoted kinsman that there was more in Horne Fisher than had ever met the eye. It was clear that his outbreak by the family fireside had been but the culmination of a long course of brooding and studying on the question. The talent he retained through life for studying his subject, and even somebody else's subject, had long been concentrated on this idea of championing a new peasantry against a new plutocracy. He spoke to a crowd with eloquence and replied to an individual with humour; two political arts that seemed to come to him naturally. He certainly knew much more about rural problems than either Hughes the Reform candidate or Verner the Constitutional candidate. And he probed those problems with a human curiosity, and went below the surface in a way that neither of them dreamed of doing. He soon became the voice of popular feelings that are never found in the popular press. New angles of criticism, arguments that had never before been uttered by an educated voice, tests and comparisons that had been made only in dialect by men drinking in the little local public-houses, crafts half-forgotten that had come down by sign of hand and tongue from remote ages when their fathers were free—all this created a curious and double excitement.

It startled the well-informed by being a new and fantastic idea they had never encountered. It startled the ignorant by being an old and familiar idea they never thought to have seen revived. Men saw things in a new light; and knew not even whether it was the sunset or the dawn.

Practical grievances were there to make the movement formidable. As Fisher went to and fro among the

The Fool of the Family

cottages and country inns, it was borne in on him without difficulty that Sir Francis Verner was a very bad landlord. Nor was the story of his acquisition of the land any more ancient and dignified than he had supposed; the story was well known in the county and in most respects was obvious enough. Hawker, the old squire, had been a loose, unsatisfactory sort of person; had been on bad terms with his first wife (who had died, as some said, of neglect), and had then married a flashy South American Jewess with a fortune. But he must have worked his way through this fortune also with marvellous rapidity, for he had been compelled to sell the estate to Verner, and had gone to live in South America, possibly on his wife's estates. But Fisher noticed that the laxity of the old squire was far less hated than the efficiency of the new squire. Verner's history seemed to be full of smart bargains and financial flutters, that left other people short of money and temper. But though he heard a great deal about Verner, there was one thing that continually eluded him; something that nobody knew; that even Saltoun had not known. He could not find out how Verner had originally made his money.

"He must have kept it specially dark," said Horne Fisher to himself. "It must be something he's really ashamed of. Hang it all, what *is* a man ashamed of nowadays?"

And as he pondered on the possibilities they grew darker and more distorted in his mind; he thought vaguely of things remote and repulsive, strange forms of slavery or sorcery, and then of ugly things yet more unnatural but nearer home. The figure of Verner seemed to be blackened and transfigured in his imagination, and to stand against varied backgrounds and strange skies.

As he strode up a village street, brooding thus, his eyes encountered a complete contrast in the face of his other rival, the Reform candidate. Eric Hughes, with his blown blond hair and eager undergraduate face, was just getting into his motor-car and saying a few final words to his agent, a sturdy, grizzled man named Gryce. Eric Hughes waved his hand in a friendly fashion; but Gryce eyed him with some hostility. Eric Hughes was a young

The Man Who Knew Too Much

man with genuine political enthusiasms, but he knew that political opponents are people with whom one may have to dine any day. But Mr. Gryce was a grim little local Radical, a champion of the chapel, and one of those happy people whose work is also their hobby. He turned his back, as the motor-car drove away, and walked briskly up the sunlit high street of the little town, whistling, with political papers sticking out of his pocket.

Fisher looked pensively after the resolute figure for a moment, and then as if by an impulse began to follow it. Through the busy market-place, amid the baskets and barrows of market day, under the painted wooden sign of the Green Dragon, up a dark side entry, under an arch, and through a tangle of crooked cobbled streets the two threaded their way, the square strutting figure in front and the lean lounging figure behind him, like his shadow in the sunshine. At length they came to a brown brick house with a brass plate, on which was Mr. Gryce's name, and that individual turned and beheld his pursuer with a stare.

"Could I have a word with you, sir?" asked Horne Fisher politely. The agent stared still more, but assented civilly, and led the other into an office littered with leaflets and hung all round with highly coloured posters, which linked the name of Hughes with all the higher interests of humanity.

"Mr. Horne Fisher, I believe," said Mr. Gryce. "Much honoured by the call, of course. Can't pretend to congratulate you on entering the contest, I'm afraid; you won't expect that. Here we've been keeping the old flag flying for freedom and reform; and you come in and break the battle-line."

For Mr. Elijah Gryce abounded in military metaphors and in denunciations of militarism. He was a square-jawed, blunt-featured man with a pugnacious cock of the eyebrow. He had been pickled in the politics of that country-side from boyhood; he knew everybody's secrets; and electioneering was the romance of his life.

"I suppose you think I'm devoured with ambition," said Horne Fisher in his rather listless voice, "aiming at a dictatorship and all that. Well, I think I can clear

The Fool of the Family

myself of the charge of mere selfish ambition. I only want certain things done. I don't want to do them. I very seldom want to do anything. And I've come here to say that I'm quite willing to retire from the contest, if you can convince me that we really want to do the same thing."

The agent of the Reform party looked at him with an odd and slightly puzzled expression, and before he could reply Fisher went on in the same level tones:

"You'd hardly believe it, but I keep a conscience concealed about me; and I am in doubt about several things. For instance, we both want to turn Verner out of Parliament; but what weapon are we to use? I've heard a lot of gossip against him, but is it right to act on mere gossip? Just as I want to be fair to you, so I want to be fair to him. If some of the things I heard were true, he ought to be turned out of Parliament and every other club in London. But I don't want to turn him out of Parliament if they aren't true."

At this point the light of battle sprang into Mr. Gryce's eyes; and he became voluble, not to say violent. He at any rate had no doubt that the stories were true; he could testify to his own knowledge that they were true. Verner was not only a hard landlord but a mean landlord, a robber as well as a rack-renter; any gentleman would be justified in hounding him out. He had cheated old Wilkins out of his freehold by a trick fit for a pickpocket; he had driven old Mother Biddle to the workhouse; he had stretched the law against Long Adam the poacher till all the magistrates were ashamed of him.

"So if you'll serve under the old banner," concluded Mr. Gryce more genially, "and turn out a swindling tyrant like that, I'm sure you'll never regret it."

"And if that is the truth," said Horne Fisher, "are you going to tell it?"

"What do you mean? Tell the truth?" demanded Gryce.

"I mean you are going to tell the truth as you have just told it," replied Fisher. "You are going to placard this town with the wickedness done to old Wilkins. You are going to fill the newspapers with the infamous story

The Man Who Knew Too Much

of Mrs. Biddle. You are going to denounce Verner from a public platform, naming him for what he did and naming the poacher he did it to. And you're going to find out by what trade this man made the money with which he bought the estate; and when you know the truth, as I said before, of course you are going to tell it. Upon those terms I come under the old flag, as you call it, and haul down my little pennon."

The agent was eyeing him with a curious expression, surly but not entirely unsympathetic.

"Well," he said, slowly, "you have to do these things in a regular way, you know, or people don't understand. I've had a lot of experience, and I'm afraid what you say wouldn't do. People understand slanging squires in a general way; but these personalities aren't considered fair play. Looks like hitting below the belt."

"Old Wilkins hasn't got a belt, I suppose," replied Horne Fisher. "Verner can hit him anyhow, and nobody must say a word. It's evidently very important to have a belt. But apparently you have to be rather high up in society to have one. Possibly," he added thoughtfully, "possibly the explanation of the phrase 'a belted earl,' the meaning of which has always escaped me."

"I mean those personalities won't do," returned Gryce, frowning at the table.

"And Mother Biddle and Long Adam the poacher are not personalities," said Fisher, "and I suppose we mustn't ask how Verner made all the money that enabled him to become—a personality."

Gryce was still loking at him under lowering brows, but the singular light in his eyes had brightened. At last he said in another and much quieter voice:

"Look here, sir. I like you, if you don't mind my saying so. I think you are really on the side of the people; and I'm sure you're a brave man. A lot braver than you know, perhaps. We daren't touch what you propose with a barge-pole; and so far from wanting you in the old party, we'd rather you ran your own risk by yourself. But because I like you and respect your pluck, I'll do you a good turn before we part. I don't want you to waste time barking up the wrong tree. You talk

The Fool of the Family

about how the new squire got the money to buy, and the ruin of the old squire and all the rest of it. Well, I'll give you a hint about that; a hint about something precious few people know."

"I am very grateful," said Fisher gravely. "What is it?"

"It's in two words," said the other. "The new squire was quite poor when he bought. The old squire was quite rich when he sold."

Horne Fisher looked at him thoughtfully as he turned away abruptly and busied himself with the papers on his desk. Then Fisher uttered a short phrase of thanks and farewell, and went out into the street, still very thoughtful.

His reflection seemed to end in resolution, and falling into a more rapid stride, he passed out of the little town along a road leading towards the gates of the great park, the country seat of Sir Francis Verner. A glitter of sunlight made the early winter more like a late autumn, and the dark woods were touched here and there with red and golden leaves like the last rags of a lost sunset. From a higher part of the road he had seen the long classical façade of the great house with its many windows, almost immediately beneath him, but when the road ran down under the wall of the estate, topped with towering trees behind, he realized that it was half a mile round to the lodge gate. After walking for a few minutes along the lane, however, he came to a place where the wall had cracked, and was in process of repair. As it was, there was a great gap in the grey masonry that looked at first as black as a cavern, and only showed at a second glance the twilight of the twinkling trees. There was something fascinating about that unexpected gate, like the opening of a fairy tale.

Horne Fisher had in him something of the aristocrat, which is very near to the anarchist. It was characteristic of him that he turned into this dark and irregular entry as casually as into his own front door, merely thinking that it would be a short cut to the house. He made his way through the dim wood for some distance and with some difficulty, until there began to shine through the trees a level light, in lines of silver, which he did not at

The Man Who Knew Too Much

first understand. The next moment he had come out into the daylight at the top of a steep bank, at the bottom of which a path ran round the rim of a large ornamental lake. The sheet of water which he had seen shimmering through the trees was of considerable extent, but was walled in on every side with woods which were not only dark but decidedly dismal. At one end of the path was a classical statue of some nameless nymph, and at the other end it was flanked by two classical urns; but the marble was all weather-stained and streaked with green and grey. A hundred other signs, smaller but more significant, told him that he had come on some outlying corner of the grounds neglected and seldom visited. In the middle of the lake was what appeared to be an island, and on the island what appeared to be meant for a classical temple, not open like a temple of the winds, but with a blank wall between its Doric pillars. We may say it only seemed like an island, because a second glance revealed a low causeway of flat stones running up to it from the shore, and turning it into a peninsula. And certainly it only seemed like a temple; for nobody knew better than Horne Fisher that no god had ever dwelt in that shrine.

"That's what makes all this classical landscape-gardening so desolate," he said to himself. "More desolate than Stonehenge or the Pyramids. We don't believe in Egyptian mythology, but the Egyptians did; and I suppose even the Druids believed in Druidism. But the eighteenth century gentleman who built these temples didn't believe in Venus or Mercury any more than we do; that's why the reflection of those pale pillars in the lake is truly only the shadow of a shade. They were men of the Age of Reason; they, who filled their gardens with these stone nymphs, had less hope than any men in all history of really meeting a nymph in the forest."

His monologue stopped abruptly with a sharp noise like a thunder-crack that rolled in dreary echoes round the dismal mere. He knew at once what it was; somebody had fired off a gun. But as to the meaning of it he was momentarily staggered; and strange thoughts thronged into his mind. The next moment he laughed,

The Fool of the Family

for he saw lying a little way along the path below him the dead bird that the shot had brought down.

At the same moment, however, he saw something else which interested him rather more. A ring of dense trees ran round the back of the island temple, framing the façade of it in dark foliage, and he could have sworn he saw a stir as of something moving among the leaves. The next moment his suspicion was confirmed, for a rather ragged figure came from under the shadow of the temple and began to move along the causeway that led to the bank. Even at that distance the figure was conspicuous by its great height, and Fisher could see that the man carried a gun under his arm. There came back into his memory at once the name of Long Adam the poacher.

With a rapid sense of strategy he sometimes showed, Fisher sprang from the bank and raced round the lake to the head of the little pier of stones. If once a man reached the mainland he could easily vanish into the woods. But when Fisher began to advance along the stones towards the island the man was cornered in a blind alley, and could only back towards the temple. Putting his broad shoulders against it, he stood as if at bay. He was a comparatively young man, with fine lines in his lean face and figure and a mop of ragged red hair. The look in his eyes might well have been disquieting to anyone left alone with him on an island in the middle of a lake.

"Good morning," said Horne Fisher pleasantly. "I thought at first you were a murderer. But it seems unlikely somehow that the partridge rushed between us and died for love of me, like the heroines in the romances, so I suppose you are a poacher?"

"I suppose you would call me a poacher," answered the man, and his voice was something of a surprise coming from such a scarecrow; it had that hard fastidiousness to be found in those who have made a fight for their own refinement among rough surroundings. "I consider I have a perfect right to shoot game in this place. But I am well aware that people of your sort take me for a thief, and I suppose you will try to land me in jail."

The Man Who Knew Too Much

"There are preliminary difficulties," replied Fisher. "To begin with, the mistake is flattering, but I am not a gamekeeper. Still less am I three gamekeepers, who would be, I imagine, about your fighting weight. But I confess I have another reason for not wanting to jail you."

"And what is that?" asked the other.

"Only that I quite agree with you," answered Fisher. "I don't exactly say you have a right to poach, but I never could see that it was as wrong as being a thief. It seems to me against the whole normal notion of property that a man should own something because it flies across his garden. He might as well own the wind or think he could write his name on a morning cloud. Besides, if we want poor people to respect property, we must give them some property to respect. You ought to have some land of your own, and I'm going to give you some if I can."

"Going to give me some land!" repeated Long Adam.

"I apologize for addressing you as if you were a public meeting," said Fisher, "but I am an entirely new kind of public man who says the same thing in public and in private. I've said this to a hundred huge crowded meetings throughout the county, and I say it to you on this queer little island in this dismal pond. I would cut up a big estate like this into small estates for everybody, even for poachers. I would do in England as they did in Ireland : buy the big men out, if possible, get them out anyhow. A man like you ought to have a little place of his own. I don't say you could keep pheasants, but you might keep chickens."

The man stiffened suddenly, and he seemed at once to blanch and flame at the promise as if it were a threat.

"Chickens!" he repeated, with a passion of contempt.

"Why do you object?" asked the placid candidate. "Because keeping hens is rather a mild amusement for a poacher? What about poaching eggs?"

"Because I am not a poacher," cried Adam in a rending voice that rang round the hollow shrines and urns like the echoes of his gun. "Because the partridge

The Fool of the Family

lying dead over there is my partridge. Because the land you are standing on is my land. Because my own land was only taken from me by a crime, and a worse crime than poaching. This has been a single estate for hundreds and hundreds of years, and if you or any meddlesome mountebanks come here and talk of cutting it up like a cake, if I ever hear a word more of you and your levelling lies——"

"You seem to be a rather turbulent public meeting," observed Horne Fisher; "but do go on. What will happen if I try to divide this estate decently among decent people?"

The poacher had recovered a grim composure as he replied:

"There will be no partridge to rush in between."

With that he turned his back, evidently resolved to say no more, and walked past the temple to the extreme end of the islet, where he stood staring into the water. Fisher followed him, but when his repeated question evoked no answer, turned back towards the shore. In doing so he took a second and closer look at the artificial temple, and noted some curious things about it. Most of these theatrical things were as thin as theatrical scenery, and he expected the classic shrine to be a shallow thing, a mere shell or mask. But there was some substantial bulk of it behind, buried in the trees, which had a grey labyrinthine look like serpents of stone, and lifted a load of leafy towers to the sky. But what arrested Fisher's eye was that in this bulk of grey-white stone behind there was a single door with great rusty bolts outside; the bolts, however, were not shot across so as to secure it. Then he walked round the small building and found no other opening except one small grating, like a ventilator, high up in the wall.

He retraced his steps thoughtfully along the causeway to the banks of the lake, and sat down on the stone steps between the two sculptured funereal urns. Then he lit a cigarette and smoked it in ruminant manner; eventually he took out a notebook and wrote down various phrases, numbering and re-numbering them till they stood in the following order:

The Man Who Knew Too Much

(1) "Squire Hawker disliked his first wife.
(2) "He married his second wife for her money.
(3) "Long Adam says the estate is really his.
(4) "Long Adam hangs round the island temple, which looks like a prison.
(5) "Squire Hawker was not poor when he gave up the estate.
(6) "Verner was poor when he got the estate."

He gazed at these notes with a gravity which gradually turned to a hard smile, threw away his cigarette, and resumed his search for a short cut to the great house. He soon picked up the path which, winding among clipped hedges and flower-beds, brought him in front of its long Palladian façade. It had the usual appearance of being, not a private house, but a sort of public building sent into exile in the provinces.

He first found himself in the presence of the butler, who really looked much older than the building; for the architecture was dated as Georgian; but the man's face, under a highly unnatural brown wig, was wrinkled with what might have been centuries. Only his prominent eyes were alive and alert, as if with protest. Fisher glanced at him, and then stopped and said:

"Excuse me, weren't you with the late squire, Mr. Hawker?"

"Yes, sir," said the man gravely. "Usher is my name. What can I do for you?"

"Only take me in to Sir Francis Verner," replied the visitor.

Sir Francis Verner was sitting in an easy chair beside a small table in a large room hung with tapestries. On the table were a small flask and glass, with the green glimmer of a liqueur, and a cup of black coffee. He was clad in a quiet grey suit, with a moderately harmonious purple tie; but Fisher saw something about the turn of his fair moustache and the lie of his flat hair. It suddenly revealed that his name was Franz Werner.

"You are Mr. Horne Fisher," he said. "Won't you sit down?"

"No, thank you," replied Fisher. "I fear this is not

The Fool of the Family

a friendly occasion, and I will remain standing. Possibly you know that I am already standing—standing for Parliament, in fact."

"I am aware we are political opponents," replied Verner, raising his eyebrows. "But I think it would be better if we fought in a sporting spirit, in a spirit of English fair play."

"Much better," assented Fisher. "It would be much better if you were English, and very much better if you had ever played fair. But what I've come to say can be said very shortly. I don't quite know how we stand with the law about that old Hawker story, but my chief object is to prevent England being entirely ruled by people like you. So, whatever the law would say, I will say no more if you will retire from the election at once."

"You are evidently a lunatic," said Verner.

"My psychology may be a little abnormal," replied Horne Fisher in a rather hazy manner. "I am subject to dreams, especially day-dreams. Sometimes what is happening to me grows vivid in a curious double way, as if it had happened before. Have you ever had that mystical feeling that things have happened before?"

"I hope you are a harmless lunatic," said Verner.

But Fisher was still staring in an absent fashion at the golden gigantic figures and traceries of brown and red in the tapestries on the walls. Then he looked again at Verner and resumed:

"I have a feeling that this interview has happened before, here, in this tapestried room, and we are two ghosts revisiting a haunted chamber. But it was Squire Hawker who sat where you sit, and it was you who stood where I stand."

He paused a moment, and then added with simplicity:

"I suppose I am a blackmailer too."

"If you are," said Sir Francis, "I promise you you shall go to jail."

But his face had a shade on it that looked like the reflection of the green wine gleaming on the table. Horne Fisher regarded him steadily and answered quietly enough.

"Blackmailers do not always go to jail. Sometimes

The Man Who Knew Too Much

they go to Parliament. But though Parliament is rotten enough already, you shall not go there if I can help it. I am not so criminal as you were in bargaining with crime. You made a squire give up his country seat. I only ask you to give up your parliamentary seat."

Sir Francis Verner sprang to his feet and looked about for one of the bell-ropes of the old-fashioned curtained room.

"Where is Usher?" he cried, with a livid face.

"And who is Usher?" said Fisher softly. "I wonder how much Usher knows of the truth."

Verner's hand fell from the bell-rope, and after standing for a moment with rolling eyes he strode abruptly from the room. Fisher went out by the other door by which he had entered and, seeing no sign of Usher, let himself out and betook himself again towards the town.

That night he put an electric torch in his pocket and set out alone in the darkness to add the last links to his argument. There was much that he did not yet know, but he thought he knew where he could find the knowledge. The night closed dark and stormy, and the black gap in the wall looked blacker than ever; the wood seemed to have grown thicker and darker in a day. If the deserted lake, with its black woods and grey urns and images, had looked desolate even by daylight, under the night and the growing storm it seemed still more like the pool of Acheron in the land of lost souls. As he stepped carefully along the jetty of stones he seemed to be travelling further and further into the abyss of night, and to have left behind him the last points from which it would be possible to signal to the land of the living. The lake seemed to have grown larger than a sea, but a sea of black and slimy waters that slept with abominable serenity, as if they had washed out the world. There was so much of this nightmare sense of extension and expansion that he was strangely surprised to come to his desert island so soon. But he knew it for a place of inhuman silence and solitude, and he felt as if he had been walking for years.

Nerving himself to a more normal mood, he paused under one of the dark dragon trees that branched out

The Fool of the Family

above him, and, taking out his torch, turned in the direction of the door at the back of the temple. It was unbolted as before, and the thought stirred faintly in him that it was slightly open, though only by a crack. The more he thought of it, however, the more certain he grew that this was but one of the common illusions of light coming from a different angle. He studied in a more scientific spirit the details of the door, with its rusty bolts and hinges, when he became conscious of something very near him; indeed, nearly above his head. Something was dangling from the trees that was not a broken branch. For some seconds he stood as still as stone and as cold. What he saw above him were the legs of a man hanging, presumably of a dead man hanged. But the next moment he knew better. The man was literally alive and kicking, and an instant after he had dropped to the ground and turned on the intruder. Simultaneously three or four other trees seemed to come to life in the same fashion. Five or six other figures had fallen on their feet from those unnatural nests. It was as if the place were an island of monkeys. But a moment after they had made a stampede towards him; and when they laid their hands on him he knew that they were men.

With the electric torch in his hand he struck the foremost of them so furiously in the face that the man stumbled and rolled over on the slimy grass; but the torch was broken and extinguished, leaving everything in a denser obscurity. He flung another man flat against the temple wall, so that he slid to the ground; but a third and a fourth carried Fisher off his feet and began to bear him, struggling, towards the doorway. Even in the bewilderment of the battle he was conscious that the door was standing open. Someone was summoning the roughs from inside.

The moment they were within they hurled him upon a sort of bench or bed with violence but with no damage, for the settee, or whatever it was, seemed to be comfortably cushioned for his reception. Their violence had in it a great element of haste, and before he could rise they had all rushed for the door to escape. Whatever bandits they were that infested this desert island, they were

The Man Who Knew Too Much

obviously uneasy about their job and very anxious to be quit of it. He had the flying fancy that regular criminals would hardly be in such a panic. The next moment the great door crashed to, and he could hear the bolts shriek as they shot into their place and the feet of the retreating men scampering and stumbling along the causeway. But rapidly as it happened, it did not happen before Fisher had done something that he wanted to do. Unable to rise from his sprawling attitude in that flash of time, he had shot out one of his long legs and hooked it round the ankle of the last man disappearing through the door. The man swayed and toppled over inside the prison chamber, and the door closed between him and his fleeing companions. Clearly they were in too much haste to realize that they had left one of their company behind.

The man sprang to his feet again and hammered and kicked furiously at the door. Fisher's sense of humour began to recover from the rough and tumble, and he sat up on his sofa with something of his native nonchalance. But as he listened to the captive beating on the door of the prison a new and curious reflection came to him.

The natural course for a man thus wishing to attract his friends' attention would be to call out, to shout as well as kick. This man was making as much noise as he could with his feet and hands, but not a sound came from his throat. Why couldn't he speak?

At first he thought the man might be gagged; which was manifestly absurd. Then his fancy fell back on the ugly idea that the man was dumb. He hardly knew why it was so ugly an idea, but it affected his imagination in a dark and disproportionate fashion. There seemed to be something creepy about the idea of being left alone in a dark room with a deaf mute. It was almost as if such a defect were a deformity. It was almost as if it went with other and worse deformities. It was as if the shape he could not trace in the darkness were some shape that should not see the sun.

Then he had a flash of sanity, and also of insight. The explanation was very simple, but rather interesting. Obviously the man did not use his voice because he did not wish his voice to be recognized. He hoped to escape

The Fool of the Family

from that dark place before Fisher found out who he was. And who was he? One thing at least was clear. He was one or other of the four or five men with whom Fisher had already talked in those parts and in the development of that strange story.

"Now, I wonder who you are," he said aloud, with all his old lazy urbanity. "I suppose it's no good trying to throttle you in order to find out; it would be displeasing to pass the night with a corpse. Besides, I might be the corpse. I've got no matches, and I've smashed my torch, so I can only speculate. Who could you be, now? Let us think?"

The man thus genially addressed had desisted from drumming on the door and retreated sullenly into a corner as Fisher continued to address him in a flowing monologue.

"Probably you are the poacher who says he isn't a poacher. He says he's a landed proprietor; but he will permit me to inform him that, whatever he is, he's a fool. What hope can there ever be of a free peasantry in England if the peasants themselves are such snobs as to want to be gentlemen? How can we make a democracy with no democrats? As it is, you want to be a landlord, and so you consent to be criminal. And in that, you know, you are rather like somebody else. And, now I think of it, perhaps you are somebody else."

There was a silence broken only by breathing from the corner and the murmur of the rising storm, that came in through the small grating above the man's head. Horne Fisher continued:

"Are you only a servant—perhaps that rather sinister old servant who was butler to Hawker and Verner? If so, you are certainly the only link between the two periods. But, if so, why do you degrade yourself to serve this dirty foreigner, when you at least saw the last of a genuine national gentry? People like you are generally at least patriotic. Doesn't England mean anything to you, Mr. Usher? All of which eloquence is possibly wasted, as perhaps you are not Mr. Usher.

"More likely you are Verner himself; and it's no good wasting eloquence to make you ashamed of yourself; nor

The Man Who Knew Too Much

is it any good to curse you for corrupting England; nor are you the right person to curse. It is the English who deserve to be cursed, and are cursed, because they allowed such vermin to crawl into the high places of their heroes and their kings. I won't dwell on the idea that you're Verner or the throttling might begin after all. Is there anyone else you could be? Surely you're not some servant of the other rival organization. I can't believe you're Gryce, the agent; and yet Gryce had a spark of the fanatic in his eye too, and men will do extraordinary things in these paltry feuds of politics. Or, if not the servant, is it the . . . no, I can't believe it . . . not the red blood of manhood and liberty . . . not the democratic ideal. . . ."

He sprang up in excitement, and at the same moment a growl of thunder came through the grating beyond. The storm had broken, and with it a new light broke on his mind. There was something else that might happen in a moment.

"Do you know what that means?" he cried. "It means that God Himself may hold a candle to show me your infernal face."

Then next moment came a crash of thunder, but before the thunder a white light had filled the whole room for a single split second.

Fisher had seen two things in front of him. One was the black and white pattern of the iron grating against the sky; the other was the face in the corner. It was the face of his brother.

Nothing came from Horne Fisher's lips except a Christian name, which was followed by a silence more dreadful than the dark. At last the other figure stirred and sprang up, and the voice of Harry Fisher was heard for the first time in that horrible room.

"You've seen me, I suppose," he said, "and we may as well have a light now. You could have turned it on at any time if you'd found the switch."

He pressed a button in the wall, and all the details of that room sprang into something stronger than daylight. Indeed, the details were so unexpected that for a moment they turned the captive's rocking mind from the last

The Fool of the Family

personal revelation. The room, so far from being a dungeon cell, was more like a drawing-room, even a lady's drawing-room, except for some boxes of cigars and bottles of wine that were stacked, with books and magazines, on a side table. A second glance showed him that the more masculine fittings were quite recent, and that the more feminine background was quite old. His eye caught a strip of faded tapestry which startled him into speech to the momentary oblivion of bigger matters.

"This place was furnished from the great house," he said.

"Yes," replied the other, "and I think you know why."

"I think I do," said Horne Fisher, "and before I go on to more extraordinary things, I will say what I think. Squire Hawker played both the bigamist and the bandit. His first wife was not dead when he married the Jewess; she was imprisoned on this island. She bore a child here, who now haunts his birth-place under the name of Long Adam. A bankrupt company-promoter named Verner discovered the secret, and blackmailed the squire into surrendering the estate. That's all quite clear, and very easy. And now let me go on to something more difficult. And that is for you to explain what the devil you are doing kidnapping your born brother."

After a pause Henry Fisher answered.

"I suppose you didn't expect to see me," he said. "But, after all, what could you expect?"

"I'm afraid I don't follow," said Horne Fisher.

"I mean what else could you expect, after making such a muck of it?" said his brother sulkily. "We all thought you were so clever. How could we know you were going to be—well, really, such a rotten failure."

"This is rather curious," said the candidate, frowning. "Without vanity, I was not under the impression that my candidature was a failure. All the big meetings were successful, and crowds of people have promised me votes."

"I should jolly well think they had," said Harry grimly. "You've made a landslide with your confounded

The Man Who Knew Too Much

acres and a cow, and Verner can hardly get a vote anywhere. Oh, it's too rotten for anything."

"What on earth do you mean?"

"Why, you lunatic," cried Harry in tones of ringing sincerity, "you didn't suppose you were meant to *win* the seat, did you? Oh, it's too childish! I tell you Verner's *got* to get in. Of course he's got to get in. He's to have the Exchequer next session, and there's the Egyptian Loan and Lord knows what else. We only wanted you to split the Reform vote, because accidents might happen after Hughes had made a score at Barkington."

"I see," said Fisher, "and you, I think, are a pillar and ornament of the Reform party. As you say, I am not clever."

The appeal to party loyalty fell on deaf ears; for the Pillar of Reform was brooding on other things At last he said in a more troubled voice:

"I didn't want you to catch me; I knew it would be a shock. But I tell you what, you never would have caught me if I hadn't come here myself, to see they didn't ill-treat you, and to make sure everything was as comfortable as it could be." There was even a sort of break in his voice as he added: "I got those cigars because I know you like them"

Emotions are queer things; and the idiocy of this concession suddenly softened Horne Fisher like an unfathomable pathos.

"Never mind, old chap," he said, "we'll say no more about it. I'll admit that you're really as kind-hearted and affectionate a scoundrel and hypocrite as ever sold himself to ruin his country. There, I can't say handsomer than that. Thank you for the cigars, old man; I'll have one if you don't mind."

By the time that Horne Fisher had ended his telling of this story to Harold March, they had come out into one of the public parks, and taken a seat on a rise of ground overlooking wide green spaces under a blue and empty sky; and there was something incongruous in the words with which the narration ended.

"I have been in that room ever since," said Horne

The Fool of the Family

Fisher. "I am in it now. I won the election, but I never went to the House. My life has been a life in that little room on that lonely island. Plenty of books and cigars and luxuries; plenty of knowledge and interest and information; but never a voice out of that tomb to reach the world outside. I shall probably die there."

And he smiled as he looked across the vast green park to the grey horizon.

VIII.—THE VENGEANCE OF THE STATUE

It was on the sunny veranda of a seaside hotel, overlooking a pattern of flower-beds and a strip of blue sea, that Horne Fisher and Harold March had their final explanation, which might be called an explosion.

Harold March, now famous as one of the first political writers of his time, had come to the little table and sat down at it with a subdued excitement smouldering in his somewhat cloudy and dreamy blue eyes. In the newspapers which he tossed from him on to the table there was enough to explain some if not all of his emotion. Public affairs in every department had reached a crisis. The Government which had stood so long that men were used to it, as they are used to a hereditary despotism, had begun to be accused of blunders and even of financial abuses. Some said that the experiment of attempting to establish a peasantry in the west of England, on the lines of an early fancy of Horne Fisher's, had resulted in nothing but dangerous quarrels with more industrial neighbours. There had been particular complaints of the ill-treatment of harmless foreigners, chiefly Asiatics, who happened to be employed in the new scientific works constructed on the coast. Indeed the new power which had arisen in Siberia, backed by Japan and other powerful allies, was inclined to take the matter up in the interests of its exiled subjects, and there had been wild talk about ambassadors and ultimatums. But something much more serious, in its personal interest for March himself, seemed to fill his meeting with his friend with a mixture of embarrassment and indignation.

Perhaps it increased his annoyance that there was a certain unusual liveliness about the usually languid figure of Fisher. The ordinary image of him in March's mind was that of a pallid and bald-browed gentleman, who

The Vengeance of the Statue

seemed to be prematurely old as well as prematurely bald. He was remembered as a man who expressed the opinions of a pessimist in the language of a lounger. Even now March could not be certain whether the change was merely a sort of masquerade of sunshine, or that effect of clear colours and clean-cut outlines that is always visible on the parade of a marine resort, relieved against the blue dado of the sea. But Fisher had a flower in his buttonhole, and his friend could have sworn he carried his cane with something almost like the swagger of a fighter. With such clouds gathering over England, the pessimist seemed to be the only man who carried his own sunshine.

"Look here," said Harold March abruptly, "you've been no end of a friend to me, and I never was so proud of a friendship before; but there's something I must get off my chest. The more I found out the less I understood how you could stand it. And I tell you I'm going to stand it no longer."

Horne Fisher gazed across at him gravely and attentively, but rather as if he were a long way off.

"You know I always liked you," said Fisher quietly, "but I also respect you, which is not always the same thing. You may possibly guess that I like a good many people I don't respect. Perhaps it is my tragedy; perhaps it is my fault. But you are very different, and I promise you this: that I will never try to keep you as somebody to be liked, at the price of your not being respected."

"I know you are magnanimous," said March after a silence, "and yet you tolerate and perpetuate everything that is mean." Then after another silence, he added: "Do you remember when we first met, when you were fishing in that brook in the affair of the target? And do you remember you said that, after all, it might do no harm if I could blow the whole tangle of this society to hell with dynamite?"

"Yes, and what of that?" asked Fisher.

"Only that I'm going to blow it to hell with dynamite," said Harold March, "and I think it right to give you fair warning. For a long time I didn't believe things were as bad as you said they were. But I never

The Man Who Knew Too Much

felt as if I could have bottled up what you knew, supposing you really knew it. Well, the long and short of it is that I've got a conscience, and now, at last, I've also got a chance. I've been put in charge of a big independent paper, with a free hand, and we're going to open a cannonade on corruption."

"That will be—Attwood, I suppose," said Fisher reflectively. "Timber merchant. Knows a lot about China."

"He knows a lot about England," said March doggedly, "and I know it too, we're not going to hush it up any longer. The people of this country have a right to know how they're ruled—or rather ruined. The Chancellor *is* in the pocket of the money-lenders and has to do as he is told; otherwise he's bankrupt and a bad sort of bankruptcy too, with nothing but cards and actresses behind it. The Prime Minister *was* in the petrol contract business, and deep in it too. The Foreign Minister is a wreck of drink and drugs. When you say that plainly about a man who may send thousands of Englishmen to die for nothing, you're called personal. If a poor engine-driver gets drunk and sends thirty or forty people to death nobody complains of the exposure being personal. The engine-driver is not a person."

"I quite agree with you," said Fisher calmly. "You are perfectly right."

"If you agree with us, why the devil don't you act with us?" demanded his friend. "If you think it's right why don't you do what's right? It's awful to think of a man of your abilities simply blocking the road to reform."

"We have often talked about that," replied Fisher with the same composure. "The Prime Minister is my father's friend. The Foreign Minister married my sister. The Chancellor of the Exchequer is my first cousin. I mention the genealogy in some detail just now because I am enjoying an emotion that is entirely new to me; a happy sensation I never remember having had before."

"What the devil do you mean?"

"I am feeling proud of my family," said Horne Fisher.

Harold March stared at him with round blue eyes, and

The Vengeance of the Statue

seemed too much mystified even to ask a question. Fisher leaned back in his chair in his lazy fashion, and smiled as he continued:

"Look here, my dear fellow. Let me ask a question in turn. You imply that I have always known these things about my unfortunate kinsmen. So I have. Do you suppose that Attwood hasn't always known them? Do you suppose he hasn't always known you, as an honest man who would say these things when he got a chance? Why does Attwood unmuzzle you like a dog at this moment, after all these years? I know why he does; I knew a good many things, far too many things. And therefore, as I have the honour to remark, I am proud of my family at last."

"But why?" repeated March rather feebly.

"I am proud of the Chancellor because he gambled, and the Foreign Minister because he drank, and the Prime Minister because he took a commission on a contract," said Fisher firmly. "I am proud of them because they did these things, and can be denounced for them, and know they can be denounced for them, and *are standing firm for all that.* I take off my hat to them because they are defying blackmail, and refusing to smash their country to save themselves. I salute them as if they were going to die on the battlefield."

After a paused, he continued:

"And it will be a battlefield too, and not a metaphorical one. We have yielded to foreign financiers so long that now it is war or ruin. Even the people, even the country people, are beginning to suspect that they are being ruined. That is the meaning of the regrettable incidents in the newspapers."

"The meaning of the outrages on Orientals?" asked March.

"The meaning of the outrages on Orientals," replied Fisher, "is that the financiers have introduced Chinese labour into this country with the deliberate intention of reducing workmen and peasants to starvation. Our unhappy politicians have made concession after concession, and now they are asking concessions which amount to our ordering a massacre of our own poor. If we do not

The Man Who Knew Too Much

fight now, we shall never fight again. They will have put England in an economic position of starving in a week. But we are going to fight now; I shouldn't wonder if there were an ultimatum in a week and an invasion in a fortnight. All the past corruption and cowardice is hampering us, of course. The west country is pretty stormy and doubtful even in a military sense, and the Irish regiments there, that are supposed to support us by the new treaty, are pretty well in mutiny, for of course this infernal coolie capitalism is being pushed in Ireland too. But it's to stop now, and if the Government message of reassurance gets through to them in time they may turn up after all by the time the enemy lands. For my poor old gang is going to stand to its guns at last. Of course it's only natural that when they have been whitewashed for half a century as paragons, their sins should come back on them at the very moment when they are behaving like men for the first time in their lives. Well, I tell you, March, I know them inside out, and I know they are behaving like heroes. Every man of them ought to have a statue, and on the pedestal words like those of the noblest ruffian of the Revolution: '*Que mon nom soit flétri; que la France soit libre.*'"

"Good God," cried March, "shall we never get to the bottom of your mines and counter-mines?"

After a silence Fisher answered in a lower voice, looking his friend in the eyes.

"Did you think there was nothing but evil at the bottom of them?" he asked gently. "Did you think I had found nothing but filth in the deep seas into which fate has thrown me? Believe me, you never know the best about men till you know the worst about them. It does not dispose of their strange human souls to know that they were exhibited to the world as impossible impeccable waxworks, who never looked after a woman or knew the meaning of a bribe. Even in a palace life can be lived well, and even in a parliament life can be lived with occasional efforts to live it well. I tell you it is as true of these rich fools and rascals as it is true of every poor footpad and pickpocket: that only Gods knows how good they have tried to be. God alone knows what the

The Vengeance of the Statue

conscience can survive, or how a man who has lost his honour will still try to save his soul."

There was another silence, and March sat staring at the table, and Fisher at the sea. Then Fisher suddenly sprang to his feet and caught up his hat and stick with all his new alertness and even pugnacity.

"Look here, old fellow," he cried, "let us make a bargain. Before you open your campaign for Attwood come down and stay with us for one week to hear what we're really doing. I mean with the Faithful Few, formerly known as the Old Gang, occasionally to be described as the Low Lot. There are really only five of us that are quite fixed and organizing the national defence, and we're living like a garrison in a sort of broken-down hotel in Kent. Come and see what we're really doing and what there is to be done, and do us justice. And after that, with unalterable love and affection for you, publish and be damned."

Thus it came about that in the last week before war, when events moved most rapidly, Harold March found himself one of a sort of small house-party of the people he was proposing to denounce. They were living simply enough, for people with their tastes, in an old brown brick inn faced with ivy and surrounded by rather dismal gardens. At the back of the building the garden ran up very steeply to a road along the ridge above, and a zig-zag path scaled the slope in sharp angles, turning to and fro amid evergreens so sombre that they might rather be called ever-black. Here and there up the slope were statues having all the cold monstrosity of such minor ornaments of the eighteenth century, and a whole row of them ran as on a terrace along the last bank at the bottom, opposite the back door. This detail fixed itself first in March's mind merely because it figured in the first conversation he had with one of the Cabinet Ministers.

The Cabinet Ministers were rather older than he had expected to find them. The Prime Minister no longer looked a boy, though he still looked a little like a baby. But it was one of those old and venerable babies, and the baby had soft grey hair. Everything about him was

149

The Man Who Knew Too Much

soft, to his speech and his way of walking; but over and above that his chief function seemed to be sleep. People left alone with him got so used to his eyes being closed that they were almost startled when they realized in the stillness that the eyes were wide open, and even watching. One thing at least would always make the old gentleman open his eyes. The one thing he really cared for in this world was his hobby of armour and weapons, especially Eastern weapons, and he would talk for hours about Damascus blades and Arab swordsmanship. Lord James Herries, the Chancellor of the Exchequer, was a short, dark, sturdy man with a very sallow face and a very sullen manner, which contrasted with the gorgeous flower in his buttonhole and his festive trick of being always slightly over-dressed. It was something of a euphemism to call him a well-known man about town. There was perhaps more mystery in the question of how a man who lived for pleasure seemed to get so little pleasure out of it. Sir David Archer, the Foreign Secretary, was the only one of them who was a self-made man, and the only one of them who looked like an aristocrat. He was tall and thin and very handsome, with a grizzled beard; his grey hair was very curly, and even rose in front in two rebellious ringlets that seemed to the fanciful to tremble like the antennæ of some giant insect, or to stir sympathetically with the restless tufted eyebrows over his rather haggard eyes. For the Foreign Secretary made no secret of his somewhat nervous condition, whatever might be the cause of it.

"Do you know that mood when one could scream because a mat is crooked?" he said to March as they walked up and down in the back garden below the line of dingy statues. "Women get into it when they've worked too hard, and I've been working pretty hard lately, of course. It drives me mad when Herries will wear his hat a little on one side; habit of looking like a gay dog. Some time, I swear, I'll knock it off. That statue of Britannia over there isn't quite straight; it sticks forward a bit, as if the lady were going to topple over. The damned thing is that it doesn't topple over and be done with it. See, it's clamped with an iron prop. Don't

The Vengeance of the Statue

be surprised if I get up in the middle of the night to hike it down."

They paced the path for a few moments in silence, and then he continued: "It's odd those little things seem specially big when there are bigger things to worry about. We'd better go in and do some work."

Horne Fisher evidently allowed for all the neurotic possibilities of Archer and the dissipated habits of Herries, and, whatever his faith in their present firmness, did not unduly tax their time and attention, even in the case of the Prime Minister. He had got the consent of the latter to finally committing the important documents, with the orders to the western armies, to the care of a less conspicuous and more solid person—an uncle of his named Horne Hewitt, a rather colourless country squire who had been a good soldier, and was the military adviser of the committee. He was charged with expediting the Government pledge, along with the concerted military plans, to the half-mutinous command in the west, and the still more urgent task of seeing that it did not fall into the hands of the enemy, who might appear at any moment from the east. Over and above this military official, the only other person present was a police official, a certain Dr. Prince, originally a police surgeon and now a distinguished detective, sent to be a bodyguard to the group. He was a square-faced man with big spectacles and a grimace that expressed the intention of keeping his mouth shut. Nobody else shared their captivity except the hotel proprietor, a crusty Kentish man with a crab-apple face, one or two of his servants, and another servant privately attached to Lord James Herries. He was a young Scotchman named Campbell, who looked much more distinguished than his bilious-looking master, having chestnut hair and a long saturnine face with large but fine features. He was probably the one really efficient person in the house.

After about four days of the informal council, March had come to feel a sort of grotesque sublimity about these dubious figures, defiant in the twilight of danger, as if they were hunchbacks and cripples left alone to defend a town. All were working hard, and he himself looked

The Man Who Knew Too Much

up from writing a page of memoranda in a private room, to see Horne Fisher standing in the doorway accoutred as if for travel. He fancied that Fisher looked a little pale, and after a moment that gentleman shut the door behind him and said quietly:

"Well, the worst has happened. Or nearly the worst"

"The enemy has landed," cried March, and sprang erect out of his chair.

"Oh, I knew the enemy would land," said Fisher with composure. "Yes, he's landed, but that's not the worst that could happen. The worst is that there's a leak of some sort, even from this fortress of ours. It's been a bit of a shock to me, I can tell you, though I suppose it's illogical. After all, I was full of admiration at finding three honest men in politics. I ought not to be full of astonishment if I find only two."

He ruminated a moment and then said, in such a fashion that Mark could hardly tell if he were changing the subject or no:

"It's hard at first to believe that a fellow like Herries, who had pickled himself in vice like vinegar, can have any scruple left. But about that I've noticed a curious thing. Patriotism is not the first virtue. Patriotism rots into Prussianism when you pretend it is the first virtue. But patriotism is sometimes the last virtue. A man will swindle or seduce who will not sell his country. But who knows?"

"But what is to be done?" cried March indignantly.

"My uncle has the papers safe enough," replied Fisher, "and is sending them west to-night; but somebody is trying to get at them from outside, I fear with the assistance of somebody inside. All I can do at present is to try and head off the man outside, and I must get away now and do it. I shall be back in about twenty-four hours. While I'm away I want you to keep an eye on these people and find out what you can. Au revoir."

He vanished down the stairs, and from the window March could see him mount a motor-cycle and trail away towards the neighbouring town.

On the following morning March was sitting in the window-seat of the old inn parlour, which was oak

The Vengeance of the Statue

panelled and ordinarily rather dark; but on that occasion it was full of the white light of a curiously clear morning; the moon had shone brilliantly for the last two or three nights. He was himself somewhat in shadow in the corner of the window-seat, and Lord James Herries, coming in hastily from the garden behind, did not see him. Lord James clutched the back of a chair as if to steady himself, and sitting down abruptly at the table, littered with the last meal, poured himself out a tumbler of brandy and drank it. He sat with his back to March, but his yellow face appeared in a round mirror beyond, and the tinge of it was like that of some horrible malady. As March moved, he started violently and faced round.

"My God," he cried, "have you seen what's outside?"

"Outside," repeated the other, glancing over his shoulder at the garden.

"Oh, go and look for yourself," cried Herries in a sort of fury. "Hewitt's murdered and his papers stolen, that's all."

He turned his back again and sat down with a thud; his square shoulders were shaking. Harold March darted out of the doorway into the back garden with its steep slope of statues.

The first thing he saw was Dr. Prince, the detective, peering through his spectacles at something on the ground, the second was the thing he was peering at. Even after the sensational news he had heard inside, the sight was something of a sensation.

The monstrous stone image of Britannia was lying prone and face downwards on the garden path, and there stuck out at random from underneath it, like the legs of a smashed fly, an arm clad in a white shirt sleeve and a leg clad in a khaki trouser, and hair of the unmistakable sandy grey that belonged to Horne Fisher's unfortunate uncle. There were pools of blood, and the limbs were quite stiff in death.

"Couldn't this have been an accident?" said March, finding words at last.

"Look for yourself, I say," repeated the harsh voice of Herries, who had followed him with restless movements out of the door. "The papers are gone, I tell you. The

The Man Who Knew Too Much

fellow tore the coat off the corpse and cut the papers out of the inner pocket. There's the coat over there on the bank, with the great slash in it."

"But wait a minute," said the detective Prince quietly. "In that case there seems to be something of a mystery. A murderer might somehow have managed to throw the statue down on him, as he seems to have done. But I bet he couldn't easily have lifted it up again. I've tried, and I'm sure it would want three men at least. Yet we must suppose, on that theory, that the murderer first knocked him down as he walked past, using the statue as a stone club, then lifted it up again, took him out and deprived him of his coat, then put him back again in the posture of death and neatly replaced the statue. I tell you, it's physically impossible. And how else could he have unclothed a man covered with that stone monument? It's worse than the conjurer's trick, when a man shuffles a coat off with his wrists tied."

"Could he have thrown down the statue after he'd stripped the corpse?" asked March.

"And why?" asked Prince sharply. "If he'd killed his man and got his papers, he'd be away like the wind. He wouldn't potter about in a garden excavating the pedestals of statues. Besides—hallo, who's that up there?"

High on the ridge above them, drawn in dark thin lines against the sky, was a figure looking so long and lean as to be almost spidery. The dark silhouette of the head showed two small tufts like horns; and they could almost have sworn that the horns moved.

"Archer!" shouted Herries, with sudden passion, and called to him with curses to come down. The figure drew back at the first cry, with an agitated movement so abrupt as almost to be called an antic. The next moment the man seemed to reconsider and collect himself, and began to come down the zigzag garden path, but with obvious reluctance, his feet falling in slower and slower rhythm. Through March's mind was throbbing the phrases that this man himself had used—about going mad in the middle of the night and wrecking the stone figure. Just so, he could fancy, the maniac who had done such a thing

The Vengeance of the Statue

might climb the crest of the hill in that feverish dancing fashion, and look down on the wreck he had made. But the wreck he had made here was not only a wreck of stone.

When the man emerged at last on to the garden path, with the full light on his face and figure, he was walking slowly indeed but easily, and with no appearance of fear.

"This is a terrible thing," he said. "I saw it from above; I was taking a stroll along the ridge."

"Do you mean that you saw the murder?" demanded March, "or the accident? I mean, did you see the statue fall?"

"No," said Archer. "I mean, I saw the statue fallen."

Prince seemed to be paying but little attention; his eye was riveted on an object lying on the path a yard or two from the corpse. It seemed to be a rusty iron bar bent crooked at one end.

"One thing I don't understand," he said, "is all this blood. The poor fellow's skull isn't smashed; most likely his neck is broken; but blood seems to have spouted as if all his arteries were severed. I was wondering if some other instrument—that iron thing, for instance; but I don't see that even that is sharp enough. I suppose nobody knows what it is."

"I know what it is," said Archer, in his deep but somewhat shaky voice. "I've seen it in my nightmares. It was the iron clamp or prop on the pedestal, stuck on to keep the wretched image upright when it began to wobble, I suppose. Anyhow, it was always stuck in the stonework there, and I suppose it came out when the thing collapsed."

Dr. Prince nodded, but he continued to look down at the pools of blood and the bar of iron.

"I'm certain there's something more underneath all this," he said at last. "Perhaps something more underneath the statue. I have a huge sort of hunch that there is. We are four men now, and between us we can lift that great tombstone there."

They all bent their strength to the business; there was

The Man Who Knew Too Much

a silence save for heavy breathing; and then, after an instant of the tottering and staggering of eight legs, the great carven column of rock was rolled away, and the body lying in its shirt and trousers was fully revealed. The spectacles of Dr. Prince seemed almost to enlarge with a restrained radiance like great eyes, for other things were revealed also. One was that the unfortunate Hewitt had a deep gash across the jugular, which the triumphant doctor instantly identified as having been made with a sharp steel edge like a razor. The other was that immediately under the bank lay littered three shining scraps of steel, each nearly a foot long, one pointed and another fitted into a gorgeously jewelled hilt or handle. It was evidently a sort of long Oriental knife, long enough to be called a sword, but with a curious wavy edge, and there was a touch or two of blood on the point.

"I should have expected more blood, hardly on the point," observed Dr. Prince thoughtfully, "but this is certainly the instrument. The slash was certainly made with a weapon shaped like this; and probably the slashing of the pocket as well. I suppose the brute threw in the statue, by way of giving him a public funeral."

March did not answer; he was mesmerized by the strange stones that glittered on the strange sword-hilt; and their possible significance was broadening upon him like a dreadful dawn. It was a curious Asiatic weapon. He knew what name was connected in his memory with curious Asiatic weapons. Lord James spoke his secret thought for him, and yet it startled him like an irrelevance.

"Where is the Prime Minister?" Herries had cried suddenly, and somehow like the bark of a dog at some discovery.

Dr. Prince turned on him his goggles and his grim face, and it was grimmer than ever.

"I cannot find him anywhere," he said. "I looked for him at once, as soon as I found the papers were gone. That servant of yours, Campbell, made a most efficient search; but there are no traces."

There was a long silence, at the end of which Herries uttered another cry, but upon an entirely new note.

The Vengeance of the Statue

"Well, you needn't look for him any longer," he said, "for here he comes, along with your friend Fisher. They look as if they'd been for a little walking tour."

The two figures approaching up the path were indeed those of Fisher, splashed with the mire of travel and carrying a scratch like that of a bramble across one side of his bald forehead, and of the great and grey-haired statesman who looked like a baby and was interested in eastern swords and swordsmanship. But beyond this bodily recognition, March could make neither head nor tail of their presence or demeanour; which seemed to give a final touch of nonsense to the whole nightmare. The more closely he watched them, as they stood listening to the revelations of the detective, the more puzzled he was by their attitude. Fisher seemed grieved at the death of his uncle, but hardly shocked at it; the older man seemed almost openly thinking about something else, and neither had anything to suggest about a further pursuit of the fugitive spy and murderer, in spite of the prodigious importance of the documents he had stolen. When the detective had gone off to busy himself with that department of the business, to telephone and write his report, when Herries had gone back, probably to the brandy bottle, and the Prime Minister had blandly sauntered away towards a comfortable arm-chair in another part of the garden, Horne Fisher spoke directly to Harold March.

"My friend," he said, "I want you to come with me at once; there is no one else I can trust so much as that. The journey will take us most of the day, and the chief business cannot be done till nightfall. So we can talk things over thoroughly on the way. But I want you to be with me; for I rather think it is my hour."

March and Fisher both had motor-bicycles; and the first half of their day's journey consisted in coasting eastward amid the unconversational noise of those uncomfortable engines. But when they came out beyond Canterbury into the flats of eastern Kent, Fisher stopped at a pleasant little public-house beside a sleepy stream, and they sat down to eat and to drink and to speak almost for the first time. It was a brilliant afternoon; birds were

The Man Who Knew Too Much

singing in the wood behind, and the sun shone full on their ale-bench and table; but the face of Fisher in the strong sunlight had a gravity never seen on it before.

"Before we go any further," he said, "there is something you ought to know. You and I have seen some mysterious things, and got to the bottom of them before now; and it's only right that you should get to the bottom of this one. But in dealing with the death of my uncle, I must begin at the other end from where our old detective yarns began. I will give you the steps of deduction presently, if you want to listen to them; but I did not reach the truth of this by steps of deduction. I will first of all tell you the truth itself; because I knew the truth from the first. The other cases I approached from the outside; but in this case I was inside. I myself was the very core and centre of everything."

Something in the speaker's pendant eyelids and grave grey eyes suddenly shook March to his foundations, and he cried distractedly: "I don't understand!" as men do when they fear that they do understand. There was no sound for a space but the happy chatter of the birds, and then Horne Fisher said calmly:

"It was I who killed my uncle. If you particularly want more, it was I who stole the State papers from him."

"Fisher!" cried his friend, in a strangled voice.

"Let me tell you the whole thing before we part," continued the other, "and let me put it, for the sake of clearness, as we used to put our old problems. Now there are two things that are puzzling people about that problem, aren't there? The first is how the murderer managed to slip off the dead man's coat, when he was already pinned to the ground with that stone incubus. The other, which is much smaller and less puzzling, is the fact of the sword that cut his throat being slightly stained at the point, instead of a good deal more stained at the edge. Well, I can dispose of the first question easily. Horne Hewitt took off his own coat before he was killed. I might say he took off his coat to be killed."

The Vengeance of the Statue

"Do you call that an explanation!" exclaimed March. "The words seem more meaningless than the facts."

"Well, let us go on to the other facts," continued Fisher equably. "The reason that particular sword is not stained at the edge with Hewitt's blood is that it was not used to kill Hewitt."

"But the doctor," protested March, "declared distinctly that the wound was made by that particular sword."

"I beg your pardon," replied Fisher. "He did not declare that it was made by that particular sword. He declared it was made by a sword of that particular pattern."

"But it was quite a queer and exceptional pattern," argued March. "Surely it is far too fantastic a coincidence to imagine!"

"It was a fantastic coincidence," reflected Horne Fisher. "It's extraordinary what coincidences do sometimes occur. By the oddest chance in the world, by one chance in a million, it so happened that another sword of exactly the same shape was in the same garden at the same time. It may be partly explained by the fact that I brought them both into the garden myself. . . . Come, my dear fellow, surely you can see now what it means! Put those two things together; there were two duplicate swords, and he took off his coat for himself. It may assist your speculations to recall the fact that I am not exactly an assassin."

"A duel!" exclaimed March, recovering himself. "Of course, I ought to have thought of that. But who was the spy who stole the papers?"

"My uncle was the spy who stole the papers," replied Fisher, "or who tried to steal the papers when I stopped him—in the only way I could. The papers, that should have gone west to reassure our friends and give them the plans for repelling the invasion, would in a few hours have been in the hands of the invader. What could I do? To have denounced one of our friends at this moment would have been to play into the hands of your friend Attwood, and all the party of panic and slavery. Besides, it may be that a man over forty has a sub-

The Man Who Knew Too Much

conscious desire to die as he has lived, and that I wanted in a sense to carry my secrets to the grave. Perhaps a hobby hardens with age, and my hobby has been silence. Perhaps I feel that I have killed my mother's brother, but I have saved my mother's name. Anyhow, I chose a time when I knew you were all asleep, and he was walking alone in the garden. I saw all the stone statues standing in the moonlight; and I myself was like one of those stone statues walking. In a voice that was not my own I told him of his treason and demanded the papers, and when he refused I forced him to take one of the two swords. The swords were among some specimens sent down here for the Prime Minister's inspection; he is a collector, you know; they were the only equal weapons I could find. To cut an ugly tale short, we fought there on the path in front of the Britannia statue; he was a man of great strength, but I had somewhat the advantage in skill. His sword grazed my forehead almost at the moment when mine sank into the joint in his neck. He fell against the statue, like Cæsar against Pompey's, hanging on to the iron rail; his sword was already broken. When I saw the blood from that deadly wound everything else went from me; I dropped my sword, and ran as if to lift him up. As I bent towards him something happened too quick for me to follow. I do not know whether the iron bar was rotted with rust and came away in his hand, or whether he rent it out of the rock with his ape-like strength; but the thing was in his hand, and with his dying energies he swung it over my head as I knelt there unarmed beside him. I looked up wildly to avoid the blow, and saw above us the great bulk of Britannia leaning outwards like the figure-head of a ship. The next instant I saw it was leaning an inch or two more than usual, and all the skies with their outstanding stars seemed to be leaning with it. For the third second it was as if the skies fell; and in the fourth I was standing in the quiet garden, looking down on that flat ruin of stone and bone at which you were looking down to-day. He had plucked out the last prop that held up the British goddess, and she had fallen and crushed the traitor in her fall. I turned and darted for the coat which I knew to

The Vengeance of the Statue

contain the package, ripped it up with my sword, and raced away up the garden path to where my motor-bike was waiting on the road above. I had every reason for haste, but I fled without looking back at the statue and the body, and I think the thing I fled from was the sight of that appalling allegory.

"Then I did the rest of what I had to do. All through the night and into the daybreak and the daylight I went humming through the villages and markets of South England like a travelling bullet, till I came to the headquarters in the west where the trouble was. I was just in time. I was able to placard the place, so to speak, with the news that the Government had not betrayed them, and that they would find supports if they push eastward against the enemy. There's no time to tell you all that happened, but I tell you it was the day of my life. A triumph like a torchlight procession, with torchlights that might have been firebrands. The mutinies simmered down; the men of Somerset and the western counties came pouring into the market-places—the men who died with Arthur and stood firm with Alfred. The Irish regiments rallied to them, after a scene like a riot, and marched eastward out of the town singing Fenian songs. There was all that is not understood about the dark laughter of that people, in the delight with which, even when marching with the English to the defence of England, they shouted at the top of their voices: 'High upon the gallows tree stood the noble-hearted three. . . . With England's cruel cord about them cast.' However, the chorus was 'God Save Ireland,' and we could all have sung that just then, in one sense or another.

"But there was another side to my mission. I carried the plans of the defence, and to a great extent, luckily, the plans of the invasion also. I won't worry you with strategies; but we knew where the enemy had pushed forward the great battery that covered all his movements; and though our friends from the west could hardly arrive in time to intercept the main movement, they might get within long artillery range of the battery and shell it, if they only knew exactly where it was. They could hardly tell that, unless somebody round about here sent up some

The Man Who Knew Too Much

sort of signal. But somehow, I rather fancy that somebody will."

With that he got up from the table, and they remounted their machines, and went eastward into the advancing twilight of evening. The levels of the landscape were repeated in flat strips of floating cloud, and the last colours of day clung to the circle of the horizon. Receding farther and farther behind them was the semicircle of the last hills, and it was quite suddenly that they saw afar off the dim line of the sea. It was not a strip of bright blue as they had seen it from the sunny veranda, but of a sinister and smoky violet, a tint that seemed ominous and dark. Here Horne Fisher dismounted once more.

"We must walk the rest of the way," he said, "and the last bit of all I must walk alone."

He bent down and began to unstrap something from his bicycle. It was something that had puzzled his companion all the way, in spite of what held him to more interesting riddles; it appeared to be several lengths of pole strapped together and wrapped up in paper. Fisher took it under his arm and began to pick his way across the turf. The ground was growing more tumbled and irregular, and he was walking towards a mass of thickets and small woods; night grew darker every moment.

"We must not talk any more," said Fisher. "I will whisper to you when you are to halt. Don't try to follow me then, for it will only spoil the show; one man can barely crawl safely to the spot, and two would certainly be caught."

"I would follow you anywhere," replied March, "but I would halt, too, if that is better."

"I know you would," said his friend in a low voice. "Perhaps you're the only man I ever quite trusted in this world."

A few paces farther on they came to the end of a great ridge or mound, looking monstrous against the dim sky, and Fisher stopped with a gesture. He caught his companion's hand and wrung it with a violent tenderness, and then darted forward into the darkness. March could

The Vengeance of the Statue

faintly see his figure crawling along under the shadow of the ridge, then he lost sight of it, and then he saw it again standing an another mound two hundred yards away. Beside him stood a singular erection made apparently of two rods. He bent over it and there was the flare of a light; all March's schoolboy memories woke in him, and he knew what it was. It was the stand of a rocket. The confused incongruous memories still possessed him up to the very moment of a fierce but familiar sound, and an instant after the rocket left its perch and went up into endless space like a starry arrow aimed at the stars. March thought suddenly of the signs of the last days, and knew he was looking at the apocalyptic meteor of something like a day of judgment.

Far up in the infinite heavens the rocket stooped and sprang into scarlet stars. For a moment the whole landscape out to the sea and back to the crescent of the wooded hills was like a lake of ruby light, of a red strangely rich and glorious, as if the world were steeped in wine rather than blood, or the earth were an earthly paradise, over which paused for ever the sanguine moment of morning.

"God save England!" cried Fisher with a tongue like the peal of a trumpet. "And now it is for God to save."

As darkness sank again over land and sea there came another sound; far away in the passes of the hills behind them the guns spoke, like the baying of great hounds. Something that was not a rocket, that came not hissing but screaming, went over Harold March's head and expanded beyond the mound into light and deafening din, staggering the brain with unbearable brutalities of noise. Another came, and then another, and the world was full of uproar and volcanic vapour and chaotic light. The artillery of the west country and the Irish had located the great enemy battery and were pounding it to pieces.

In the mad excitement of that moment March peered through the storm, looking again for the long lean figure that stood beside the stand of the rocket. Then another flash lit up the whole ridge. The figure was not there.

The Man Who Knew Too Much

Before the fires of the rocket had faded from the sky, long before the first gun had sounded from the distant hills, a splutter of rifle fire had flashed and flickered all around from the hidden trenches of the enemy. Something lay in the shadow at the foot of the ridge, as stiff as the stick of the fallen rocket, and the man who knew too much knew what is worth knowing.

THE TREES OF PRIDE

CHAPTER I

THE TALE OF THE PEACOCK TREES

SQUIRE VANE was an elderly schoolboy of English education and Irish extraction. His English education, at one of the great public schools, had preserved his intellect perfectly and permanently at the stage of boyhood. But his Irish extraction subconsciously upset in him the proper solemnity of an old boy, and sometimes gave him back the brighter outlook of a naughty boy. He had a bodily impatience which played tricks with him almost against his will, and had already rendered him rather too radiant a failure in civil and diplomatic service. Thus it is true that compromise is the key of British policy, especially as effecting an impartiality among the religions of India; but Vane's attempt to meet the Moslem half-way by kicking off one boot at the gates of the mosque, was felt not so much to indicate true impartiality as something that could only be called an aggressive indifference. Again, it is true that an English aristocrat can hardly enter fully into the feelings of either party in a quarrel between a Russian Jew and an Orthodox procession carrying relics; but Vane's idea that the procession might carry the Jew as well, himself a venerable and historic relic, was misunderstood on both sides. In short, he was a man who particularly prided himself on having no nonsense about him; with the result that he was always doing nonsensical things. He seemed to be standing on his head merely to prove that he was hard-headed.

He had just finished a hearty breakfast, in the society of his daughter, at a table under a tree in his garden by the Cornish coast. For, having a glorious circulation,

The Man Who Knew Too Much

he insisted on as many outdoor meals as possible, though spring had barely touched the woods and warmed the seas round that southern extremity of England. His daughter Barbara, a good-looking girl with heavy red hair and a face as grave as one of the garden statues, still sat almost motionless as a statue when her father rose. A fine tall figure in light clothes, with his white hair and moustache flying backwards rather fiercely from a face that was good-humoured enough, for he carried his very wide Panama hat in his hand, he strode across the terraced garden, down some stone steps flanked with old ornamental urns to a more woodland path fringed with little trees, and so down a zigzag road which descended the craggy cliff to the shore, where he was to meet a guest arriving by boat. A yacht was already in the blue bay, and he could see a boat pulling towards the little paved pier.

And yet in that short walk between the green turf and the yellow sands he was destined to find his hard-headedness provoked into a not unfamiliar phase which the world was inclined to call hot-headedness. The fact was that the Cornish peasantry, who composed his tenantry and domestic establishment, were far from being people with no nonsense about them. There was, alas! a great deal of nonsense about them; with ghosts, witches and traditions as old as Merlin, they seemed to surround him with a fairy ring of nonsense. But the magic circle had one centre; there was one point to which the curving conversation of the rustics always returned. It was a point that always pricked the Squire to exasperation, and even in this short walk he seemed to strike it everywhere. He paused before descending the steps from the lawn to speak to the gardener about potting some foreign shrubs, and the gardener seemed to be gloomily gratified, in every line of his leathery brown visage, at the chance of indicating that he had formed a low opinion of foreign shrubs.

"We wish you'd get rid of what you've got here, sir," he observed, digging doggedly. "Nothing'll grow right with them here."

"Shrubs!" said the Squire, laughing. "You don't call the peacock trees shrubs, do you? Fine tall trees—you ought to be proud of them."

The Trees of Pride

"Ill weeds grow apace," observed the gardener. "Weeds can grow big as houses when somebody plants them." Then he added: "Him that sowed tares in the Bible, Squire."

"Oh, blast your——" began the Squire, and then replaced the more apt and alliterative word "Bible" by the general word "superstition." He was himself a robust rationalist, but he went to church to set his tenants an example. Of what, it would have puzzled him to say.

A little way along the lower path by the trees he encountered a wood-cutter, one Martin, who was more explicit, having more of a grievance. His daughter was at that time seriously ill with a fever recently common on that coast, and the Squire, who was a kind-hearted gentleman, would normally have made allowances for low spirits and loss of temper. But he came near to losing his own again when the peasant persisted in connecting his tragedy with the traditional monomania about the foreign trees.

"If she were well enough I'd move her," said the woodcutter, "as we can't move them, I suppose. I'd just like to get my chopper into them and feel 'em come crashing down."

"One would think they were dragons," said Vane.

"And that's about what they look like," replied Martin. "Look at 'em!"

The woodman was naturally a rougher and even wilder figure than the gardener. His face also was brown, and looked like an antique parchment, and it was framed in an outlandish arrangement of raven beard and whiskers, which was really a fashion fifty years ago, but might have been five thousand years old or older. Phœnicians, one felt, trading on those strange shores in the morning of the world, might have combed or curled or braided their blue-black hair into some such quaint patterns. For this patch of population was as much a corner of Cornwall as Cornwall is a corner of England; a tragic and unique race, small and inter-related like a Celtic clan. The clan was older than the Vane family, though that was old as county families go. For in many such parts of England it is

The Man Who Knew Too Much

the aristocrats who are the latest arrivals. It was the sort of racial type that is supposed to be passing, and perhaps has already passed.

The obnoxious objects stood some hundred yards away from the speaker, who waved towards them with his axe; and there was something suggestive in the comparison. That coast, to begin with, stretching towards the sunset, was itself almost as fantastic as a sunset cloud. It was cut out against the emerald or indigo of the sea in graven horns and crescents that might be the cast or mould of some such crested serpents; and, beneath, was pierced and fretted by caves and crevices, as if by the boring of some such titanic worms. Over and above this draconian architecture of the earth a veil of grey woods hung thinner like a vapour; woods which the witchcraft of the sea had, as usual, both blighted and blown out of shape. To the right the trees trailed along the sea-front in a single line, each drawn out in thin wild lines like a caricature. At the other end of their extent they multiplied into a huddle of hunchbacked trees, a wood spreading towards a projecting part of the high coast. It was here that the sight appeared to which so many eyes and minds seemed to be almost automatically turning.

Out of the middle of this low and more or less level wood rose three separate stems that shot up and soared into the sky like a lighthouse out of the waves or a church spire out of the village roofs. They formed a clump of three columns close together, which might well be the mere bifurcation, or rather trifurcation, of one tree, the lower part being lost or sunken in the thick wood around. Everything about them suggested something stranger and more southern than anything even in that last peninsula of Britain which pushes out farthest towards Spain and Africa and the southern stars. Their feathery leafage had sprouted in advance of the faint mist of yellow-green around them, and it was of another and less natural green, tinged with blue, like the colours of a kingfisher. But one might fancy it the scales of some three-headed dragon towering over a herd of huddled and fleeing cattle.

"I am exceedingly sorry your girl is so unwell," said

The Trees of Pride

Vane shortly. "But really——" and he strode down the steep road with plunging strides.

The boat was already secured to the little stone jetty, and the boatman, a younger shadow of the woodcutter —and, indeed, a nephew of that useful malcontent— saluted his territorial lord with the sullen formality of the family. The Squire acknowledged it casually and had soon forgotten all such things in shaking hands with the visitor who had just come ashore. The visitor was a long, loose man, very lean to be so young, whose long, fine features seemed wholly fitted together of bone and nerve, and seemed somehow to contrast with his hair, that showed in vivid yellow patches upon his hollow temples under the brim of his white holiday hat. He was carefully dressed in exquisite taste, though he had come straight from a considerable sea-voyage; and he carried something in his hand which in his long European travels, and even longer European visits, he had almost forgotten to call a grip-sack.

Mr. Cyprian Paynter was an American who lived in Italy. There was a good deal more to be said about him, for he was a very acute and cultivated gentleman; but those two facts would, perhaps, cover most of the others. Storing his mind like a museum with the wonder of the Old World, but all lit up as by a window with the wonder of the New, he had fallen heir to something of the unique critical position of Ruskin or Pater, and was further famous as a discoverer of minor poets. He was a judicious discoverer, and he did not turn all his minor poets into major prophets. If his geese were swans, they were not all Swans of Avon. He had even incurred the deadly suspicion of classicism by differing from his young friends the Punctuist Poets, when they produced versification consisting exclusively of commas and colons. He had a more humane sympathy with the modern flame kindled from the embers of Celtic mythology, and it was in reality the recent appearance of a Cornish poet, a sort of parallel to the new Irish poets, which had brought him on this occasion to Cornwall. He was, indeed, far too well-mannered to allow a host to guess that any pleasure was being sought outside his own hospitality. He had

The Man Who Knew Too Much

a long-standing invitation from Vane, whom he had met in Cyprus in the latter's days of undiplomatic diplomacy; and Vane was not aware that relations had only been thus renewed after the critic had read "Merlin and Other Verses," by a new writer named John Treherne. Nor did the Squire even begin to realize the much more diplomatic diplomacy, by which he had been induced to invite the local bard to lunch on the very day of the American critic's arrival.

Mr. Paynter was still standing with his grip-sack, gazing in a trance of true admiration at the hollowed crags, topped by the grey grotesque wood, and crested finally by the three fantastic trees.

"It is like being shipwrecked on the coast of fairyland," he said.

"I hope you haven't been shipwrecked much," replied his host, smiling. "I fancy Jake here can look after you very well."

Mr. Paynter looked across at the boatman and smiled also. "I am afraid," he said, "our friend is not quite so enthusiastic for this landscape as I am."

"Oh, the trees, I suppose!" said the Squire wearily.

The boatman was by normal trade a fisherman; but as his house, built of black tarred timber, stood right on the foreshore a few yards from the pier, he was employed in such cases as a sort of ferryman. He was a big, black-browed youth, generally silent, but something seemed now to sting him into speech.

"Well, sir," he said, "everybody knows it's not natural. Everybody knows the sea blights trees and beats them under, when they're only just trees. These things thrive like some unholy great seaweed that don't belong to the land at all. It's like the—the blessed sea-serpent got on shore, Squire, and eating everything up."

"There is some stupid legend," said Squire Vane gruffly. "But come up into the garden; I want to introduce you to my daughter."

When, however, they reached the little table under the tree, the apparently immovable young lady had moved away after all, and it was some time before they came upon the track of her. She had risen, though languidly,

The Trees of Pride

and wandered slowly along the upper path of the terraced garden looking down on the lower path where it ran closer to the main bulk of the little wood by the sea.

Her languor was not a feebleness but rather a fullness of life, like that of a child half-awake; she seemed to stretch herself and enjoy everything without noticing anything. She passed the wood, into the grey huddle of which a single white path vanished through a black hole. Along this part of the terrace ran something like a low rampart or balustrade, embowered with flowers at intervals; and she leaned over it, looking down at another glimpse of the glowing sea behind the clump of trees, and on another irregular path tumbling down to the pier and the boatman's cottage on the beach.

As she gazed, sleepily enough, she saw that a strange figure was very actively climbing the path, apparently coming from the fisherman's cottage; so actively that a moment afterwards it came out between the trees, and stood upon the path just below her. It was not only a figure strange to her, but one somewhat strange in itself. It was that of a man still young, and seeming somehow younger than his own clothes, which were not only shabby but antiquated; clothes common enough in texture, yet carried in an uncommon fashion. He wore what was presumably a light waterproof, perhaps through having come off the sea; but it was held at the throat by one button, and hung, sleeves and all, more like a cloak than a coat. He rested one bony hand on a black stick; under the shadow of his broad hat his black hair hung down in a tuft or two. His face, which was swarthy but rather handsome in itself, wore something that may have been a slightly embarrassed smile, but had too much the appearance of a sneer.

Whether this apparition was a tramp or a trespasser, or a friend of some of the fishers or wood-cutters, Barbara Vane was quite unable to guess. He removed his hat, still with his unaltered and rather sinister smile, and said civilly: "Excuse me. The Squire asked me to call." Here he caught sight of Martin, the woodman, who was shifting along the path, thinning the thin trees; and the stranger made a familiar salute with one finger.

The Man Who Knew Too Much

The girl did not know what to say. "Have you—have you come about cutting the wood?" she asked at last.

"I would I were so honest a man," replied the stranger. "Martin is, I fancy, a distant cousin of mine; we Cornish folk just round here are nearly all related, you know; but I do not cut wood. I do not cut anything, except, perhaps, capers. I am, so to speak, a *jongleur*."

"A what?" asked Barbara.

"A minstrel, shall we say?" answered the new-comer, and looked up at her more steadily. During a rather odd silence their eyes rested on each other. What she saw has been already noted, though by her, at any rate, not in the least understood. What he saw was a decidedly beautiful woman with a statuesque face and hair that shone in the sun like a helmet of copper.

"Do you know," he went on, "that in this old place, hundreds of years ago, a *jongleur* may really have stood where I stand, and a lady may really have looked over that wall and thrown him money?"

"Do you want money?" she asked, all at sea.

"Well," drawled the stranger, "in the sense of lacking it, perhaps, but I fear there is no place now for a minstrel, except a nigger minstrel. I must apologize for not blacking my face"

She laughed a little in her bewilderment, and said: "Well, I hardly think you need do that."

"You think the natives here are dark enough already, perhaps," he observed calmly "After all, we are aborigines, and are treated as such."

She threw out some desperate remark about the weather or the scenery, and wondered what would happen next.

"The prospect is certainly beautiful," he assented, in the same enigmatic manner. "There is only one thing in it I am doubtful about."

While she stood in silence he slowly lifted his black stick like a long black finger and pointed it at the peacock trees above the wood. And a queer feeling of disquiet fell on the girl, as if he were, by that mere gesture, doing a destructive act and could send a blight upon the garden.

The Trees of Pride

The strained and almost painful silence was broken by the voice of Squire Vane, loud even while it was still distant.

"We couldn't make out where you'd got to, Barbara," he said. "This is my friend, Mr. Cyprian Paynter." The next moment he saw the stranger and stopped, a little puzzled.

It was only Mr. Cyprian Paynter himself who was equal to the situation. He had seen months ago a portrait of the new Cornish poet in some American literary magazine, and he found himself, to his surprise, the introducer instead of the introduced.

"Why, Squire," he said in considerable astonishment, "don't you know Mr. Treherne? I supposed, of course, he was a neighbour."

"Delighted to see you, Mr. Treherne," said the Squire, recovering his manners with a certain genial confusion. "So pleased you were able to come. This is Mr. Paynter—my daughter," and, turning with a certain boisterous embarrassment, he led the way to the table under the tree.

Cyprian Paynter followed, inwardly revolving a puzzle which had taken even his experience by surprise. The American, if intellectually an aristocrat, was still socially and subconsciously a democrat. It had never crossed his mind that the poet should be counted lucky to know the squire and not the squire to know the poet. The honest patronage in Vane's hospitality was something which made Paynter feel he was, after all, an exile in England.

The Squire, anticipating the trial of luncheon with a strange literary man, had dealt with the case tactfully from his own standpoint. County society might have made the guest feel like a fish out of water; and, except for the American critic and the local lawyer and doctor, worthy middle-class people who fitted into the picture, he had kept it as a family party. He was a widower, and when the meal had been laid out on the garden table, it was Barbara who presided as hostess. She had the new poet on her right hand and it made her very uncomfortable. She had practically offered that fallacious *jongleur* money, and it did not make it easier to offer him lunch.

The Man Who Knew Too Much

"The whole countryside's gone mad," announced the Squire, by way of the latest local news. "It's about this infernal legend of ours."

"I collect legends," said Paynter, smiling. "You must remember I haven't yet had a chance to collect yours. And this," he added, looking round at the romantic coast, "is a fine theatre for anything dramatic."

"Oh, it's dramatic in its way," admitted Vane, not without a faint satisfaction. "It's all about those things over there we call the peacock trees—I suppose, because of the queer colour of the leaf, you know, though I have heard they make a shrill noise in a high wind that's supposed to be like the shriek of a peacock; something like a bamboo in the botanical structure, perhaps. Well, those trees are supposed to have been brought over from Barbary by my ancestor Sir Walter Vane, one of the Elizabethan patriots or pirates, or whatever you call them. They say that at the end of his last voyage the villagers gathered on the beach down there and saw the boat standing in from the sea, and the new trees stood up in the boat like a mast, all gay with leaves out of season, like green bunting. And as they watched they thought at first that the boat was steering oddly, and then that it wasn't steering at all; and when it drifted to the shore at last every man in that boat was dead, and Sir Walter Vane, with his sword drawn, was leaning up against the tree trunk, as stiff as the tree."

"Now this is rather curious," remarked Paynter thoughtfully. "I told you I collected legends, and I fancy I can tell you the beginning of the story of which that is the end, though it comes hundreds of miles across the sea."

He tapped meditatively on the table with his thin, taper fingers, like a man trying to recall a tune. He had, indeed, made a hobby of such fables, and he was not without vanity about his artistic touch in telling them.

"Oh, do tell us your part of it!" cried Barbara Vane, whose air of sunny sleepiness seemed in some vague degree to have fallen from her.

The American bowed across the table with a serious

The Trees of Pride

politeness, and then began playing idly with a quaint ring on his long finger as he talked.

"If you go down to the Barbary Coast, where the last wedge of the forest narrows down between the desert and the great tideless sea, you will find the natives still telling a strange story about a saint of the Dark Ages. There, on the twilight border of the Dark Continent, you feel the Dark Ages. I have only visited the place once, though it lies, so to speak, opposite to the Italian city where I lived for years, and yet you would hardly believe how the topsy-turvydom and transmigration of this myth somehow seemed less mad than they really are, with the wood loud with lions at night and that dark red solitude beyond. They say that the hermit St. Securis, living there among trees, grew to love them like companions; since, though great giants with many arms like Briareus, they were the mildest and most blameless of the creatures; they did not devour like the lions, but rather opened their arms to all the little birds. And he prayed that they might be loosened from time to time to walk like other things. And the trees were moved upon the prayers of Securis, as they were at the songs of Orpheus. The men of the desert were stricken from afar with fear, seeing the saint walking with a walking grove, like a schoolmaster with his boys. For the trees were thus freed under strict conditions of discipline. They were to return at the sound of the hermit's bell, and, above all, to copy the wild beasts in walking only—to destroy and devour nothing. Well, it is said that one of the trees heard a voice that was not the saint's; that in the warm green twilight of one summer evening it became conscious of something sitting and speaking in its branches in the guise of a great bird, and it was that which once spoke from a tree in the guise of a great serpent. As the voice grew louder among its murmuring leaves the tree was torn with a great desire to stretch out and snatch at the birds that flew harmlessly about their nests, and pluck them to pieces. Finally, the tempter filled the tree-top with his own birds of pride, the starry pageant of the peacocks. And the spirit of the brute overcame the

The Man Who Knew Too Much

spirit of the tree, and it rent and consumed the blue-green birds till not a plume was left, and returned to the quiet tribe of trees. But they say that when spring came all the other trees put forth leaves, but this put forth feathers of a strange hue and pattern. And by that monstrous assimilation the saint knew of the sin, and he rooted that one tree to the earth with a judgment, so that evil should fall on any who removed it again. That, Squire, is the beginning in the deserts of the tale that ended here, almost in this garden."

"And the end is about as reliable as the beginning, I should say," said Vane. "Yours is a nice plain tale for a small tea-party; a quiet little bit of still-life, that is."

"What a queer, horrible story," exclaimed Barbara. "It makes one feel like a cannibal."

"*Ex Africa,*" said the lawyer, smiling. "It comes from a cannibal country. I think it's the touch of the tar-brush, that nightmare feeling that you don't know whether the hero is a plant or a man or a devil. Don't you feel it sometimes in ' Uncle Remus '? "

"True," said Paynter. "Perfectly true" And he looked at the lawyer with a new interest. The lawyer, who had been introduced as Mr. Ashe, was one of those people who are more worth looking at than most people realize when they look. If Napoleon had been red-haired, and had bent all his powers with a curious contentment upon the petty lawsuits of a province, he might have looked much the same; the head with the red hair was heavy and powerful; the figure in its dark, quiet clothes was comparatively insignificant, as was Napoleon's. He seemed more at ease in the Squire's society than the doctor, who, though a gentleman, was a shy one, and a mere shadow of his professional brother.

"As you truly say," remarked Paynter, "the story seems touched with quite barbarous elements, probably negro. Originally, though, I think there was really a hagiological story about some hermit, though some of the higher critics say St. Securis never existed, but was only an allegory of arboriculture, since his name is the Latin for an axe."

The Trees of Pride

"Oh, if you come to that," remarked the poet Treherne, "you might as well say Squire Vane doesn't exist, and that he's only an allegory for a weathercock." Something a shade too cool about this sally drew the lawyer's red brows together. He looked across the table and met the poet's somewhat equivocal smile.

"Do I understand, Mr. Treherne," asked Ashe, "that you support the miraculous claims of St. Securis in this case. Do you, by any chance, believe in the walking trees?"

"I see men as trees walking," answered the poet, "like the man cured of blindness in the Gospel. By the way, do I understand that you support the miraculous claims of that—thaumaturgist?"

Paynter intervened swiftly and suavely. "Now that sounds a fascinating piece of psychology. You see men as trees?"

"As I can't imagine why men should walk, I can't imagine why trees shouldn't," answered Treherne.

"Obviously, it is the nature of the organism," interposed the medical guest, Dr. Burton Brown; "it is necessary in the very type of vegetable structure."

"In other words, a tree sticks in the mud from year's end to year's end," answered Treherne. "So do you stop in your consulting-room from ten to eleven every day. And don't you fancy a fairy, looking in at your window for a flash after having just jumped over the moon and played mulberry bush with the Pleiades, would think you were a vegetable structure, and that sitting still was the nature of the organism?"

"I don't happen to believe in fairies," said the doctor rather stiffly, for the *argumentum ad hominem* was becoming too common. A sulphurous subconscious anger seemed to radiate from the dark poet.

"Well, I should hope not, doctor," began the Squire, in his loud and friendly style, and then stopped, seeing the other's attention arrested. The silent butler waiting on the guests had appeared behind the doctor's chair, and was saying something in the low, level tones of the well-trained servant. He was so smooth a specimen of the type that others never noticed, at first, that he also

The Man Who Knew Too Much

repeated the dark portrait, however varnished, so common in this particular family of Cornish Celts. His face was sallow and even yellow, and his hair indigo black. He went by the name of Miles. Some felt oppressed by the tribal type in this tiny corner of England. They felt somehow as if all these dark faces were the masks of a secret society.

The doctor rose with a half apology. "I must ask pardon for disturbing this pleasant party; I am called away on duty. Please don't let anybody move. We have to be ready for these things, you know. Perhaps Mr. Treherne will admit that my habits are not so very vegetable, after all." With this Parthian shaft, at which there was some laughter, he strode away very rapidly across the sunny lawn to where the road dipped down towards the village.

"He is very good among the poor," said the girl with an honourable seriousness.

"A capital fellow," agreed the Squire. "Where is Miles? You will have a cigar, Mr. Treherne?" And he got up from the table; the rest followed, and the group broke up on the lawn.

"Remarkable man, Treherne," said the American to the lawyer conversationally.

"Remarkable is the word," assented Ashe rather grimly. "But I don't think I'll make any remark about him."

The Squire, too impatient to wait for the yellow-faced Miles, had betaken himself indoors for the cigars, and Barbara found herself once more paired off with the poet, as she floated along the terrace garden; but this time, symbolically enough, upon the same level of lawn. Mr. Treherne looked less eccentric after having shed his curious cloak, and seemed a quieter and more casual figure.

"I didn't mean to be rude to you just now," she said abruptly.

"And that's the worst of it," replied the man of letters, "for I'm horribly afraid I did mean to be rude to you. When I looked up and saw you up there something surged up in me that was in all the revolutions of history. Oh,

The Trees of Pride

there was admiration in it too! Perhaps there was idolatry in all the iconoclasts."

He seemed to have a power of reaching rather intimate conversation in one silent and cat-like bound, as he had scaled the steep road, and it made her feel him to be dangerous, and perhaps unscrupulous. She changed the subject sharply, not without a movement towards gratifying her own curiosity.

"What *did* you mean by all that about walking trees?" she asked. "Don't tell me you really believe in a magic tree that eats birds!"

"I should probably surprise you," said Treherne gravely, "more by what I don't believe than by what I do."

Then, after a pause, he made a general gesture towards the house and garden. "I'm afraid I don't believe in all this; for instance, in Elizabethan houses and Elizabethan families and the way estates have been improved, and the rest of it. Look at our friend the woodcutter now." And he pointed to the man with the quaint black beard, who was still plying his axe upon the timber below.

"That man's family goes back for ages, and it was far richer and freer in what you call the Dark Ages than it is now. Wait till the Cornish peasant writes a history of Cornwall."

"But what in the world," she demanded, "has this to do with whether you believe in a tree eating birds?"

"Why should I confess what I believe in?" he said, a muffled drum of mutiny in his voice. "The gentry came here and took our land and took our labour and took our customs. And now, after exploitation, a viler thing, education! They must take our dreams!"

"Well, this dream was rather a nightmare, wasn't it?" asked Barbara, smiling; and the next moment grew quite grave, saying almost anxiously: "But here's Dr. Brown back again. Why, he looks quite upset."

The doctor, a black figure on the green lawn, was indeed coming towards them at a very vigorous walk. His body and gait were much younger than his face, which seemed prematurely lined as with worry; his brow

The Man Who Knew Too Much

was bald, and projected from the straight, dark hair behind it. He was visibly paler than when he left the lunch table.

"I am sorry to say, Miss Vane," he said, "that I am the bearer of bad news to poor Martin, the woodman here. His daughter died half an hour ago."

"Oh," cried Barbara warmly, "I am *so* sorry!"

"So am I," said the doctor, and passed on rather abruptly; he ran down the stone steps between the stone urns; and they saw him in talk with the woodcutter. They could not see the woodcutter's face. He stood with his back to them, but they saw something that seemed more moving than any change of countenance. The man's hand holding the axe rose high above his head, and for a flash it seemed as if he would have cut down the doctor. But in fact he was not looking at the doctor. His face was set towards the cliff where, sheer out of the dwarf forest, rose, gigantic and gilded by the sun, the trees of pride.

The strong brown hand made a movement and was empty. The axe went circling swiftly through the air, its head showing like a silver crescent against the grey twilight of the trees. It did not reach its tall objective, but fell among the undergrowth, shaking up a flying litter of birds. But in the poet's memory, full of primal things, something seemed to say that he had seen the birds of some pagan augury, the axe of some pagan sacrifice.

A moment after the man made a heavy movement forward, as if to recover his tool; but the doctor put a hand on his arm.

"Never mind that now," they heard him say sadly and kindly. "The Squire will excuse you any more work, I know."

Something made the girl look at Treherne. He stood gazing, his head a little bent, and one of his black elf-locks had fallen forward over his forehead. And again she had the sense of a shadow over the grass; she almost felt as if the grass were a host of fairies, and that the fairies were not her friends.

The Trees of Pride

CHAPTER II

THE WAGER OF SQUIRE VANE

It was more than a month before the legend of the peacock trees was again discussed in the Squire's circle. It fell out one evening, when his eccentric taste for meals in the garden had gathered the company round the same table, now lit with a lamp and laid out for dinner in a glowing spring twilight. It was even the same company, for in the few weeks intervening they had insensibly grown more and more into each other's lives, forming a little group like a club. The American æsthete was of course the most active agent, his resolution to pluck out the heart of the Cornish poet's mystery leading him again and again to influence his flighty host for such reunions. Even Mr. Ashe, the lawyer, seemed to have swallowed his half-humorous prejudices; and the doctor, though a rather sad and silent, was a companionable and considerate man. Paynter had even read Treherne's poetry aloud, and he read admirably; he had also read other things, not aloud, grubbing up everything in the neighbourhood, from guidebooks to epitaphs, that could throw a light on local antiquities. And it was that evening when the lamplight and the last daylight had kindled the colours of the wine and silver on the table under the tree, that he announced a new discovery.

"Say, Squire," he remarked, with one of his rare Americanisms, "about those bogey trees of yours; I don't believe you know half the tales told round here about them. It seems they have a way of eating things. Not that I have any ethical objection to eating things," he continued, helping himself elegantly to green cheese. "But I have more or less, broadly speaking, an objection to eating people."

"Eating people!" repeated Barbara Vane.

"I know a globe-trotter mustn't be fastidious," replied

The Man Who Knew Too Much

Mr. Paynter. "But I repeat firmly, an objection to eating people. The peacock trees seem to have progressed since the happy days of innocence when they only ate peacocks. If you ask the people here—the fisherman who lives on that beach, or the man that mows this very lawn in front of us—they'll tell you tales taller than any tropical one I brought you from the Barbary Coast. If you ask them what happened to the fisherman Peters, who got drunk on All Hallows Eve, they'll tell you he lost his way in that little wood, tumbled down asleep under the wicked trees, and then—evaporated, vanished, was licked up like dew by the sun. If you ask them where Harry Hawke is, the widow's little son, they'll just tell you he's swallowed; that he was dared to climb the trees and sit there all night, and did it. What the trees did God knows; the habits of a vegetable ogre leave one a little vague. But they even add the agreeable detail that a new branch appears on the tree when somebody has petered out in this style."

"What new nonsense is this?" cried Vane. "I know there's some crazy yarn about the trees spreading fever, though every educated man knows why these epidemics return occasionally. And I know they say you can tell the noise of them among other trees in a gale, and I dare say you can. But even Cornwall isn't a lunatic asylum, and a tree that dines on a passing tourist——"

"Well, the two tales are reconcilable enough," put in the poet quietly. "If there were a magic that killed men when they came close, it's likely to strike them with sickness when they stand far off. In the old romance the dragon, that devours some people, often blasts others with a sort of poisonous breath."

Ashe looked across at the speaker steadily, not to say stonily.

"Do I understand," he inquired, "that you swallow the swallowing trees too?"

Treherne's dark smile was still on the defensive; his fencing always annoyed the other, and he seemed not without malice in the matter.

"Swallowing is a metaphor," he said, "about me, if not about the trees. And metaphors take us at once into

The Trees of Pride

dreamland—no bad place, either. This garden, I think, gets more and more like a dream at this corner of the day and night, that might lead us anywhere."

The yellow horn of the moon had appeared silently and as if suddenly over the black horns of the sea-wood, seeming to announce as night something which till then had been evening. A night breeze came in between the trees and raced stealthily across the turf, and as they ceased speaking they heard, not only the seething grass, but the sea itself move and sound in all the cracks and caves round them and below them and on every side. They all felt the note that had been struck—the American as an art critic and the poet as a poet; and the Squire, who believed himself boiling with an impatience purely rational, did not really understand his own impatience. In him, more perhaps than the others—more certainly than he knew himself—the sea-wind went to the head like wine.

"Credulity is a curious thing," went on Treherne in a low voice. "It is more negative than positive, and yet it is infinite. Hundreds of men will avoid walking under a ladder; they don't know where the door of the ladder will lead. They don't really think God would throw a thunderbolt at them for such a thing. They don't know what would happen, that is just the point; but yet they step aside as from a precipice. So the poor people here may or may not believe anything; they don't go into those trees at night."

"I walk under a ladder whenever I can," cried Vane, in quite unnecessary excitement.

"You belong to a Thirteen Club," said the poet. "You walk under a ladder on Friday to dine thirteen at a table, everybody spilling the salt. But even you don't go into those trees at night."

Squire Vane stood up, his silver hair flaming in the wind.

"I'll stop all night in your tom-fool wood and up your tom-fool trees," he said. "I'll do it for twopence or two thousand pounds, if anyone will take the bet."

Without waiting for reply, he snatched up his wide white hat and settled it on with a fierce gesture, and had

The Man Who Knew Too Much

gone off in great leonine strides across the lawn before anyone at the table could move.

The stillness was broken by Miles, the butler, who dropped and broke one of the plates he carried. He stood looking after his master with his long, angular chin thrust out, looking yellower where it caught the yellow light of the lamp below. His face was thus sharply in shadow, but Paynter fancied for a moment it was convulsed by some passion passing surprise. But the face was quite as usual when it turned, and Paynter realized that a night of fancies had begun, like the cross purposes of the *Midsummer Night's Dream*.

The wood of the strange trees, towards which the Squire was walking, lay so far forward on the headland, which ultimately almost overhung the sea, that it could be approached by only one path, which shone clearly like a silver ribbon in the twilight. The ribbon ran along the edge of the cliff, where the single row of deformed trees ran beside it all the way, and eventually plunged into the closer mass of trees by one natural gateway, a mere gap in the wood, looking dark, like a lion's mouth. What became of the path inside could not be seen, but it doubtless led round the hidden roots of the great central trees. The Squire was already within a yard or two of this dark entry when his daughter rose from the table and took a step or two after him as if to call him back.

Treherne had also risen, and stood as if dazed at the effect of his idle defiance. When Barbara moved he seemed to recover himself, and stepping after her, said something which Paynter did not hear. He said it casually and even distantly enough, but it clearly suggested something to her mind; for, after a moment's thought, she nodded and walked back, not towards the table, but apparently towards the house. Paynter looked after her with a momentary curiosity, and when he turned again the Squire had vanished into the hole in the wood.

"He's gone," said Treherne, with a clang of finality in his tones, like the slamming of a door.

"Well, suppose he has?" cried the lawyer, roused at the voice. "The Squire can go into his own wood, I suppose! What the devil's all the fuss about, Mr.

The Trees of Pride

Paynter? Don't tell me *you* think there's any harm in that plantation of sticks."

"No, I don't," said Paynter, throwing one leg over another and lighting a cigar. "But I shall stop here till he comes out."

"Very well," said Ashe shortly, "I'll stop with you, if only to see the end of this farce."

The doctor said nothing, but he also kept his seat and accepted one of the American's cigars. If Treherne had been attending to the matter he might have noted, with his sardonic superstition, a curious fact—that, while all three men were tacitly condemning themselves to stay out all night if necessary, all, by one blank omission or oblivion, assumed that it was impossible to follow their host into the wood just in front of them. But Treherne, though still in the garden, had wandered away from the garden-table, and was pacing along the single line of trees against the dark sea. They had in their regular interstices, showing the sea as through a series of windows, something of the look of the ghost or skeleton of a cloister, and he, having thrown his coat once more over his neck, like a cape, passed to and fro like the ghost of some not very sane monk.

All these men, whether sceptics or mystics, looked back for the rest of their lives on that night as on something unnatural. They sat still or started up abruptly, and paced the great garden in long detours, so that it seemed that no three of them were together at a time, and none knew who would be his companion; yet their rambling remained within the same dim and mazy space. They fell into snatches of uneasy slumber; these were very brief, and yet they felt as if the whole sitting, strolling, or occasional speaking had been parts of a single dream.

Paynter woke once, and found Ashe sitting opposite him at a table otherwise empty; his face dark in shadow and his cigar-end like the red eye of a Cyclops. Until the lawyer spoke, in his steady voice, Paynter was positively afraid of him. He answered at random and nodded again; when he again woke the lawyer was gone, and what was opposite him was the bald, pale brow of the

The Man Who Knew Too Much

doctor; there seemed suddenly something ominous in the familiar fact that he wore spectacles. And yet the vanishing Ashe had only vanished a few yards away, for he turned at that instant and strolled back to the table. With a jerk Paynter realized that his nightmare was but a trick of sleep or sleeplessness, and spoke in his natural voice, but rather loud.

"So you've joined us again; where's Treherne?"

"Oh, still revolving, I suppose, like a polar bear under those trees on the cliff," replied Ashe, motioning with his cigar, "looking at what an older (and you will forgive me for thinking a somewhat better) poet called the wine-dark sea. It really has a sort of purple shade; look at it."

Paynter looked; he saw the wine-dark sea and the fantastic trees that fringed it, but he did not see the poet; the cloister was already emptied of its restless monk.

"Gone somewhere else," he said, with futility far from characteristic. "He'll be back here presently. This is an interesting vigil, but a vigil loses some of its intensity when you can't keep awake. Ah! Here's Treherne; so we're all mustered, as the politician said when Mr. Colman came late for dinner. No, the doctor's off again; how restless we all are!" The poet had drawn near, his feet were falling soft on the grass, and was gazing at them with a singular attentiveness.

"It will soon be over," he said.

"What?" snapped Ashe very abruptly.

"The night, of course," replied Treherne in a motionless manner. "The darkest hour has passed."

"Didn't some other minor poet remark," inquired Paynter flippantly, "that the darkest hour before the dawn——? My God, what was that? It was like a scream."

"It was a scream," replied the poet. "The scream of a peacock."

Ashe stood up, his strong face pale against his red hair, and said furiously: "What the devil do you mean?"

"Oh, perfectly natural causes, as Dr. Brown would say," replied Treherne. "Didn't the Squire tell us the

The Trees of Pride

trees had a shrill note of their own when the wind blew? The wind's beating up again from the sea; I shouldn't wonder if there was a storm before dawn."

Dawn indeed came gradually with a growing noise of wind, and the purple sea began to boil about the dark volcanic cliffs. The first change in the sky showed itself only in the shapes of the wood and the single stems growing darker but clearer; and above the grey clump, against a glimpse of growing light, they saw aloft the evil trinity of the trees. In their long lines there seemed to Paynter something faintly serpentine and even spiral. He could almost fancy he saw them slowly revolving as in some cyclic dance, but this, again, was but a last delusion of dreamland, for a few seconds later he was again asleep. In dreams he toiled through a tangle of inconclusive tales, each filled with the same stress and noise of sea and seawind; and above and outside all other voices, the wailing of the Trees of Pride.

When he woke it was broad day, and a bloom of early light lay on wood and garden and on fields and farms for miles away. The comparative common sense that daylight brings even to the sleepless drew him alertly to his feet, and showed him all his companions standing about the lawn in similar attitudes of expectancy. There was no need to ask what they were expecting. They were waiting to hear the nocturnal experiences, comic or commonplace or whatever they might prove to be, of that eccentric friend, whose experiment (whether from some subconscious fear or some fancy of honour) they had not ventured to interrupt. Hour followed hour, and still nothing stirred in the wood save an occasional bird. The Squire, like most men of his type, was an early riser, and it was not likely that he would in this case sleep late; it was much more likely, in the excitement in which he had left them, that he would not sleep at all. Yet it was clear that he must be sleeping, perhaps by some reaction from a strain. By the time the sun was high in heaven Ashe the lawyer, turning to the others, spoke abruptly and to the point.

"Shall we go into the wood now?" asked Paynter, and almost seemed to hesitate.

The Man Who Knew Too Much

"I will go in," said Treherne simply. Then, drawing up his dark head in answer to their glances, he added:

"Oh, do not trouble yourselves. It is never the believer who is afraid."

For the second time they saw a man mount the white curling path and disappear into the grey tangled wood, but this time they did not have to wait long to see him again.

A few minutes later he reappeared in the woodland gateway, and came slowly towards them across the grass. He stopped before the doctor, who stood nearest, and said something. It was repeated to the others, and went round the ring with low cries of incredulity. The others plunged into the wood and returned wildly, and were seen speaking to others again who gathered from the house; the wild wireless telegraphy which is the education of countryside communities spread it farther and farther before the fact itself was fully realized; and before nightfall a quarter of the county knew that Squire Vane had vanished like a burst bubble.

Widely as the wild story was repeated, and patiently as it was pondered, it was long before there was even the beginning of a sequel to it. In the interval Paynter had politely removed himself from the house of mourning, or rather of questioning, but only so far as the village inn; for Barbara Vane was glad of the traveller's experience and sympathy, in addition to that afforded her by the lawyer and doctor as old friends of the family. Even Treherne was not discouraged from his occasional visits with a view to helping the hunt for the lost man. The five held many counsels round the old garden table, at which the unhappy master of the house had dined for the last time; and Barbara wore her old mask of stone, if it was now a more tragic mask. She had shown no passion after the first morning of discovery, when she had broken forth once, speaking strangely enough in the view of some of her hearers.

She had come slowly out of the house, to which her own or some one else's wisdom had relegated her during the night of the wager; and it was clear from her face that somebody had told her the truth; Miles, the butler,

The Trees of Pride

stood on the steps behind her; and it was probably he.

"Do not be much distressed, Miss Vane," said Dr. Brown, in a low and rather uncertain voice. "The search in the wood has hardly begun. I am convinced we shall find—something quite simple."

"The doctor is right," said Ashe, in his firm tones; "I myself——"

"The doctor is not right," said the girl, turning a white face on the speaker, "I know better. The poet is right. The poet is always right. Oh, he has been here from the beginning of the world, and seen wonders and terrors that are all round our path, and only hiding behind a bush or a stone. You and your doctoring and your science—why, you have only been here for a few fumbling generations; and you can't conquer even your own enemies of the flesh. Oh, forgive me, doctor, I know you do splendidly; but the fever comes in the village, and the people die and die for all that. And now it's my poor father. God help us all! The only thing left is to believe in God; for we can't help believing in devils." And she left them, still walking quite slowly, but in such a fashion that no one could go after her.

The spring had already begun to ripen into summer, and spread a green tent from the tree over the garden table, when the American visitor, sitting there with his two professional companions, broke the silence by saying what had long been in his mind.

"Well," he said, "I suppose whatever we may think it wise to say, we have all begun to think of a possible conclusion. It can't be put very delicately anyhow; but, after all, there's a very necessary business side to it. What are we going to do about poor Vane's affairs, apart from himself? I suppose you know," he added, in a low voice to the lawyer, "whether he made a will?"

"He left everything to his daughter unconditionally," replied Ashe. "But nothing can be done with it. There's no proof whatever that he's dead."

"No legal proof?" remarked Paynter dryly.

A wrinkle of irritation had appeared in the big bald brow of Dr. Brown; and he made an impatient movement.

The Man Who Knew Too Much

"Of course he's dead," he said. "What's the sense of all this legal fuss? We were watching this side of the wood, weren't we? A man couldn't have flown off those high cliffs over the sea; he could only have fallen off. What else can he be but dead?"

"I speak as a lawyer," returned Ashe, raising his eyebrows. "We can't presume his death, or have an inquest or anything till we find the poor fellow's body, or some remains that may reasonably be presumed to be his body."

"I see," observed Paynter quietly. "You speak as a lawyer; but I don't think it's very hard to guess what you think as a man."

"I own I'd rather be a man than a lawyer," said the doctor, rather roughly. "I'd no notion the law was such an ass. What's the good of keeping the poor girl out of her property, and the estate all going to pieces? Well, I must be off, or my patients will be going to pieces too."

And with a curt salutation he pursued his path down to the village.

"That man does his duty, if anybody does," remarked Paynter. "We must pardon his—shall I say manners or manner?"

"Oh, I bear him no malice," replied Ashe good-humouredly, "but I'm glad he's gone, because—well, because I don't want him to know yet how jolly right he is." And he leaned back in his chair and stared up at the roof of green leaves.

"You are sure," said Paynter, looking at the table, "that Squire Vane is dead?"

"More than that," said Ashe, still staring at the leaves. "I'm sure of how he died."

"Ah!" said the American, with an intake of breath, and they remained for a moment, one gazing at the tree and the other at the table.

"*Sure* is perhaps too strong a word," continued Ashe. "But my conviction will want some shaking. I don't envy the counsel for the defence."

"The counsel for the defence," repeated Paynter, and looked up quickly at his companion. He was struck again

The Trees of Pride

by the man's Napoleonic chin and jaw, as he had been when they first talked of the legend of St. Securis.

"Then," he began, "you don't think the trees——"

"The trees be damned!" snorted the lawyer. "The tree had two legs on that evening. What our friend the poet," he added, with a sneer, "would call a walking tree. Apropos of our friend the poet, you seemed surprised that night to find he was not walking poetically by the sea all the time, and I fear I affected to share your ignorance. I was not so sure then as I am now."

"Sure of what?" demanded the other.

"To begin with," said Ashe, "I'm sure our friend the poet followed Vane into the wood that night, for I saw him coming out again."

Paynter leaned forward, suddenly pale with excitement, and struck the wooden table so that it rattled.

"Mr. Ashe, you're wrong," he cried. "You're a wonderful man and you're wrong. You've probably got tons of true convincing evidence, and you're wrong. I know this poet; I know him as a poet; and that's just what you don't. I know you think he gave you crooked answers, and seemed to be all smiles and black looks at once; but you don't understand the type. I know now why you don't understand the Irish. Sometimes you think it's soft, and sometimes sly, and sometimes murderous, and sometimes uncivilized; and all the time it's only civilized; quivering with the sensitive irony of understanding all that you don't understand."

"Well," said Ashe shortly, "we'll see who's right."

"We will," cried Cyprian, and rose suddenly from the table. All the drooping pose of the æsthete had dropped from him; his Yankee accent rose high, like a horn of defiance, and there was nothing about him but the New World.

"I guess I will look into this myself," he said, stretching his long limbs like an athlete. "I search that little wood of yours to-morrow. It's a bit late, or I'd do it now."

"The wood has been searched," said the lawyer, rising also.

"Yes," drawled the American. "It's been searched

The Man Who Knew Too Much

by servants, policemen, local policemen, and quite a lot of people; and do you know I have a notion that nobody round here is likely to have searched it at all."

"And what are you going to do with it?" asked Ashe.

"What I bet they haven't done," replied Cyprian. "I'm going to climb a tree."

And with a quaint air of renewed cheerfulness he took himself away at a rapid walk to his inn.

He appeared at daybreak next morning outside the Vane Arms with all the air of one setting out on his travels in distant lands. He had a field-glass slung over his shoulder, and a very large sheath-knife buckled by a belt round his waist, and carried with the cool bravado of the bowie-knife of a cowboy. But in spite of this backwoodsman's simplicity, or perhaps rather because of it, he eyed with rising relish the picturesque plan and sky-line of the antiquated village, and especially the wooden square of the old inn-sign that hung over his head; a shield, of which the charges seemed to him a mere medley of blue dolphins, gold crosses and scarlet birds. The colours and cubic corners of that painted board pleased him like a play or a puppet-show. He stood staring and straddling for some moments on the cobbles of the little market-place; then he gave a short laugh and began to mount the steep streets towards the high park and garden beyond. From the high lawn, above the tree and table, he could see on one side the land stretch away past the house into a great rolling plain, which under the clear edges of the dawn seemed dotted with picturesque details. The woods here and there on the plain looked like green hedgehogs, as grotesque as the incongruous beasts found unaccountably walking in the blank spaces of mediæval maps. The land, cut up into coloured fields, recalled the heraldry of the signboard; this also was at once ancient and gay. On the other side the ground to seaward swept down and then up again to the famous or infamous wood; the square of strange trees lay slightly tilted on the slope, also suggesting, if not a map, at least a bird's-eye view. Only the triple centrepiece of the peacock trees rose clear of the sky-line; and these stood up in tranquil sunlight

The Trees of Pride

as things almost classical, a triangular temple of the winds. They seemed pagan in a newer and more placid sense; and he felt a newer and more boyish curiosity and courage for the consulting of the oracle. In all his wanderings he had never walked so lightly. For the connoisseur of sensations had found something to do at last; he was fighting for a friend.

He was brought to a standstill once, however, and that at the very gateway of the garden of the trees of knowledge. Just outside the black entry of the wood, now curtained with greener and larger leafage, he came on a solitary figure. It was Martin, the woodcutter, wading in the bracken and looking about him in rather a lost fashion. The man seemed to be talking to himself.

"I dropt it here," he was saying. "But I'll never work with it again I reckon. Doctor wouldn't let me pick it up, when I wanted to pick it up; and now they've got it, like they've got the Squire. Wood and iron, wood and iron, but eating it's nothing to them."

"Come!" said Paynter kindly, remembering the man's domestic trouble. "Miss Vane will see you have anything you want, I know. And look here, don't brood on all those stories about the Squire. Is there the slightest trace of the trees having anything to do with it? Is there even this extra branch the idiots talked about?"

There had been growing on Paynter the suspicion that the man before him was not perfectly sane; yet he was much more startled by the sudden and cold sanity that looked for an instant out of the woodman's eyes, as he answered in his ordinary manner.

"Well, sir, did you count the branches before?"

Then he seemed to relapse; and Paynter left him wandering and wavering in the undergrowth; and entered the wood like one across whose sunny path a shadow has fallen for an instant.

Diving under the wood, he was soon threading a leafy path which, even under that summer sun, shone only with an emerald twilight, as if it were on the floor of the sea. It wound about more snakily than he had supposed, as if resolved to approach the central trees as if

The Man Who Knew Too Much

they were the heart of the maze at Hampton Court. They were the heart of the maze for him, anyhow; he sought them as straight as a crooked road would carry him; and, turning a final corner, he beheld for the first time the foundations of those towers of vegetation he had as yet only seen from above, as they stood waist-high in the woodland. He found the suspicion correct which supposed that tree branched from one great root, like a candelabrum; the fork, though stained and slimy with green fungoids, was quite near the ground, and offered a first foothold. He put his foot in it, and without a flash of hesitation went aloft, like Jack climbing the Beanstalk.

Above him the green roof of leaves and boughs seemed sealed like a firmament of foliage; but, by bending and breaking the branches to right and left he slowly forced a passage upwards; and had at last, and suddenly, the sensation of coming out on the top of the world. He felt as if he had never been in the open air before. Sea and land lay in a circle below and about him, as he sat astride a branch of the tall tree; he was almost surprised to see the sun still comparatively low in the sky; as if he were looking over a land of eternal sunrise.

"Silent upon a peak in Darien," he remarked, in a needlessly loud and cheerful voice; and though the claim, thus expressed, was illogical, it was not inappropriate. He did feel as if he were a primitive adventurer just come to the New World, instead of a modern traveller just come from it.

"I wonder," he proceeded, "whether I am really the first that ever burst into this silent tree. It looks like it. Those——"

He stopped and sat on his branch quite motionless, but his eyes were turned on a branch a little below it, and they were brilliant with a vigilance, like those of a man watching a snake.

What he was looking at might, at first sight, have been a large white fungus spreading on the smooth and monstrous trunk; but it was not. Leaning down dangerously from his perch, he detached it from the twig on which it had caught, and then sat holding it in his

The Trees of Pride

hand and gazing at it. It was Squire Vane's white Panama hat, but there was no Squire Vane under it. Paynter felt a nameless relief in the very fact that there was not.

There in the clear sunlight and sea air, for an instant, all the tropical terrors of his own idle tale surrounded and suffocated him. It seemed indeed some demon tree of the swamps; a vegetable serpent that fed on men. Even the hideous farce in the fancy of digesting a whole man with the exception of his hat, seemed only to simplify the nightmare. And he found himself gazing dully at one leaf of the tree, which happened to be turned towards him, so that the odd markings, which had partly made the legend, really looked a little like the eye in a peacock's feather. It was as if the sleeping tree had opened one eye upon him.

With a sharp effort he steadied himself in mind and posture on the bough; his reason returned, and he began to descend with the hat in his teeth. When he was back in the underworld of the wood, he studied the hat again and with closer attention. In one place in the crown there was a hole or rent, which certainly had not been there when it had last lain on the table under the garden tree. He sat down, lit a cigarette, and reflected for a long time.

A wood, even a small wood, is not an easy thing to search minutely; but he provided himself with some practical tests in the matter. In one sense the very density of the thicket was a help; he could at least see where anyone had strayed from the path, by broken and trampled growths of every kind. After many hours' industry, he had made a sort of new map of the place; and had decided beyond doubt that some person or persons had so strayed, for some purpose, in several defined directions. There was a way burst through the bushes, making a short cut across a loop of the wandering path; there was another forking out from it as an alternative way into the central space. But there was one especially which was unique, and which seemed to him, the more he studied it, to point to some essential of the mystery.

One of these beaten and broken tracks went from the

The Man Who Knew Too Much

space under the peacock trees outwards into the wood for about twenty yards and then stopped. Beyond that point not a twig was broken nor a leaf disturbed. It had no exit, but he could not believe that it had no goal. After some further reflection, he knelt down and began to cut away grass and clay with his knife, and was surprised at the ease with which they detached themselves. In a few moments a whole section of the soil lifted like a lid; it was a round lid and presented a quaint appearance, like a flat cap with green feathers. For though the disc itself was made of wood, there was a layer of earth on it with the live grass still growing there. And the removal of the round lid revealed a round hole, black as night and seemingly bottomless. Paynter understood it instantly. It was rather near the sea for a well to be sunk, but the traveller had known wells sunk even nearer. He rose to his feet with the great knife in his hand, a frown on his face, and his doubts resolved. He no longer shrank from naming what he knew. This was not the first corpse that had been thrown down a well; here, without stone or epitaph, was the grave of Squire Vane. In a flash all the mythological follies about saints and peacocks were forgotten; he was knocked on the head, as with a stone club, by the human common sense of crime.

Cyprian Paynter stood long by the well in the wood, walked round it in meditation, examined its rim and the ring of grass about it, searched the surrounding soil thoroughly, came back and stood beside the well once more. His researches and reflections had been so long that he had not realized that the day had passed and that the wood and the world around it were beginning already to be steeped in the enrichment of evening. The day had been radiantly calm; the sea seemed to be as still as the well, and the well was as still as a mirror. And then, quite without warning, the mirror moved of itself like a living thing.

In the well in the wood the water leapt and gurgled, with a grotesque noise like something swallowing, and then settled again with a second sound. Cyprian could not see into the well clearly, for the opening, from where he stood, was an ellipse, a mere slit, and half masked by

The Trees of Pride

thistles and rank grass like a green beard. For where he stood now was three yards away from the well, and he had not yet himself realized that he had sprung back all that distance from the brink, when the water spoke.

CHAPTER III

THE MYSTERY OF THE WELL

CYPRIAN PAYNTER did not know what he expected to see rise out of the well—the corpse of the murdered man or merely the spirit of the fountain. Anyhow, neither of them rose out of it, and he recognized after an instant that this was, after all, perhaps the more natural course of things. Once more he pulled himself together, walked to the edge of the well and looked down. He saw, as before, a dim glimmer of water, at that depth no brighter than ink; he fancied he still heard a faint convulsion and murmur, but it gradually subsided to an utter stillness. Short of suicidally diving in, there was nothing to be done. He realized that, with all his equipment, he had not even brought anything like a rope or basket, and at length decided to return for them. As he retraced his steps to the entrance, he recurred to, and took stock of, his more solid discoveries. Somebody had gone into the wood, killed the Squire and thrown him down the well. He did not admit for a moment that it was his friend the poet; but if the latter had actually been seen coming out of the wood the matter was serious. As he walked the rapidly darkening twilight was cloven with red gleams, that made him almost fancy for a moment that some fantastic criminal had set fire to the tiny forest as he fled. A second glance showed him nothing but one of those red sunsets in which such serene days sometimes close.

As he came out of the gloomy gate of trees into the full glow he saw a dark figure standing quite still in the

The Man Who Knew Too Much

dim bracken, on the spot where he had left the woodcutter. It was not the woodcutter.

It was topped by a tall black hat of a funereal type, and the whole figure stood so black against the field of crimson fire that edged the sky-line that he could not for an instant understand or recall it. When he did, it was with an odd change in the whole channel of his thoughts.

"Dr. Brown!" he cried. "Why, what are you doing up here?"

"I have been talking to poor Martin," answered the doctor, and made a rather awkward movement with his hand towards the road down to the village. Following the gesture, Paynter dimly saw another dark figure walking away in the blood-red distance. He also saw that the hand motioning was really black, and not merely in shadow; and, coming nearer, found the doctor's dress was really funereal, down to the detail of the dark gloves. It gave the American a small but queer shock, as if this were actually an undertaker come up to bury the corpse that could not be found.

"Poor Martin's been looking for his chopper," observed Dr. Brown, "but I told him I'd picked it up and kept it for him. Between ourselves, I hardly think he's fit to be trusted with it." Then, seeing the glance at his black garb, he added: "I've just been to a funeral. Did you know there's been another loss? Poor Jake the fisherman's wife, down in the cottage on the shore, you know. This infernal fever, of course."

As they both turned, facing the red evening light, Paynter instinctively made a closer study, not merely of the doctor's clothes, but of the doctor. Dr. Burton Brown was a tall, alert man, neatly dressed, who would otherwise have had an almost military air but for his spectacles and an almost painful intellectualism in his lean brown face and bald brow. The contrast was clinched by the fact that, while his face was of the ascetic type generally conceived as clean-shaven, he had a strip of dark moustache cut too short for him to bite, and yet a mouth that often moved as if trying to bite it. He might have been a very intelligent army surgeon, but he had more the

The Trees of Pride

look of an engineer or one of those services that combine a military silence with a more than military science. Paynter had always respected something ruggedly reliable about the man, and after a little hesitation he told him all the discoveries.

The doctor took the hat of the dead Squire in his hand, and examined it with frowning care. He put one finger through the hole in the crown and moved it meditatively. And Paynter realized how fanciful his own fatigue must have made him; for so silly a thing as the black finger waggling through the rent in that frayed white relic unreasonably displeased him. The doctor soon made the same discovery with professional acuteness, and applied it much further. For when Paynter began to tell him of the moving water in the well he looked at him a moment through his spectacles, and then said.

"Did you have any lunch?"

Paynter for the first time realized that he had, as a fact, worked and thought furiously all day without food.

"Please don't fancy I mean you had too much lunch," said the medical man, with mournful humour. "On the contrary, I mean you had too little. I think you are a bit knocked out, and your nerves exaggerate things. Anyhow, let me advise you not to do any more to-night There's nothing to be done without ropes or some sort of fishing tackle, if with that; but I think I can get you some of the sort of grappling irons the fishermen use for dragging. Poor Jake's got some, I know; I'll bring them round to you to-morrow morning. The fact is, I'm staying there for a bit as he's rather in a state, and I think it's better for me to ask for the things and not a stranger. I am sure you'll understand."

Paynter understood sufficiently to assent, and hardly knew why he stood vacantly watching the doctor make his way down the steep road to the shore and the fisher's cottage. Then he threw off thoughts he had not examined, or even consciously entertained, and walked slowly and rather heavily back to the Vane Arms.

The doctor, still funereal in manner, though no longer so in costume, appeared punctually under the wooden sign

The Man Who Knew Too Much

next morning, laden with what he had promised; an apparatus of hooks and a hanging net for hoisting up anything sunk to a reasonable depth. He was about to proceed on his professional round, and said nothing further to deter the American from proceeding on his own very unprofessional experiment as a detective. That buoyant amateur had indeed recovered most if not all of yesterday's buoyancy, was now well fitted to pass any medical examination, and returned with all his own energy to the scene of yesterday's labours.

It may well have brightened and made breezier his second day's toil that he had not only the sunlight and the birds singing in the little wood, to say nothing of a more scientific apparatus to work with, but also human companionship, and that of the most intelligent type. After leaving the doctor and before leaving the village he had bethought himself of seeking the little court or square where stood the quiet brown house of Andrew Ashe, solicitor; and the operations of dragging were worked in double harness. Two heads were peering over the well in the wood: one yellow-haired, lean and eager; the other red-haired, heavy and pondering; and if it be true that two heads are better than one, it is truer that four hands are better than two. In any case, their united and repeated efforts bore fruit at last, if anything so hard and meagre and forlorn can be called a fruit. It weighed loosely in the net as it was lifted, and rolled out on the grassy edge of the well; it was a bone.

Ashe picked it up and stood with it in his hand, frowning.

"We want Dr. Brown here," he said. "This may be the bone of some animal. Any dog or sheep might fall into a hidden well." Then he broke off, for his companion was already detaching a second bone from the net.

After another half-hour's effort Paynter had occasion to remark: "It must have been rather a large dog." There were already a heap of such white fragments at his feet.

"I have seen nothing yet," said Ashe, speaking more plainly, "that is certainly a human bone."

The Trees of Pride

"I fancy this must be a human bone," said the American.

And he turned away a little as he handed the other a skull.

There was no doubt of what sort of skull; there was the one unique curve that holds the mystery of reason, and underneath it the two black holes that had held human eyes. But just above that on the left was another and smaller black hole, which was not an eye.

Then the lawyer said, with something like an effort: "We may admit it is a man without admitting it is—any particular man. There may be something, after all, in that yarn about the drunkard; he may have tumbled into the well. Under certain conditions, after certain natural processes, I fancy, the bones might be stripped in this way, even without the skill of any assassin. We want the doctor again."

Then he added suddenly, and the very sound of his voice suggested that he hardly believed his own words.

"Haven't you got poor Vane's hat there?"

He took it from the silent American's hand, and with a sort of hurry fitted it on the bony head.

"Don't!" said the other involuntarily.

The lawyer had put his finger, as the doctor had done, through the hole in the hat, and it lay exactly over the hole in the skull.

"I have the better right to shrink," he said steadily, but in a vibrant voice. "I think I am the older friend."

Paynter nodded without speech, accepting the final identification. The last doubt, or hope, had departed, and he turned to the dragging apparatus, and did not speak till he had made his last find.

The singing of the birds seemed to grow louder about them, and the dance of the green summer leaves was repeated beyond in the dance of the green summer sea. Only the great roots of the mysterious trees could be seen, the rest being far aloft, and all round it was a wood of little, lively and happy things. They might have been two innocent naturalists, or even two children fishing for efts or tittlebats on that summer holiday, when Paynter pulled up something that weighed in the net more heavily than

The Man Who Knew Too Much

any bone. It nearly broke the meshes, and fell against a mossy stone with a clang.

"Truth lies at the bottom of a well," cried the American, with lift in his voice. "The woodman's axe."

It lay, indeed, flat and gleaming in the grasses by the well in the wood, just as it had lain in the thicket where the woodman threw it in the beginning of all these things. But on one corner of the bright blade was a dull brown stain.

"I see," said Ashe, "the woodman's axe, and therefore the woodman. Your deductions are rapid."

"My deductions are reasonable," said Paynter. "Look here, Mr. Ashe; I know what you're thinking. I know you distrust Treherne; but I'm sure you will be just for all that. To begin with, surely the first assumption is that the woodman's axe is used by the woodman. What have you to say to it?"

"I say 'No' to it," replied the lawyer. "The last weapon a woodman would use would be a woodman's axe; that is if he is a sane man."

"He isn't," said Paynter quietly; "you said you wanted the doctor's opinion just now. The doctor's opinion on this point is the same as my own. We both found him meandering about outside there; it's obvious this business has gone to his head, at any rate. If the murderer were a man of business like yourself, what you say might be sound. But this murderer is a mystic. He was driven by some fanatical fad about the trees. It's quite likely he thought there was something solemn and sacrificial about the axe, and would have liked to cut off Vane's head before a crowd, like Charles the First's. He's looking for the axe still, and probably thinks it a holy relic."

"For which reason," said Ashe, smiling, "he instantly chucked it down a well."

Paynter laughed.

"You have me there certainly," he said. "But I think you have something else in your mind. You'll say, I suppose, that we were all watching the wood; but were we? Frankly, I could almost fancy the peacock trees

The Trees of Pride

did strike me with a sort of sickness—a sleeping sickness."

"Well," admitted Ashe, "you have me there too. I'm afraid I couldn't swear I was awake all the time; but I don't put it down to magic trees—only to a private hobby of going to bed at night. But look here, Mr. Paynter; there's another and better argument against any outsider from the village or countryside having committed the crime. Granted he might have slipped past us somehow, and gone for the Squire. But why should he go for him in the wood? How did he know he was in the wood? You remember how suddenly the poor old boy bolted into it, on what a momentary impulse. It's the last place where one would normally look for such a man in the middle of the night. No, it's an ugly thing to say, but we, the group round that garden table, were the only people who knew. Which brings me back to the one point in your remarks which I happen to think perfectly true."

"What was that?" inquired the other.

"That the murderer was a mystic," said Ashe. "But a cleverer mystic than poor old Martin."

Paynter made a murmur of protest, and then fell silent.

"Let us talk plainly," resumed the lawyer. "Treherne had all those mad motives you yourself admit against the woodcutter. He had the knowledge of Vane's whereabouts, which nobody can possibly attribute to the woodcutter. But he had much more. Who taunted and goaded the Squire to go into the wood at all? Treherne. Who practically prophesied, like an infernal quack astrologer, that something would happen to him if he did go into the wood? Treherne. Who was, for some reason, no matter what, obviously burning with rage and restlessness all that night, kicking his legs impatiently to and fro on the cliff, and breaking out with wild words about it being all over soon? Treherne. And on top of all this, when I walked closer to the wood, whom did I see slip out of it swiftly and silently like a shadow, but turning his face once to the moon? On my oath and on my honour—Treherne."

The Man Who Knew Too Much

"It is awful," said Paynter, like a man stunned. "What you say is simply awful."

"Yes," said Ashe seriously, "very awful, but very simple. Treherne knew where the axe was originally thrown. I saw him, on that day he lunched here first, watching it like a wolf, while Miss Vane was talking to him. On that dreadful night he could easily have picked it up as he went into the wood. He knew about the well, no doubt; who was so likely to know any old traditions about the peacock trees? He hid the hat in the trees, where perhaps he hoped (though the point is unimportant) that nobody would dare to look. Anyhow, he hid it, simply because it was the one thing that would not sink in the well. Mr. Paynter, do you think I would say this of any man in mere mean dislike? Could any man say it of any man unless the case were complete, as this is complete?"

"It is complete," said Paynter, very pale. "I have nothing left against it but a faint, irrational feeling; a feeling that, somehow or other, if poor Vane could stand alive before us at this moment, he might tell some other and even more incredible tale."

Ashe made a mournful gesture.

"Can these dry bones live?" he said.

"Lord, Thou knowest," answered the other mechanically. "Even these dry bones——"

And he stopped suddenly with his mouth open, a blinding light of wonder in his pale eyes.

"See here," he said hoarsely and hastily. "You have said the word. What does it mean? What can it mean? Dry? Why are these bones dry?"

The lawyer started and stared down at the heap.

"Your case complete!" cried Paynter, in mounting excitement. "Where is the water in the well? The water I saw leap like a flame? Why did it leap? Where is it gone to? Complete! We are buried under riddles."

Ashe stooped, picked up a bone and looked at it.

"You are right," he said, in a low and shaken voice; "this bone is as dry—as a bone."

"Yes, I am right," replied Cyprian. "And your mystic is still as mysterious—as a mystic."

The Trees of Pride

There was a long silence. Ashe laid down the bone, picked up the axe and studied it more closely. Beyond the dull stain at the corner of the steel there was nothing unusual about it save a broad white rag wrapped round the handle, perhaps to give a better grip. The lawyer thought it worth noting, however, that the rag was certainly newer and cleaner than the chopper. But both were quite dry.

"Mr. Paynter," he said at last, "I admit you have scored, in the spirit if not in the letter. In strict logic, this greater puzzle is not a reply to my case. If this axe has not been dipped in water, it has been dipped in blood; and the water jumping out of the well is not an explanation of the poet jumping out of the wood. But I admit that morally and practically it does make a vital difference. We are now faced with a colossal contradiction, and we don't know how far it extends. The body might have been broken up or boiled down to its bones by the murderer, though it may be hard to connect it with the conditions of the murder. It might conceivably have been so reduced by some property in the water and soil, for decomposition varies vastly with these things. I should not dismiss my strong prima facie case against the likely person because of these difficulties. But here we have something entirely different. That the bones themselves should remain dry in a well full of water, or a well that yesterday was full of water—that brings us to the edge of something beyond which we can make no guess. There is a new factor, enormous and quite unknown. While we can't fit together such prodigious facts, we can't fit together a case against Treherne or against anybody. No; there is only one thing to be done now. Since we can't accuse Treherne, we must appeal to him. We must put the case against him frankly before him, and trust he has an explanation—and will give it. I suggest we go back and do it now."

Paynter, beginning to follow, hesitated a moment, and then said: "Forgive me for a kind of liberty; as you say, you are an older friend of the family. I entirely agree with your suggestion, but before you act on your present suspicions, do you know, I think Miss Vane ought to be

The Man Who Knew Too Much

warned a little? I rather fear all this will be a new shock to her."

"Very well," said Ashe, after looking at him steadily for an instant. "Let us go across to her first."

From the opening of the wood they could see Barbara Vane writing at the garden table, which was littered with correspondence, and the butler with his yellow face waiting behind her chair. As the lengths of grass lessened between them, and the little group at the table grew larger and clearer in the sunlight, Paynter had a painful sense of being part of an embassy of doom. It sharpened when the girl looked up from the table and smiled on seeing them.

"I should like to speak to you rather particularly if I may," said the lawyer, with a touch of authority in his respect; and when the butler was dismissed he laid open the whole matter before her, speaking sympathetically, but leaving out nothing, from the strange escape of the poet from the wood to the last detail of the dry bones out of the well. No fault could be found with any one of his tones or phrases, and yet Cyprian, tingling in every nerve with the fine delicacy of his nation about the other sex, felt as if she were faced with an inquisitor. He stood about uneasily, watched the few coloured clouds in the clear sky and the bright birds darting about the wood, and he heartily wished himself up the tree again.

Soon, however, the way the girl took it began to move him to perplexity rather than pity. It was like nothing he had expected, and yet he could not name the shade of difference. The final identification of her father's skull, by the hole in the hat, turned her a little pale, but left her composed; this was, perhaps, explicable, since she had from the first taken the pessimistic view. But during the rest of the tale there rested on her broad brows under her copper coils of hair a brooding spirit that was itself a mystery. He could only tell himself that she was less merely receptive, either firmly or weakly, than he would have expected. It was as if she revolved, not their problem, but her own. She was silent a long time, and said at last:

"Thank you, Mr. Ashe, I am really very grateful for

The Trees of Pride

this. After all, it brings things to the point where they must have come sooner or later." She looked dreamily at the wood and sea, and went on: "I've not only had myself to consider, you see; but if you're really thinking *that,* it's time I spoke out, without asking anybody. You say, as if it were something very dreadful, 'Mr. Treherne was in the wood that night.' Well, it's not quite so dreadful to me, you see, because I know he was. In fact, we were there together."

"Together!" repeated the lawyer.

"We were together," she said quietly, "because we had a right to be together."

"Do you mean," stammered Ashe, surprised out of himself, "that you were engaged?"

"Oh, no," she said. "We were married."

Then, amid a startled silence, she added, as a kind of afterthought:

"In fact, we are still."

Strong as was his composure, the lawyer sat back in his chair with a sort of solid stupefaction at which Paynter could not help smiling.

"You will ask me, of course," went on Barbara in the same measured manner, "why we should be married secretly, so that even my poor father did not know. Well, I answer you quite frankly to begin with; because, if he had known, he would certainly have cut me off with a shilling. He did not like my husband, and I rather fancy you don't like him either. And when I tell you this, I know perfectly well what you will say—the usual adventurer getting hold of the usual heiress. It is quite reasonable, and, as it happens, it is quite wrong. If I had deceived my father for the sake of the money, or even for the sake of a man, I should be a little ashamed to talk to you about it. And I think you can see that I am not ashamed."

"Yes," said the American, with a grave inclination, "yes, I can see that."

She looked at him thoughtfully for a moment, as if seeking words for an obscure matter, and then said:

"Do you remember, Mr. Paynter, that day you first lunched here and told us about the African trees? Well,

The Man Who Knew Too Much

it was my birthday; I mean my first birthday. I was born then, or woke up or something. I had walked in this garden like a somnambulist in the sun. I think there are many such somnambulists in our set and our society; stunned with health, drugged with good manners, fitting their surroundings too well to be alive. Well, I came alive somehow; and you know how deep in us are the things we first realize when we were babies and began to take notice. I began to take notice. One of the first things I noticed was your own story, Mr. Paynter. I feel as if I heard of St. Securis as children hear of Santa Claus, and as if that big tree were a bogey I still believed in. For I do still believe in such things, or rather I believe in them more and more; I feel certain my poor father drove on the rocks by disbelieving, and you are all racing to ruin after him. That is why I do honestly want the estate, and that is why I am not ashamed of wanting it. I am perfectly certain, Mr. Paynter, that nobody can save this perishing land and this perishing people but those who understand. I mean who understand a thousand little signs and guides in the very soil and lie of the land, and traces that are almost trampled out. My husband understands, and I have begun to understand; my father would never have understood. There are powers, there is the spirit of a place, there are presences that are not to be put by. Oh, don't fancy I am sentimental and hanker after the good old days. The old days were not all good; that is just the point, and we must understand enough to know the good from the evil. We must understand enough to save the traces of a saint or a sacred tradition, or, where a wicked god has been worshipped, to destroy his altar and to cut down his grove."

"His grove," said Paynter automatically, and looked towards the little wood, where the sun-bright birds were flying.

"Mrs. Treherne," said Ashe, with a formidable quietness, "I am not so unsympathetic with all this as you may perhaps suppose. I will not even say it is all moonshine, for it is something better. It is, if I may say so, honeymoonshine. I will never deny the saying that it

The Trees of Pride

makes the world go round, if it makes people's heads go round too. But there are other sentiments, madam, and other duties. I need not tell you your father was a good man, and that what has befallen him would be pitiable, even as the fate of the wicked. This is a horrible thing, and it is chiefly among horrors that we must keep our common sense. There are seasons for everything, and when my old friend lies butchered, do not come to me with even the most beautiful fairy tales about a saint and his enchanted grove."

"Well, and you!" she cried, and rose radiantly and swiftly. "With what kind of fairy tales do you come to me? In what enchanted groves are *you* walking? You come and tell me that Mr. Paynter found a well where the water danced and then disappeared; but of course miracles are all moonshine! You tell me you yourself fished bones from under the same water, and every bone was as dry as a biscuit; but, for heaven's sake, let us say nothing that makes anybody's head go round! Really, Mr. Ashe, you must try to preserve your common sense!"

She was smiling, but with blazing eyes; and Ashe got to his feet with an involuntary laugh of surrender.

"Well, we must be going," he said. "May I say that a tribute is really due to your new transcendental training? If I may say so, I always knew you had brains; and you've been learning to use them."

The two amateur detectives went back to the wood for the moment, that Ashe might consider the removal of the unhappy Squire's remains. As he pointed out, it was now legally possible to have an inquest, and, even at that early stage of investigations, he was in favour of having it at once.

"I shall be the coroner," he said, "and I think it will be a case of 'some person or persons unknown.' Don't be surprised; it is often done to give the guilty a false security. This is not the first time the police have found it convenient to have the inquest first and the inquiry afterwards."

But Paynter had paid little attention to the point; for his great gift of enthusiasm, long wasted on arts and

The Man Who Knew Too Much

affectations, was lifted to inspiration by the romance of real life into which he had just walked. He was really a great critic; he had a genius for admiration, and his admiration varied fittingly with everything he admired.

"A splendid girl and a splendid story," he cried. "I feel as if I were in love again myself, not so much with her as with Eve or Helen of Troy, or some such tower of beauty in the morning of the world. Don't you love all heroic things, that gravity and great candour, and the way she took one step from a sort of throne to stand in a wilderness with a vagabond? Oh, believe me, it is she who is the poet; she has the higher reason, and honour and valour are at rest in her soul."

"In short, she is uncommonly pretty," replied Ashe, with some cynicism. "I knew a murderess rather well who was very much like her, and had just that coloured hair."

"You talk as if a murderer could be caught red-haired instead of red-handed," retorted Paynter. "Why, at this very minute, you could be caught red-haired yourself. Are you a murderer, by any chance?"

Ashe looked up quickly, and then smiled.

"I'm afraid I'm a connoisseur in murderers, as you are in poets," he answered, "and I assure you they are of all colours in hair as well as temperament. I suppose it's inhumane, but mine is a monstrously interesting trade, even in a little place like this. As for that girl, of course I've known her all her life, and—— but—but that is just the question. Have I known her all her life? Have I known her at all? Was she even there to be known? You admire her for telling the truth; and so she did, by God, when she said that some people wake up late, who have never lived before. Do we know what they might do—we, who have only seen them asleep?"

"Great heavens!" cried Paynter. "You don't dare suggest that she——"

"No, I don't," said the lawyer, with composure, "but there are other reasons. . . . I don't suggest anything fully, till we've had our interview with this poet of yours. I think I know where to find him."

They found him, in fact, before they expected him,

The Trees of Pride

sitting on the bench outside the Vane Arms, drinking a mug of cider and waiting for the return of his American friend; so it was not difficult to open conversation with him. Nor did he in any way avoid the subject of the tragedy; and the lawyer, seating himself also on the long bench that fronted the little market-place, was soon putting the last developments as lucidly as he had put them to Barbara.

"Well," said Treherne at last, leaning back and frowning at the signboard, with the coloured birds and dolphins, just above his head; "suppose somebody did kill the Squire. He'd killed a good many people with his hygiene and his enlightened landlordism."

Paynter was considerably uneasy at this alarming opening; but the poet went on quite coolly, with his hands in his pockets and his feet thrust out into the street.

"When a man has the power of a Sultan in Turkey, and uses it with the ideas of a spinster in Tooting, I often wonder that nobody puts a knife in him. I wish there were more sympathy for murderers, somehow. I'm very sorry the poor old fellow's gone myself; but you gentlemen always seem to forget there are any other people in the world. He's all right; he was a good fellow, and his soul, I fancy, has gone to the happiest paradise of all."

The anxious American could read nothing of the effect of this in the dark Napoleonic face of the lawyer, who merely said: "What do you mean?"

"The fool's paradise," said Treherne, and drained his pot of cider.

The lawyer rose. He did not look at Treherne, or speak to him; but looked and spoke straight across him to the American, who found the utterance not a little unexpected.

"Mr. Paynter," said Ashe, "you thought it rather morbid of me to collect murderers; but it's fortunate for your own view of the case that I do. It may surprise you to know that Mr. Treherne has now, in my eyes, entirely cleared himself of suspicion. I have been intimate with several assassins, as I remarked; but there's one thing none of them ever did. I never knew a murderer

The Man Who Knew Too Much

talk about the murder, and then at once deny it and defend it. No, if a man is concealing his crime, why should he go out of his way to apologize for it?"

"Well," said Paynter, with his ready appreciation, "I always said you were a remarkable man; and that's certainly a remarkable idea."

"Do I understand," asked the poet, kicking his heels on the cobbles, "that both you gentlemen have been kindly directing me towards the gallows?"

"No," said Paynter thoughtfully. "I never thought you guilty; and even supposing I had, if you understand me, I should never have thought it quite so guilty to be guilty. It would not have been for money or any mean thing, but for something a little wilder and worthier of a man of genius. After all, I suppose, the poet has passions like great unearthly appetites; and the world has always judged more gently of his sins. But now that Mr. Ashe admits your innocence, I can honestly say I have always affirmed it."

The poet rose also. "Well, I am innocent, oddly enough," he said. "I think I can make a guess about your vanishing well, but of the death and dry bones I know no more than the dead—if so much. And, by the way, my dear Paynter"—and he turned two bright eyes on the art critic—"I will excuse you from excusing me for all the things I haven't done; and you, I hope, will excuse me if I differ from you altogether about the morality of poets. As you suggest, it is a fashionable view, but I think it is a fallacy. No man has less right to be lawless than a man of imagination. For he has spiritual adventures, and can take his holidays when he likes. I could picture the poor Squire carried off to elfland whenever I wanted him carried off, and that wood needed no crime to make it wicked for me. That red sunset the other night was all that a murder would have been to many men. No, Mr. Ashe; show, when next you sit in judgment, a little mercy to some wretched man who drinks and robs because he must drink beer to taste it, and take it to drink it. Have compassion on the next batch of poor thieves, who have to hold things in order to have them. But if ever you find *me* stealing one small

The Trees of Pride

farthing, when I can shut my eyes and see the city of El Dorado, then "—and he lifted his head like a falcon—"show me no mercy, for I shall deserve none."

"Well," remarked Ashe, after a pause, "I must go and fix things up for the inquest. Mr. Treherne, your attitude is singularly interesting; I really almost wish I could add you to my collection of murderers. They are a varied and extraordinary set."

"Has it ever occurred to you," asked Paynter, "that perhaps the men who have never committed murder are a varied and very extraordinary set? Perhaps every plain man's life holds the real mystery, the secret of sins avoided."

"Possibly," replied Ashe. "It would be a long business to stop the next man in the street and ask him what crimes he never committed and why not. And I happen to be busy, so you'll excuse me."

"What," asked the American, when he and the poet were alone, "is this guess of yours about the vanishing water?"

"Well, I'm not sure I'll tell you yet," answered Treherne, something of the old mischief coming back into his dark eyes. "But I'll tell you something else, which may be connected with it; something I couldn't tell until my wife had told you about our meeting in the wood." His face had grown grave again, and he resumed after a pause:

"When my wife started to follow her father I advised her to go back first to the house, to leave it by another door and to meet me in the wood in half an hour. We often made these assignations, of course, and generally thought them great fun; but this time the question was serious, and I didn't want the wrong thing done in a hurry. It was a question whether anything could be done to undo an experiment we both vaguely felt to be dangerous, and she especially thought, after reflection, that interference would make things worse. She thought the old sportsman, having been dared to do something, would certainly not be dissuaded by the very man who had dared him or by a woman whom he regarded as a child. She left me at last in a sort of despair, but I lingered with

The Man Who Knew Too Much

a last hope of doing something, and drew doubtfully near to the heart of the wood; and there, instead of the silence I expected, I heard a voice. It seemed as if the Squire must be talking to himself, and I had the unpleasant fancy that he had already lost his reason in that wood of witchcraft. But I soon found that if he was talking he was talking with two voices. Other fancies attacked me, as that the other was the voice of the tree or the voices of the three trees talking together, and with no man near. But it was not the voice of the tree. The next moment I knew the voice, for I had heard it twenty times across the table. It was the voice of that doctor of yours; I heard it as certainly as you hear my voice now."

After a moment's silence, he resumed: "I left the wood, I hardly knew why, and with wild and bewildered feelings; and as I came out into the faint moonshine I saw that old lawyer standing quietly, but staring at me like an owl. At least, the light touched his red hair with fire, but his square old face was in shadow. But I knew, if I could have read it, that it was the face of a hanging judge."

He threw himself on the bench again, smiled a little, and added: "Only, like a good many hanging judges, I fancy, he was waiting patiently to hang the wrong man."

"And the right man——" said Paynter mechanically. Treherne shrugged his shoulders, sprawling on the ale-bench, and played with his empty pot.

CHAPTER IV

THE CHASE AFTER THE TRUTH

SOME time after the inquest, which had ended in the inconclusive verdict which Mr. Andrew Ashe had himself predicted and achieved, Paynter was again sitting on the bench outside the village inn, having on the little table

The Trees of Pride

in front of it a tall glass of light ale, which he enjoyed much more as local colour than as liquor. He had but one companion on the bench, and that a new one, for the little market-place was empty at that hour, and he had lately, for the rest, been much alone. He was not unhappy, for he resembled his great countryman, Walt Whitman, in carrying a kind of universe with him like an open umbrella; but he was not only alone, but lonely. For Ashe had gone abruptly up to London, and since his return had been occupied obscurely with legal matters, doubtless bearing on the murder. And Treherne had long since taken up his position openly at the great house as the husband of the great lady, and he and she were occupied with sweeping reforms on the estate. The lady especially, being of the sort whose very dreams "drive at practice," was landscape gardening as with the gestures of a giantess. It was natural, therefore, that so sociable a spirit as Paynter should fall into speech with the one other stranger who happened to be staying at the inn, evidently a bird of passage like himself. This man, who was smoking a pipe on the bench beside him, with his knapsack before him on the table, was an artist come to sketch on that romantic coast; a tall man in a velvet jacket, with a shock of tow-coloured hair, a long fair beard, but eyes of dark brown, the effect of which contrast reminded Paynter vaguely, he hardly knew why, of a Russian. The stranger carried his knapsack into many picturesque corners; he obtained permission to set up his easel in that high garden where the late Squire had held his al fresco banquets. But Paynter had never had an opportunity of judging of the artist's work, nor did he find it easy to get the artist even to talk of his art. Cyprian himself was always ready to talk of any art, and he talked of it excellently, but with little response. He gave his own reasons for preferring the Cubists to the cult of Picasso, but his new friend seemed to have but a faint interest in either. He insinuated that perhaps the Neo-Primitives were after all only thinning their line, while the true Primitives were rather tightening it; but the stranger seemed to receive the insinuation without any marked reaction of feeling. When Paynter had even gone

The Man Who Knew Too Much

back as far into the past as the Post-Impressionists to find a common ground, and not found it, other memories began to creep back into his mind. He was just reflecting, rather darkly, that after all the tale of the peacock trees needed a mysterious stranger to round it off, and this man had much the air of being one, when the mysterious stranger himself said suddenly:

"Well, I think I'd better show you the work I'm doing down here."

He had his knapsack before him on the table, and he smiled rather grimly as he began to unstrap it. Paynter looked on with polite expressions of interest, but was considerably surprised when the artist unpacked and placed on the table, not any recognisable works of art, even of the most Cubist description, but (first) a quire of foolscap closely written with notes in black and red ink, and (second), to the American's extreme amazement, the old woodman's axe with the linen wrapper, which he had himself found in the well long ago.

"Sorry to give you a start, sir," said the Russian artist, with a marked London accent. "But I'd better explain straight off that I'm a policeman."

"You don't look it," said Paynter.

"I'm not supposed to," replied the other. "Mr. Ashe brought me down here from the Yard to investigate; but he told me to report to you when I'd got anything to go on. Would you like to go into the matter now?

"When I took this matter up," explained the detective, "I did it at Mr. Ashe's request, and largely, of course, on Mr. Ashe's lines. Mr. Ashe is a great criminal lawyer; with a beautiful brain, sir, as full as the Newgate Calendar. I took, as a working notion, his view that only you five gentlemen round the table in the Squire's garden were acquainted with the Squire's movements. But you gentlemen, if I may say so, have a way of forgetting certain other things and other people which we are rather taught to look for first. And as I followed Mr. Ashe's inquiries through the stages you know already, through certain suspicions I needn't discuss because they've been dropped, I found the thing shaping after all towards something, in the end, which I think we should

The Trees of Pride

have considered at the beginning. Now, to begin with, it is not true that there were five men round the table. There were six."

The creepy conditions of that garden vigil vaguely returned upon Paynter; and he thought of a ghost, or something more nameless than a ghost. But the deliberate speech of the detective soon enlightened him.

"There were six men and five gentlemen, if you like to put it so," he proceeded. "That man Miles the butler saw the Squire vanish as plainly as you did; and I soon found that Miles was a man worthy of a good deal of attention."

A light of understanding dawned on Paynter's face. "So that was it, was it?" he muttered. "Does all our mythological mystery end with a policeman collaring a butler? Well, I agree with you he is far from an ordinary butler, even to look at; and the fault in imagination is mine. Like many faults in imagination, it was simply snobbishness."

"We don't go quite so fast as that," observed the officer, in an impassive manner. "I only said I found the inquiry pointing to Miles; and that he was well worthy of attention. He was much more in the old Squire's confidence than many people supposed; and when I cross-examined him he told me a good deal that was worth knowing. I've got it all down in these notes here; but at the moment I'll only trouble you with one detail of it. One night this butler was just outside the Squire's dining-room door, when he heard the noise of a violent quarrel. The Squire was a violent gentleman, from time to time; but the curious thing about this scene was that the other gentleman was the more violent of the two. Miles heard him say repeatedly that the Squire was a public nuisance, and that his death would be a good riddance for everybody. I only stop now to tell you that the other gentleman was Dr. Burton Brown, the medical man of this village.

"The next examination I made was that of Martin, the woodcutter. Upon one point at least his evidence is quite clear, and is, as you will see, largely confirmed by other witnesses. He says first that the doctor prevented him from recovering his axe, and this is corro-

The Man Who Knew Too Much

borated by Mr. and Mrs. Treherne. But he says further that the doctor admitted having the thing himself; and this again finds support in other evidence by the gardener, who saw the doctor, some time afterwards, come by himself and pick up the chopper. Martin says that Dr. Brown repeatedly refused to give it up, alleging some fanciful excuse every time. And, finally, Mr. Paynter, we will hear the evidence of the axe itself."

He laid the woodman's tool on the table in front of him, and began to rip up and unwrap the curious linen covering round the handle.

"You will admit this is an odd bandage," he said. "And that's just the odd thing about it, that it really is a bandage. This white stuff is the sort of lint they use in hospitals, cut into strips like this. But most doctors keep some; and I have the evidence of Jake the fisherman, with whom Dr. Brown lived for some time, that the doctor had this useful habit. And, last," he added, flattening out a corner of the rag on the table, "isn't it odd that it should be marked T.B.B.?"

The American gazed at the rudely inked initials, but hardly saw them. What he saw, as in a mirror in his darkened memory, was the black figure with the black gloves against the blood-red sunset, as he had seen it when he came out of the wood, and which had always haunted him, he knew not why.

"Of course, I see what you mean," he said, "and it's very painful for me, for I knew and respected the man. But surely, also, it's very far from explaining everything. If he is a murderer, is he a magician? Why did the well-water all evaporate in a night, and leave the dead man's bones dry as dust? That's not a common operation in the hospitals, is it?"

"As to the water, we do know the explanation," said the detective. "I didn't tumble to it at first myself, being a Cockney; but a little talk with Jake and the other fishermen about the old smuggling days put me straight about that. But I admit the dried remains still stump us all. All the same——"

A shadow fell across the table, and his talk was sharply cut short. Ashe was standing under the painted

The Trees of Pride

sign, buttoned up grimly in black, and with the face of the hanging judge, of which the poet had spoken, plain this time in the broad sunlight. Behind him stood two big men in plain clothes, very still; but Paynter knew instantly who they were.

"We must move at once," said the lawyer. "Dr. Burton Brown is leaving the village."

The tall detective sprang to his feet, and Paynter instinctively imitated him.

"He has gone up to the Treherne's, possibly to say good-bye," went on Ashe rapidly. "I'm sorry, but we must arrest him in the garden there, if necessary. I've kept the lady out of the way, I think. But you"—addressing the factitious landscape-painter—"must go up at once and rig up that easel of yours near the table and be ready. We will follow quietly, and come up behind the tree. We must be careful, for it's clear he's got wind of us, or he wouldn't be doing a bolt."

"I don't like this job," remarked Paynter, as they mounted towards the park and garden, the detective darting on ahead.

"Do you suppose I do?" asked Ashe; and, indeed, his strong, heavy face looked so lined and old that the red hair seemed unnatural, like a red wig. "I've known him longer than you, though perhaps I've suspected him longer as well."

When they topped the slope of the garden the detective had already erected his easel, though a strong breeze blowing towards the sea rattled and flapped his apparatus and blew about his fair (and false) beard in the wind. Little clouds curled like feathers were scudding seawards across the many-coloured landscape, which the American art critic had once surveyed on a happier morning; but it is doubtful if the landscape-painter paid much attention to it. Treherne was dimly discernible in the doorway of what was now his house; he would come no nearer, for he hated such a public duty more bitterly than the rest. The others posted themselves a little way behind the tree. Between the lines of these masked batteries the black figure of the doctor could be seen coming across the green lawn, travelling straight as a bullet, as he had done when

The Man Who Knew Too Much

he brought the bad news to the woodcutter. To-day he was smiling, under the dark moustache that was cut short of the upper lip, though they fancied him a little pale, and he seemed to pause a moment and peer through his spectacles at the artist.

The artist turned from his easel with a natural movement, and then in a flash had captured the doctor by the coat-collar.

"I arrest you——" he began, but Dr. Brown plucked himself free with startling promptitude, took a flying leap at the other, tore off his sham beard, tossing it into the air like one of the wild wisps of the cloud; then, with one wild kick, sent the easel flying topsy-turvy, and fled like a hare for the shore.

Even at that dazzling instant Paynter felt that this wild reception was a novelty and almost an anti-climax; but he had no time for analysis when he and the whole pack had to follow in the hunt; even Treherne bringing up the rear with a renewed curiosity and energy.

The fugitive collided with one of the policemen who ran to head him off, sending him sprawling down the slope; indeed, the fugitive seemed inspired with the strength of a wild ape. He cleared at a bound the rampart of flowers over which Barbara had once leaned to look at her future lover, and tumbled with blinding speed down the steep path up which that troubadour had climbed. Racing with the rushing wind they all streamed across the garden after him, down the path, and finally on to the seashore by the fisher's cot and the pierced crags and caverns the American had admired when he first landed. The runaway did not, however, make for the house he had long inhabited, but rather for the pier, as if with a mind to seize the boat or to swim. Only when he reached the other end of the small stone jetty did he turn, and show them the pale face with the spectacles; and they saw that it was still smiling.

"I'm rather glad of this," said Treherne, with a great sigh. "The man is mad."

Nevertheless, the naturalness of the doctor's voice, when he spoke, startled them almost as much as a shriek.

"Gentlemen," he said, "I won't protract your painful

The Trees of Pride

duties by asking you what you want; but I will ask at once for a small favour, which will not prejudice those duties in any way. I came down here rather in a hurry perhaps; but the truth is I thought I was late for an appointment." He looked dispassionately at his watch. "I find there is still some fifteen minutes. Will you wait with me here for that short time; after which I am quite at your service."

There was a bewildered silence, and then Paynter said: "For my part, I feel as if it would really be better to humour him."

"Ashe," said the doctor, with a new note of seriousness, "for old friendship, grant me this last little indulgence. It will make no difference; I have no arms or means of escape; you can search me if you like. I know you think you are doing right, and I also know you will do it as fairly as you can. Well, after all, you get friends to help you; look at our friend with the beard, or the remains of the beard. Why shouldn't I have a friend to help me? A man will be here in a few minutes in whom I put some confidence; a great authority on these things. Why not, if only out of curiosity, wait and hear his view of the case?"

"This seems all moonshine," said Ashe, "but on the chance of any light on things—even from the moon—I don't mind waiting a quarter of an hour. Who is this friend, I wonder; some amateur detective, I suppose."

"I thank you," said the doctor, with some dignity. "I think you will trust him when you have talked to him a little. And now," he added with an air of amiably relaxing into lighter matters, "let us talk about the murder."

He seated himself on a rock, and began to talk with the absurd air of a lecturer condescending to his class.

"This case," he said in a detached manner, "will be found, I suspect, to be rather unique. There is a very clear and conclusive combination of evidence against Thomas Burton Brown, otherwise myself. But there is one peculiarity about that evidence, which you may perhaps have noticed. It all comes ultimately from one source, and that a rather unusual one. Thus, the wood-

The Man Who Knew Too Much

cutter says I had his axe, but what makes him think so? He says *I* told him I had his axe; that I told him so again and again. Once more, Mr. Paynter here pulled up the axe out of the well; but how? I think Mr. Paynter will testify that *I* brought him the tackle for fishing it up, tackle he might never have got in any other way. Curious, is it not? Again, the axe is found to be wrapped in lint that was in my possession, according to the fisherman. But who showed the lint to the fisherman? I did. Who marked it with large letters as mine? I did. Who wrapped it round the handle at all? I did. Rather a singular thing to do; has anyone ever explained it?"

His words, which had been heard at first with a cold pain, were beginning to hold more and more of their attention.

"Then there is the well itself," proceeded the doctor, with the same air of insane calm. "I suppose some of you by this time know at least the secret of that. The secret of the well is simply that it is not a well. It is purposely shaped at the top so as to look like one, but it is really a sort of chimney opening from the roof of one of those caves over there; a cave that runs inland just under the wood, and indeed is connected by tunnels and secret passages with other openings miles and miles away. It is a sort of labyrinth used by smugglers and such people for ages past. This doubtless explains many of those disappearances we have heard of. But to return to the well that is not a well, in case some of you still don't know about it. When the sea rises very high at certain seasons it fills the low cave, and even rises a little way in the funnel above, making it look more like a well than ever. The noise Mr. Paynter heard was the natural eddy of a breaker from outside, and the whole experience depended on something so elementary as the tide."

The American was startled into ordinary speech.

"The tide!" he said. "And I never even thought of it! I guess that comes of living by the Mediterranean."

"The next step will be obvious enough," continued the speaker, "to a logical mind like that of Mr. Ashe, for instance. If it be asked why, even so, the tide did

The Trees of Pride

not wash away the Squire's remains that had lain there since his disappearance, there is only one possible answer. The remains had *not* lain there since his disappearance. The remains had been deliberately put there in the cavern under the wood, and put there *after* Mr. Paynter had made his first investigation. They were put there, in short, after the sea had retreated and the cave was again dry. That is why they were dry; of course, much drier than the cave. Who put them there, I wonder?"

He was gazing gravely through his spectacles over their heads into vacancy, and suddenly he smiled.

"Ah," he cried, jumping up from the rock with alacrity, "here is the amateur detective at last!"

Ashe turned his head over his shoulder, and for a few seconds did not move it again, but stood as if with a stiff neck. In the cliff just behind him was one of the clefts or cracks, into which it was everywhere cloven. Advancing from this into the sunshine, as if from a narrow door, was Squire Vane, with a broad smile on his face.

The wind was tearing from the top of the high cliff out to sea, passing over their heads, and they had the sensation that everything was passing over their heads and out of their control. Paynter felt as if his head had been blown off like a hat. But none of this gale of unreason seemed to stir a hair on the white head of the Squire, whose bearing, though self-important and bordering on a swagger, seemed if anything more comfortable than in the old days. His red face was, however, burnt like a sailor's, and his light clothes had a foreign look.

"Well, gentlemen," he said genially, "so this is the end of the legend of the peacock trees. Sorry to spoil that delightful traveller's tale, Mr Paynter, but the joke couldn't be kept up for ever. Sorry to put a stop to your best poem, Mr. Treherne, but I thought all this poetry had been going a little too far. So Dr. Brown and I fixed up a little surprise for you. And I must say, without vanity, that you look a little surprised."

"What on earth," asked Ashe at last, "is the meaning of all this?"

The Squire laughed pleasantly, and even a little apologetically.

The Man Who Knew Too Much

"I'm afraid I'm fond of practical jokes," he said, "and this I suppose is my last grand practical joke. But I want you to understand that the joke is really practical. I flatter myself it will be of very practical use to the cause of progress and common sense, and the killing of such silly superstitions everywhere. The best part of it, I admit, was the doctor's idea and not mine. All I meant to do was to pass a night in the trees, and then turn up as fresh as paint to tell you what fools you were. But Dr. Brown here followed me into the wood, and we had a little talk which rather changed my plans. He told me that a disappearance for a few hours like that would never knock the nonsense on the head; most people would never even hear of it, and those who did would say that one night proved nothing. He showed me a much better way, which had been tried in several cases where bogus miracles had been shown up. The thing to do was to get the thing really believed everywhere as a miracle, and then shown up everywhere as a sham miracle. I can't put all the arguments as well as he did, but that was the notion, I think."

The doctor nodded, gazing silently at the sand; and the Squire resumed with undiminished relish.

"We agreed that I should drop through the hole into the cave, and make my way through the tunnels, where I often used to play as a boy, to the railway station a few miles from here, and there take a train for London. It was necessary for the joke, of course, that I should disappear without being traced; so I made my way to a port, and put in a very pleasant month or two round my old haunts in Cyprus and the Mediterranean. There's no more to say of that part of the business, except that I arranged to be back by a particular time; and here I am. But I've heard enough of what's gone on round here to be satisfied that I've done the trick. Everybody in Cornwall and most people in South England have heard of the Vanishing Squire; and thousands of noodles have been nodding their heads over crystals and tarot cards at this marvellous proof of an unseen world. I reckon the Reappearing Squire will scatter their cards and smash their crystals, so that such rubbish won't appear again

The Trees of Pride

in the twentieth century. I'll make the peacock trees the laughing stock of all Europe and America."

"Well," said the lawyer, who was the first to rearrange his wits, "I'm sure we're all only too delighted to see you again, Squire; and I quite understand your explanation and your own very natural motives in the matter. But I'm afraid I haven't got the hang of everything yet. Granted that you wanted to vanish, was it necessary to put bogus bones in the cave, so as nearly to put a halter round the neck of Dr. Brown? And who put them there? The statement would appear perfectly maniacal; but so far as I can make head or tail out of anything, Dr. Brown seems to have put them there himself."

The doctor lifted his head for the first time.

"Yes; I put the bones there," he said. "I believe I am the first son of Adam who ever manufactured all the evidence of a murder charge against himself."

It was the Squire's turn to look astonished. The old gentleman looked rather wildly from one to the other.

"Bones! Murder charge!" he ejaculated. "What the devil is all this? Whose bones?"

"Your bones, in a manner of speaking," delicately conceded the doctor. "I had to make sure you had really died, and not disappeared by magic."

The Squire in his turn seemed more hopelessly puzzled than the whole crowd of his friends had been over his own escapade. "Why not?" he demanded. "I thought it was the whole point to make it look like magic. Why did you want me to die so much?"

Dr. Brown had lifted his head; and he now very slowly lifted his hand. He pointed with outstretched arm at the headland overhanging the foreshore, just above the entrance to the cave. It was the exact part of the beach where Paynter had first landed, on that spring morning when he had looked up in his first fresh wonder at the peacock trees. But the trees were gone.

The fact itself was no surprise to them; the clearance had naturally been one of the first of the sweeping changes of the Treherne regime. But though they knew it well, they had wholly forgotten it; and its significance returned on them suddenly like a sign in heaven.

The Man Who Knew Too Much

"That is the reason," said the doctor. "I have worked for that for fourteen years."

They no longer looked at the bare promontory on which the feathery trees had once been so familiar a sight; for they had something else to look at. Anyone seeing the Squire now would have shifted his opinion about where to find the lunatic in that crowd. It was plain in a flash that the change had fallen on him like a thunderbolt; that he, at least, had never had the wildest notion that the tale of the Vanishing Squire had been but a prelude to that of the vanishing trees. The next half-hour was full of his ravings and expostulations, which gradually died away into demands for explanation and incoherent questions repeated again and again. He had practically to be overruled at last, in spite of the respect in which he was held, before anything like a space and silence were made in which the doctor could tell his own story. It was perhaps a singular story, of which he alone had ever had the knowledge; and though its narration was not uninterrupted, it may be set forth consecutively in his own words.

"First, I wish it clearly understood that I believe in nothing. I do not even give the nothing I believe a name; or I should be an atheist. I have never had inside my head so much as a hint of heaven and hell. I think it most likely we are worms in the mud; but I happen to be sorry for the other worms under the wheel. And I happen myself to be a sort of worm that turns when he can. If I care nothing for piety, I care less for poetry. I'm not like Ashe here, who is crammed with criminology, but has all sorts of other culture as well. I know nothing about culture, except bacteria culture. I sometimes fancy Mr. Ashe is as much an art critic as Mr. Paynter; only he looks for his heroes, or villains, in real life. But I am a very practical man; and my stepping-stones have been simply scientific facts. In this village I found a fact—a fever. I could not classify it; it seemed peculiar to this corner of the coast; it had singular reactions of delirium and mental breakdown. I studied it exactly as I should a queer case in the hospital, and corresponded and compared notes with other men of science. But nobody had

The Trees of Pride

even a working hypothesis about it, except of course the ignorant peasantry, who said the peacock trees were in some wild way poisonous.

"Well, the peacock trees were poisonous. The peacock trees did produce the fever. I verified that fact in the plain plodding way required, comparing all the degrees and details of a vast number of cases; and there were a shocking number to compare. At the end of it I had discovered the thing as Harvey discovered the circulation of the blood. Everybody was the worse for being near the things; those who came off best were exactly the exceptions that proved the rule, abnormally healthy and energetic people like the Squire and his daughter. In other words, the peasants were right. But if I put it that way, somebody will cry : ' But do you believe it was supernatural then?' In fact, that's what you'll all say; and that's exactly what I complain of. I fancy hundreds of men have been left dead and diseases left undiscovered, by this suspicion of superstitution, this stupid fear of fear. Unless you can see daylight through the forest of facts from the first, you won't venture into the wood at all. Unless we can promise you beforehand that there shall be what you call a natural explanation, to save your precious dignity from miracles, you won't even hear the beginning of the plain tale. Suppose there isn't a natural explanation! Suppose there is, and we never find it! Suppose I haven't a notion whether there is or not! What the devil has that to do with you, or with me in dealing with the facts I do know? My own instinct is to think there is; that if my researches could be followed far enough it would be found that some horrible parody of hay-fever, some effect analogous to that of pollen, would explain all the facts. I have never found the explanation. What I have found are the facts. And the fact is that those trees on the top there dealt death right and left, as certainly as if they had been giants, standing on a hill and knocking men down in crowds with a club. It will be said that now I had only to produce my proofs and have the nuisance removed. Perhaps I might have convinced the scientific world finally, when more and more processions of dead men had passed

The Man Who Knew Too Much

through the village to the cemetery. But I had not got to convince the scientific world, but the Lord of the Manor. The Squire will pardon my saying that it was a very different thing. I tried it once; I lost my temper, and said things I do not defend; and I left the Squire's prejudices rooted anew, like the trees. I was confronted with one colossal coincidence that was an obstacle to all my aims. One thing made all my science sound like nonsense. It was the popular legend.

"Squire, if there were a legend of hay-fever, you would not believe in hay-fever. If there were a popular story about pollen, you would say that pollen was only a popular story. I had something against me heavier and more hopeless than the hostility of the learned; I had the support of the ignorant. My truth was hopelessly tangled up with a tale that the educated were resolved to regard as entirely a lie. I never tried to explain again; on the contrary, I apologized, affected a conversion to the common-sense view, and watched events. And all the time the lines of a larger if more crooked plan began to get clearer in my mind. I knew that Miss Vane, whether or no she were married to Mr. Treherne, as I afterwards found she was, was so much under his influence that the first day of her inheritance would be the last day of the poisonous trees. But she could not inherit, or even interfere, till the Squire died. It became simply self-evident, to a rational mind, that the Squire must die. But wishing to be humane as well as rational, I desired his death to be temporary.

"Doubtless my scheme was completed by a chapter of accidents, but I was watching for such accidents. Thus I had a foreshadowing of how the axe would figure in the tale when it was first flung at the trees; it would have surprised the woodman to know how near our minds were, and how I was but laying a more elaborate siege to the towers of pestilence. But when the Squire spontaneously rushed on what half the countryside would call certain death, I jumped at my chance. I followed him, and told him all that he has told you. I don't suppose he'll ever forgive me now, but that shan't prevent my saying that I admire him hugely for being what people

The Trees of Pride

would call a lunatic and what is really a sportsman. It takes rather a grand old man to make a joke in the grand style. He came down so quick from the tree he had climbed that he had no time to pull his hat off the bough it had caught in.

"At first I found I had made a miscalculation. I thought his disappearance would be taken as his death, at least after a little time; but Ashe told me there could be no formalities without a corpse. I fear I was a little annoyed, but I soon set myself to the duty of manufacturing a corpse. It's not hard for a doctor to get a skeleton; indeed, I had one, but Mr. Paynter's energy was a day too early for me, and I only got the bones into the well when he had already found it. His story gave me another chance, however; I noted where the hole was in the hat, and made a precisely corresponding hole in the skull. The reason for creating the other clues may not be so obvious. It may not yet be altogether apparent to you that I am not a fiend in human form. I could not substantiate a murder without at least suggesting a murderer, and I was resolved that if the crime happened to be traced to anybody, it should be to me. So I'm not surprised you were puzzled about the purpose of the rag round the axe, because it had no purpose, except to incriminate the man who put it there. The chase had to end with me, and when it was closing in at last the joke of it was too much for me, and I fear I took liberties with the gentleman's easel and beard. I was the only person who could risk it, being the only person who could at the last moment produce the Squire and prove there had been no crime at all. That, gentlemen, is the true story of the peacock trees; and that bare crag up there, where the wind is whistling as it would over a wilderness, is a waste place I have laboured to make, as many men have laboured to make a cathedral.

"I don't think there is any more to say, and yet something moves in my blood and I will try to say it. Could you not have trusted a little these peasants whom you already trust so much? These men are men, and they meant something; even their fathers were not wholly fools. If your gardener told you of the trees you called

The Man Who Knew Too Much

him a madman, but he did not plan and plant your garden like a madman. You would not trust your woodman about these trees, yet you trusted him with all the others. Have you ever thought what all the work of the world would be like if the poor were so senseless as you think them? But no, you stuck to your rational principle. And your rational principle was that a thing must be false because thousands of men had found it true; that *because* many human eyes had seen something it could not be there."

He looked across at Ashe with a sort of challenge, but though the sea-wind ruffled the old lawyer's red mane, his Napoleonic mask was unruffled; it even had a sort of beauty from its new benignity.

"I am too happy just now in thinking how wrong I have been," he answered, "to quarrel with you, doctor, about our theories. And yet, in justice to the Squire as well as myself, I should demur to your sweeping inference. I respect these peasants, I respect your regard for them; but their stories are a different matter. I think I would do anything for them but believe them. Truth and fancy, after all, are mixed in them, when in the more instructed they are separate; and I doubt if you have considered what would be involved in taking their word for anything. Half the ghosts of those who died of fever may be walking by now; and kind as these people are, I believe they might still burn a witch. No, doctor, I admit these people have been badly used, I admit they are in many ways our betters, but I still could not accept anything on their evidence."

The doctor bowed gravely and respectfully enough, and then, for the last time that day, they saw his rather sinister smile.

"Quite so," he said. "But you would have hanged me on their evidence."

And, turning his back on them, as if automatically, he set his face towards the village, where for so many years he had gone his round.

THE GARDEN OF SMOKE

The end of London looked very like the end of the world; and the last lamp-post of the suburbs like a lonely star in the fields of space. It also resembled the end of the world in another respect: that it was a long time coming. The girl Catharine Crawford was a good walker; she had the fine figure of the mountaineer, and there almost went with her a wind from the hills through all the grey labyrinth of London. For she came from the high villages of Westmorland, and seemed to carry the quiet colours of them in her light brown hair, her open features, irregular yet the reverse of plain, the framework of two grave and very beautiful grey eyes. But the mountaineer began to feel the labyrinth of London suburbs interminable and intolerable, swiftly as she walked. She knew little of the details of her destination, save the address of the house, and the fact that she was going there as a companion to a Mrs. Mowbray, or rather to *the* Mrs. Mowbray—a famous lady novelist and fashionable poet, married, it was said, to some matter-of-fact medical man, reduced to the permanent status of Mrs. Mowbray's husband. And when she found the house eventually, it was at the end of the very last line of houses, where the suburban gardens faded into the open fields.

The whole heavens were full of the hues of evening, though still as luminous as noon; as if in a land of endless sunset. It settled down in a shower of gold amid the twinkling leaves of the thin trees of the gardens, most of which had low fences and hedges, and lay almost as open to the yellow sky as the fields beyond. The air was so still that occasional voices, talking or laughing on distant lawns, could be heard like clear bells. One voice, more recurrent than the rest, seemed to be whistling and singing the old sailor's song of "Spanish Ladies"; it drew nearer and nearer; and when she turned into the

The Man Who Knew Too Much

last garden gate at the corner, the singer was the first figure she encountered. He stood in a garden red with very gorgeous ranks of standard roses, and against a background of the golden sky and a white cottage with touches of rather fanciful colour; the sort of cottage that is not built for cottagers.

He was a lean not ungraceful man in grey with a limp straw hat pulled forward above his dark face and black beard, out of which projected an almost blacker cigar; which he removed when he saw the lady.

"Good evening," he said politely. "I think you must be Miss Crawford. Mrs. Mowbray asked me to tell you that she would be out here in a minute or two, if you cared to look round the garden first. I hope you don't mind my smoking. I do it to kill the insects, you know, on the roses. Need I say that this is the one and only origin of all smoking? Too little credit, perhaps, is given to the self-sacrifice of my sex, from the clubmen in smoking-rooms to the navvies on scaffoldings, all steadily and firmly smoking, on the mere chance that a rose may be growing somewhere in the neighbourhood. Handicapped, like most of my comrades, with a strong natural dislike of tobacco, I contrive to conquer it and——"

He broke off, because the grey eyes regarding him were a little blank and even bleak. He spoke with gravity and even gloom; and she was conscious of humour, but was not sure that it was good-humour. Indeed she felt, at first sight, something faintly sinister about him; his face was aquiline and his figure feline, almost as in the fabulous griffin; a creature moulded of the eagle and the lion, or perhaps the leopard. She was not sure that she approved of fabulous animals.

"Are you Dr. Mowbray?" she asked, rather stiffly.

"No such luck," he replied. "I haven't got such beautiful roses, or such a beautiful—household, shall we say. But Mowbray is about the garden somewhere, spraying the roses with some low scientific instrument called a syringe. He's a great gardener; but you won't find him spraying with the same perpetual, uncomplaining patience as you'll find me smoking."

The Garden of Smoke

With these words he turned on his heel and hallooed his friend's name across the garden in a style which, along with the echo of his song, somehow suggested a ship's captain; which was indeed his trade. A stooping figure disengaged itself from a distant rose bush and came forward apologetically.

Dr. Mowbray also had a loose straw hat and a beard, but there the resemblance ended; his beard was fair and he was burly and big of shoulder; his face was good-humoured and would have been good-looking but that his blue and smiling eyes were a little wide apart; which rather increased the pleasant candour of his expression. By comparison, the more deep sunken eyes on either side of the dark captain's beak seemed to be too close together.

"I was explaining to Miss Crawford," said the latter gentleman, "the superiority of my way of curing your roses of any of their little maladies. In scientific circles the cigar has wholly superseded the syringe."

"Your cigars look as if they'd kill the roses," replied the doctor. "Why are you always smoking your very strongest cigars here?"

"On the contrary, I am smoking my mildest," answered the captain, grimly. "I've got another sort here, if anybody wants them."

He turned back the lapel of his square jacket, and showed some dangerous-looking sticks of twisted leaf in his upper waistcoat pocket. As he did so they noticed also that he had a broad leather belt round his waist, to which was buckled a big crooked knife in a leather sheath.

"Well, I prefer health to tobacco," said Mowbray, laughing. "I may be a doctor, but I take my own medicine; which is fresh air. People cultivate these tastes till they can't taste the air, or the smell of the earth, or any of the elementary things. I agree with Thoreau—that the sunrise is a better beginning of the day than tea or coffee."

"So it is; but not better than beer or rum," replied the sailor. "But it is a matter of taste, as you say. Hallo, who's this?"

As they spoke the french windows of the house opened abruptly, and a man in black came out and passed them,

The Man Who Knew Too Much

going out at the garden gate. He was walking rapidly, as if irritably, and putting his hat and gloves on as he went. Before he put on his hat he showed a head half bald and bumpy, with a semicircle of red hair; and before he put on his gloves he tore a small piece of paper into yet smaller pieces, and tossed it away among the roses by the road.

"Oh, one of Marion's friends from the Theosophical or Ethical Society, I think," said the doctor. "His name's Miall, a tradesman in the town, a chemist or something."

"He doesn't seem in the best or most ethical of tempers," observed the captain. "I thought you nature-worshippers were always serene. Well, he's released our hostess at any rate; and here she comes."

Marion Mowbray really looked like an artist, which an artist is not supposed to do. This did not come from her clinging green drapery and halo of Pre-Raphaelite brown hair, which need only have made her look like an æsthete. But in her face there was a true intensity; her keen eyes were full of distances, that is, of desires, but of desires too large to be sensuous. If such a soul was wasted by a flame, it seemed one of purely spiritual ambition. A moment after she had given her hand to the guest, with very graceful apologies, she stretched it out towards the flowers with a gesture that was quite natural, yet so decisive as to be almost dramatic.

"I simply must have some more of those roses in the house," she said, "and I've lost my scissors. I know it sounds silly, but when the fit comes over me I feel I must tear them off with my hands. Don't you love roses, Miss Crawford? I simply can't do without them sometimes."

The captain's hand had gone to his hip, and the queer crooked knife was naked in the sun; a shining but ugly shape. In a few flashes he had hacked and lopped away a long spray or two of blossom, and handed them to her with a bow, like a bouquet on the stage.

"Oh, thank you," she said rather faintly; and one could fancy, somehow, a tragic irony behind the masquerade. The next moment she recovered herself and

The Garden of Smoke

laughed a little. "It's absurd, I know; but I do so hate ugly things, and living in the London suburbs, though only on the edge of them. Do you know, Miss Crawford, the next door neighbour walks about his garden in a top-hat. Positively in a top-hat. I see it passing just above that laurel hedge about sunset; when he's come back from the city, I suppose. Think of the laurel, that we poor poets are supposed to worship," and she laughed more naturally, "and then think of my feelings, looking up and seeing it wreathed round a top-hat."

And indeed, before the party entered the house to prepare for an evening meal, Catharine had actually seen the offending head-dress appear above the hedge, a shadow of respectability in the sunshine of that romantic plot of roses.

At dinner they were served by a man in black, like a butler, and Catharine felt an unmeaning embarrassment in the mere fact. A man-servant seemed out of place in that artistic toy cottage; and there was nothing notable about the man addressed as Parker except that he seemed especially so; a tall man with a wooden face and dark flat hair like a Dutch doll's. He would have been proper enough if the doctor had lived in Harley Street; but he was too big for the suburbs. Nor was he the only incongruous element, nor the principal one. The captain, whose name seemed to be Fonblanque, still puzzled her and did not altogether please her. Her northern Puritanism found something obscurely rowdy about his attitude. It would be hardly adequate to say he acted as if he were at home; it would be truer to say he acted as if he were abroad, in a café or tavern in some foreign port. Mrs. Mowbray was a vegetarian; and though her husband lived the simple life in a rather simpler fashion, he was sufficiently sophisticated to drink water. But Captain Fonblanque had a great flagon of rum all to himself, and did not disguise his relish; and the meal ended in smoke of the most rich and reeking description. And throughout the captain continued to fence with his hostess and with the stranger with the same flippancies that had fallen from him in the garden.

"It's my childlike innocence that makes me drink and

The Man Who Knew Too Much

smoke," he explained. "I can enjoy a cigar as I could a sugar-stick; but you jaded dissipated vegetarians look down on such sugar-sticks. And rum, too, if it comes to that, is itself a sort of liquid sugar-stick. They say it makes sailors drunk; but after all, what is being drunk but another form of infantile faith and confidence? How saintly must be the innocence of a sailor who can trust himself entirely to a policeman? I do so hate this cynical, suspicious habit of being sober at all sorts of odd times, to catch other people napping."

"When you have done talking nonsense," said Mrs. Mowbray, rising, "we will go into the other room." The nonsense made no particular impression on her or on her feminine companion; but the latter still regarded the speaker with a subdued antagonism, chiefly because he really seemed in an equally subdued degree to be an antagonist. His irony was partly provocative, whether of her hosts or herself; and she was conscious of something slightly Mephistophelian about his blue-black beard and ivory yellow face amid the fumes.

In passing out, the ladies paused accidentally at the open french windows, and Catharine looked out upon the darkening lawn. She was surprised to see that clouds had already come up out of the coloured west and the twilight was troubled with rain. There was a silence, and then Catharine said, rather suddenly:

"That neighbour of yours must be very fond of his garden. Almost as fond of the roses as you are, Mrs. Mowbray."

"Why, what do you mean?" asked that lady, turning back.

"He's still standing among his flowers in the pouring rain," said Catharine, staring, "and will soon be standing in the pitch dark too. . . . I can still see his black hat in the dusk."

"Who knows," said the lady poet, softly; "perhaps a sense of beauty has really stirred in him in a strange, sudden way. If seeds under black earth can grow into those glorious roses, what will souls even under black hats grow into at last? Everything moves upwards; even our sins are steps upwards; there is nowhere any

The Garden of Smoke

downward turning in the great spiral road, the winding staircase of the stars. Perhaps the black hat may turn into the laurel wreath after all."

She glanced behind her, and saw that the two men had already strolled out of the room; and her voice fell into a tone more casual and yet confidential.

"Besides," she added, "I'm not sure he isn't right; and perhaps rain is as beautiful as sun or anything else in the wonderful wheel of things. Don't you like the smell of the damp earth, and that deep noise of all the roses drinking?"

"All the roses are teetotallers, anyhow," remarked Catharine, with a smile.

Her hostess smiled also. "I'm afraid Captain Fonblanque shocked you a little; he's rather eccentric, wearing that crooked eastern dagger just because he's travelled in the East, and drinking rum, of all ridiculous things, just to show he's a sailor. But he's an old friend, you know; I knew him well many years ago; and he's done his duty on the sea at least, and even gained distinction there. I'm afraid he's still rather on the animal plane; but at least he's a fighting animal."

"Yes, he reminds me of a pirate in a play," said Catharine, laughing. "He might be stalking round this house looking for hidden treasure of gold and silver."

Mrs. Mowbray seemed to start a little, and then stared out into the dark in silence. At last she said, in a changed voice:

"It is strange that you should say that."

"And why?" inquired her companion, in some wonder.

"Because there is a hidden treasure in this house," said Mrs. Mowbray, "and such a thief might well steal it. It's not exactly gold or silver, but it's almost as valuable, I believe, even in money. I don't know why I tell you this; but at least you can see I don't distrust you. Let's go into the other room." And she rather abruptly led the way in that direction.

Catharine Crawford was a woman whose conscious mind was full of practicality; but her unconscious mind had its own poetry, which was all on the note of purity. She loved white light and clear waters, boulders washed

The Man Who Knew Too Much

smooth in rivers, and the sweeping curves of wind. It was perhaps the poetry that Wordsworth, at his finest, found in the lakes of her own land; and in principle it could repose in the artistic austerity of Marion Mowbray's home. But whether the stage was filled too much by the almost fantastic figure of the piratical Fonblanque, or whether the summer heat, with its hint of storm, obscured such clarity, she felt an oppression. Even the rose-garden seemed more like a chamber curtained with red and green than an open place. Her own chamber was curtained in sufficiently cool and soothing colours; but she fell asleep later than usual, and then heavily.

She woke with a start from some tangled dream of which she recalled no trace; and with senses sharpened by darkness, she was vividly conscious of a strange smell. It was vaporous and heavy, not unpleasant to the nostrils, yet somehow all the more unpleasant to the nerves. It was not the smell of any tobacco she knew; and yet she connected it with those sinister black cigars to which the captain's brown finger had pointed. She thought half-consciously that he might be still smoking in the garden; and that those dark and dreadful weeds might well be smoked in the dark. But it was only half consciously that she thought or moved at all; she remembered half rising from her bed; and then remembered nothing but more dreams, which left a little more recollection in their track. They were but a medley of the smoking and the strange smell and the scents of the rose garden, but they seemed to make up a mystery as well as a medley. Sometimes the roses were themselves a sort of purple smoke. Sometimes they glowed from purple to fiery crimson, like the butts of a giant's cigars. And that garden of smoke was haunted by the pale yellow face and blue-black beard; and she awoke with the word "Bluebeard" on her mind and almost on her mouth.

Morning was so much of a relief as to be almost a surprise; the rooms were full of the white light that she loved, and which might well be the light of a primeval wonder. As she passed the half-opened door of the doctor's scientific study or consulting-room, she paused by a window, and saw the silver daybreak brightening

The Garden of Smoke

over the garden. She was idly counting the birds that began to dart by the house; and as she counted the fourth she heard the shock of a falling chair, followed by a voice crying out and cursing again and again.

The voice was strained and unnatural; but after the first few syllables she recognized it as that of the doctor.

"It's gone," he was saying. "The stuff's gone, I tell you!"

The reply was inaudible; but she already suspected that it came from the servant Parker, whose voice proved to be as baffling as was his face.

The doctor answered again in unabated agitation.

"The drug, you devil or dunce or whatever you are! The drug I told you to keep an eye on!"

This time she heard the dull tones of the other, who seemed to be saying: "There's very little of it gone, sir."

"Why has any of it gone?" cried Doctor Mowbray. "Where's my wife?"

Probably hearing the rustle of a skirt outside, he flung the door open and came face to face with Catharine, falling back before her in consternation. The room into which she now looked in bewilderment was neat and even severe, except for the fallen chair still lying on the carpet. It was fitted with bookcases, and contained a rank of bottles and phials, like those in a chemist's shop, the colours of which looked like jewels in the brilliant early daylight. One glittering green bottle bore a large label of "Poison"; but the present problem seemed to revolve round a glass vessel, rather like a decanter, which stood on the table more than half full of a dust or powder of a rich reddish brown.

Against this strict scientific background the tall servant looked more important and appropriate; in fact, she was soon conscious that he was something more intimate than a servant who waited at table. He had at least the air of a doctor's assistant; and indeed, in comparison with his distracted employer, might almost at that moment have been the attendant in a private asylum.

He was saying, as she doubtfully entered: "I am very sorry this has happened, sir. But at least I kept very

The Man Who Knew Too Much

careful note of the quantity; and I assure you there is very little gone. Not enough to do anyone much harm."

"It's the damned plague breaking out again," said the doctor hastily. "Go and see if my wife is in the dining-room"

He pulled himself together as Parker left the room, and picked up the chair that had fallen on the carpet, offering it to the girl with a gesture. Then he went and leaned on the window-sill, looking out upon the garden. She could see his large shoulders shift and shake; but there was no sound but the growing noise of the birds in the bushes. At last he said in his natural voice:

"Well, I suppose you ought to have been told. Anyhow, you'll have to be told now."

There was another silence, and then he said: "My wife is a poet, you know; a creative artist, and all that. And all enlightened people know that a genius can't be judged quite by common rules of conduct. A genius lives by a recurrent need for a sort of inspiration."

"What do you mean?" asked Catharine almost impatiently; for the preamble of excuses was a strain on her nerves.

"There's a kind of opium in that bottle," he said abruptly, "a very rare kind. She smokes it occasionally, that's all. I wish Parker would hurry up and find her."

"I can find her, I think," said Catharine, relieved by the chance of doing something; and not a little relieved also to get out of the scientific room. "I think I saw her going down the garden path."

When she went out into the rose garden it was full of the freshness of the sunrise; and all her smoky nightmares were rolled away from it. The roof of her green and crimson room seemed to have been lifted off like a lid. She went down many winding paths without seeing any living thing but the birds hopping here and there; then she came to the corner of one turning and stood still.

In the middle of the sunny path, a few yards from one of the birds, lay something crumpled like a great green rag. But it was really the rich green dress of Marion Mowbray; and beyond it was her fallen face,

The Garden of Smoke

colourless against its halo of hair and one arm thrust out, in a piteous stiffness towards the roses, as she had stretched it when Catharine saw her for the first time. Catharine gave a little cry, and the bird flashed away into a tree. Then she bent over the fallen figure, and knew, in a blast of all the trumpets of terror, why the face was colourless and why the arm was stiff.

An hour afterwards, still in that world of rigid unreality that remains long after a shock, she was but automatically, though efficiently, helping in the hundred minute and aching utilities of a house of mourning. How she had told them she hardly knew; but there was no need to tell much. Mowbray the doctor soon had bad news for Mowbray the husband, when he had been but a few moments silent and busy over the body of his wife. Then he turned away; and Catharine almost feared he would fall.

A problem confronted him still, however, even as a doctor, when he had so grimly solved his problem as a husband. His medical assistant, whom he had always had reason to trust, still emphatically asserted that the amount of the drug missing was insufficient to kill a kitten. He came down and stood with the little group on the lawn, where the dead woman had been laid on a sofa, to be examined in the best light. He repeated his assertion in the face of the examination, and his wooden face was knotted with obstinacy.

"If he is right," said Captain Fonblanque, "she must have got it from somewhere else as well, that's all. Did any strange people come here lately?"

He had taken a turn or two of pacing up and down the lawn, when he stopped with an arrested gesture.

"Didn't you say that theosophist was also a chemist?" he asked. "He may be as theosophical or ethical as he likes; but he didn't come here on a theosophical errand. No, by God, nor an ethical one."

It was agreed that this question should be followed up first; Parker was dispatched to the High Street of the neighbouring suburb; and about half an hour afterwards the black-clad figure of Mr. Miall came back into the garden, much less swiftly than he had gone out of it.

The Man Who Knew Too Much

He removed his hat out of respect for the presence of death; and his face under the ring of red hair was whiter than the dead.

But though pale, he also was firm; and that upon a point that brought the inquiry once more to a standstill. He admitted that he had once supplied that peculiar brand of opium; and did not attempt to dissipate the cloud of responsibility that rested on him so far. But he vehemently denied that he had supplied it yesterday, or even lately, or indeed for long past. And he was especially emphatic upon one point, which seemed almost to be a personal grievance: that he could not supply it, because he could not get it.

"She must have got some more somehow," cried the doctor, in dogmatic and even despotic tones, "and where could she have got it but from you?"

"And where could I have got it from anybody?" demanded the tradesman equally hotly. "You seem to think it's sold like shag. I tell you there's no more of it in England—a chemist can't get it even for desperate cases. I gave her the last I had months ago, more shame to me; and when she wanted more yesterday, I told her I not only wouldn't but couldn't. There's the scraps of the note she sent me, still lying where I tore it up in a temper."

And he pointed a dark-gloved finger at a few white specks lying here and there under the hedge. The captain strode across and silently stamped them into the black soil. He turned again, pale but composed, and said to the doctor quietly: "We must be careful, Mowbray. Poor Marion's death is more of a mystery than we thought."

"There is no mystery," said Mowbray angrily. "Out of his own mouth this fellow owns he had the stuff."

"I've no more got the stuff now than the Crown Jewels," repeated the chemist. "It's about as rare now, and more valuable than a heap of gold and silver."

Catharine's mind had a movement of recollection; and she thought, with a cold thrill, of how the same strange words about a treasure had been on the lips of the unfortunate Marion the night before. Was it possible that

The Garden of Smoke

the hidden treasure, that had dazzled the dead woman like diamonds, was only this red dust of death?

The doctor seemed to regard the hitch in the inquiry with a sort of harassed fury. He browbeat the pale chemist even more than he had browbeaten his servant about his first and smaller discovery. Indeed, Catharine began to feel about Dr. Mowbray something that can be felt at times in men of such solid amiability. She suspected that his serenity had been a strong stream or tide of steady satisfaction; and that he could bear being baffled less than more bitter men. Perhaps he was of a sort sometimes called the strong man; who is strong in fulfilling his desires, but not in controlling them. Anyhow, his desire at the moment, so concrete as to be comic in such a scene, seemed to be the desire to hang a chemist.

"Look here, Mowbray, you know how we all feel for you, but you really mustn't be so violent," remonstrated the captain. "You'll put us all in the wrong. Mr. Miall has a right to justice, not to mention law; which will probably have a hand in this business."

"If you interfere with me, Fonblanque," said the doctor, "I will say something I have never said before."

"What the devil do you mean?"

The figures in the little group on the lawn had fallen into such angry attitudes that one could almost fancy they would strike each other even in the presence of the dead, when an interruption came as soft as the note of the bird but as unexpected as a thunderbolt.

A voice from several yards away said mildly but more or less loudly: "Permit me to offer you my assistance."

They all looked round and saw the next-door neighbour's top-hat, above a large, loose, heavy-lidded face, leaning over the low fringe of laurels.

"I'm sure I can be of some little help," he said; and the next moment he had calmly taken a high stride over the low hedge, and was walking across the lawn towards them. He was a large, heavily-walking man in a loose frock coat; his clean-shaven face was at once heavy and cadaverous. He spoke in a soft and even sentimental

The Man Who Knew Too Much

tone, which contrasted with his impudence and, as it soon appeared, with his trade.

"What do you want here?" asked Dr. Mowbray sharply, when he had recovered from a sheer astonishment.

"It is you who want something. Sympathy," said the strange gentleman. "Sympathy . . . sympathy, and also light. I think I can offer both. Poor lady, I have watched her sympathetically for many months; and I think I can offer both."

"If you've been watching over the wall," said the captain frowning, "we should like to know why. These are suspicious facts here, and you seem to have behaved in a suspicious manner."

"Suspicion rather than sympathy," said the stranger, with a sigh, "is perhaps the defect in my duties. But my sorrow for this poor lady is perfectly sincere. Do you suspect me of being mixed up in her trouble?"

"Who are you?" asked the angry doctor.

"My name is Traill," said the man in the top-hat. "I have some official title; but it was never used except at the Yard. Scotland Yard, I mean. We needn't use it among neighbours."

"You are a detective, in fact?" observed the captain; but he received no reply, for the new investigator was already examining the corpse, quite respectfully, but with a professional absence of apology. After a few moments he rose again, and looked at them under the large drooping eyelids which were his most prominent features; and said simply: "It is satisfactory to let people go, Dr. Mowbray; and your druggist and your assistant can certainly go. It was not the fault of either of them that the unhappy lady died."

"Do you mean it was a suicide?" asked the other.

"I mean it was a murder," said Mr. Traill. "But I have a very sufficient reason for saying she was not killed by the druggist."

"And why not?"

"Because she was not killed by the drug," said the man from next door.

"What?" exclaimed the captain, with a slight start. "Why, how else could she have been killed?"

The Garden of Smoke

"She was killed with a short and sharp instrument, the point of which was prepared in a particular manner for the purpose," said Traill in the level tones of a lecturer. "There was apparently a struggle, but probably a short, or even a slight one. Poor lady, just look at this "; and he lifted one of the dead hands quite gently, and pointed to what appeared to be a prick or puncture on the wrist.

"A hypodermic needle, perhaps," said the doctor in a low voice; "she generally took a drug by smoking it; but she might have used a hypodermic syringe and needle, after all."

The detective shook his head, so that one could almost imagine his hanging eyelids flapping with the loose movement. "If she injected it herself," he said sadly, "she would make a clean perforation. This is more a scratch than a prick, and you can see it has torn the lace on her sleeve a little."

"But how can it have killed her," Catharine was impelled to ask, "if it was only a scratching on the wrist?"

"Ah," said Mr. Traill; and then after a short silence, "I'm sure you'll support me, Dr. Mowbray, when I say it's improbable, after all, that any mere opiate should produce that extreme rigidity in the body. The effect resembles rather that of some direct vegetable poison, especially some of those rapid oriental poisons. Poor lady, poor lady, it is really a very horrible story."

"But what is the story, do you think, in plain words?" asked the captain.

"I think," said Traill, "that when we find the dagger we shall find it a poisoned dagger. Is that plain enough, Captain Fonblanque?"

The next moment he seemed to droop again with his rather morbid and almost maudlin tone of compassion.

"Poor lady," he repeated. "She was so fond of roses, wasn't she? Strew on her roses, roses, as the poet says. I really feel somehow that it might give a sort of rest to her, even now."

He looked round the garden with his heavy half-closed eyes, and addressed Fonblanque more sympathetically.

The Man Who Knew Too Much

"It was on a happier occasion, Captain, that you last cut flowers for her; I can't help wishing it could be done again now."

Half unconsciously, the captain's hand went to where the hilt of his knife had hung; then his hand dropped, as if in abrupt recollection. But as the flap of his jacket shifted for an instant, they saw that the leather sheath was empty; and the knife was gone.

"Such a very sad story, such a terrible story," murmured the man in the top-hat distantly, as if he were talking of a novel. "Of course, it is a silly fancy about the flowers. It is not such things as that that are our duties to the dead."

The others seemed still a little bewildered; but Catharine was looking at the captain as if she had been turned to stone by a basilisk. Indeed, that moment had been for her the beginning of a monstrous interregnum of imagination, which might well be said to be full of monsters. Something of mythology had hung about the garden since her first fancy about a man like a griffin. It lasted for many days and nights, during which the detective seemed to hover over the house like a vampire; but the vampire was not the most awful of the monsters. She hardly defined to herself what she thought, or rather refused to think. But she was conscious of other unknown emotions coming to the surface and co-existing, somehow, with that sunken thought that was their contrary. For some time past the first unfriendly feelings about the captain had rather faded from her mind; even in that short space he had improved on acquaintance, and his sensible conduct in the crisis was a relief from the wild grief and anger of the husband, however natural these might be. Moreover, the very explosion of the opium secret, in accounting for the cloud upon the house, had cleared away another suspicion she had half entertained about the wife and the piratical guest. This she was now disposed to dismiss, so far at least as he was concerned; and she had lately had an additional reason for doing so. The eyes of Fonblanque had been following her about in a manner about which so humorous and therefore modest a lady was not likely to be mistaken;

The Garden of Smoke

and she was surprised to find in herself a corresponding recoil from the idea of this comedy of sentiment turning suddenly to a tragedy of suspicion. For the next few nights she again slept uneasily; and as is often the case with a crushed or suppressed thought, the doubt raged and ruled in her dreams. What might be called the Bluebeard motif ran through even wilder scenes of strange lands, full of fantastic cities and giant vegetation, through all of which passed a solitary figure with a blue beard and a red knife. It was as if this sailor not only had a wife, but a murdered wife, in every port. And there recurred again and again, like a distant but distinct voice speaking, the accents of the detective: "If only we could find the dagger, we should find it a poisoned dagger." And yet nothing could have seemed more cool and casual at the moment, on the following morning, when she did find it. She had come down from the upper rooms and gone through the french windows into the garden once more; she was about to pass down the paths among the rose bushes, when she looked round and saw the captain leaning on the garden gate. There was nothing unusual in his idle and somewhat languid attitude, but her eye was fixed, and as it were frozen, on the one bright spot where the sun again shone and shifted on the crooked blade. He was somewhat sullenly hacking with it at the wooden fence, but stopped when their eyes met.

"So you've found it again," was all that she could say.

"Yes, I've found it," he replied, rather gloomily; and then, after a pause: "I've also found several other things, including how I lost it."

"Do you mean," asked Catharine unsteadily, "that you've found out about—about Mrs. Mowbray?"

"It wouldn't be correct to say I've found it out," he answered. "Our depressing neighbour with the top-hat and the eyelids has found it out, and he's upstairs now, finding more of it out. But if you mean do I know how Marion was murdered, yes, I do; and I rather wish I didn't."

After a minute or two of objectless chipping on the fence he stuck the point of his knife into the wood and faced her abruptly in a franker fashion.

The Man Who Knew Too Much

"Look here," he said. "I should like to explain myself a little. When we first knew each other, I suppose I was very flippant. I admired your gravity and great goodness so much that I had to attack it; can you understand that? But I was not entirely flippant—no, nor entirely wrong. Think again of all the silly things that annoyed you, and of whether they have turned out so very silly? Are not rum and tobacco really more childlike and innocent than some things, my friend? Has any low sailor's tavern seen a worse tragedy than you have seen here? Mine are vulgar tastes, or, if you like, vulgar vices. But there is one thing to be said for our appetites: that they are appetites. Pleasure may be only satisfaction; but it can be satisfied. We drink it because we are thirsty; but not because we want to be thirsty. I tell you that these artists thirst for thirst. They want infinity, and they get it, poor souls. It may be bad to be drunk, but you can't be infinitely drunk; you fall down. A more horrible thing happens to them; they rise and rise, for ever. Isn't it better to fall under the table and snore than to rise through the seven heavens on the smoke of opium?"

She answered at last, with an appearance of thought and hesitation.

"There may be something in what you say, but it doesn't account for all the nonsensical things you said." She smiled a little, and added: "You said you only smoked for the good of the roses, you know. You'll hardly pretend there was any solemn truth behind that."

He started, and then stepped forward, leaving the knife standing and quivering in the fence.

"Yes, by God, there was," he cried. "It may seem the maddest thing of all, but it's true. Death and hell would not be in this house to-day, if they had only trusted to my trick of smoking the roses."

Catharine continued to look at him wildly, but his own gaze did not falter or show a shade of doubt; and he went slowly back to the fence and plucked his knife out of it. There was a long silence in the garden before either of them spoke again. He seemed to be revolving the best way of opening a difficult explanation. At last

The Garden of Smoke

he spoke; his words were not the least of the riddles of the rose-garden.

"Do you think," he asked in a low voice, "that Marion is really dead?"

"Dead!" repeated Catharine; "why, of course she's dead."

He seemed to nod in brooding acquiescence, staring, at his knife; then he added:

"Do you think her ghost walks?"

"What do you mean? Do you think so?" demanded his companion.

"No," he said. "But that drug is still disappearing."

She could only repeat, with a rather pale face: "Still disappearing?"

"In fact, it's nearly disappeared," remarked the captain; "you can come upstairs and see, if you like." He stopped and gazed at her a moment very seriously. "I know you are brave," he said. "Would you really like to see the end of this nightmare?"

"It would be a much worse nightmare if I didn't," she answered. And the captain, with a gesture at once negligent and resolved, tossed his knife among the rose bushes and turned towards the house.

She looked at him with a last flicker of suspicion.

"Why are you leaving your dagger in the garden?" she asked abruptly.

"The garden is full of daggers," said the captain, as he went upstairs.

Mounting the staircase with a catlike swiftness, he was some way ahead of the girl, in spite of her own mountaineering ease of movement. She had time to reflect that the greys and greens of the dados and decorative curtains had never seemed to her so dreary and even inhuman. And when she reached the landing and the door of the doctor's study, she met the captain again face to face. For he stood now with a face as pale as her own, and not any longer as leading her, but rather as barring her way.

"What is the matter?" she cried; and then, by a wild intuition: "Is somebody else dead?"

"Yes," replied Fonblanque; "somebody else is dead."

The Man Who Knew Too Much

In the silence they heard within the heavy and yet soft movements of the strange investigator; and Fonblanque spoke again with a new impulsiveness.

"Catharine, my friend, I think you know how I feel about you; but what I am trying to say now is not about myself. It may seem a queer thing for a man like me to say, but somehow I think you will understand. Before you go inside, remember the things outside. I don't mean my things, but yours. I mean the empty sky and all the good grey virtues and the things that are clean and strong, like the wind. Believe me, they are real, after all; more real than the cloud on this accursed house. Hold fast to them still; tell yourself that God's winds and washing rivers are really there; at least as much there as the thing in that room."

"Yes, I think I understand you," she said. "And now let me pass." Apart from the detective's presence there were but two differences in the doctor's study, as compared with the time when she stood in it last; and though they bulked very unequally to the eye, they seemed almost equal in a deadly significance. On a sofa under the window, covered with a sheet, lay something that could only be a corpse; but the very bulk of it and the way in which the folds of the sheet fell, showed her that it was not the corpse she had already seen. For herself, she had hardly need to glance at it; she knew, almost before she looked, that it was not the wife but the husband. And on the table in the centre stood the glass vessel of the opium and the other green bottle labelled "Poison"; but the opium vessel was quite empty.

The detective came forward with a mildness amounting to embarrassment, and spoke in a tone that seemed more sincerely sympathetic than his old half ironic phrases of sympathy. Without his top hat he looked much older; for his head was bald, with a fringe of grey hair behind standing out in rather neglected wisps. Irrationally enough the absence of the hat, as well as the greyness of the hair, made her feel that this man also improved on acquaintance. And indeed when he spoke to her it was in a paternal and even pathetic tone which she did not resent.

The Garden of Smoke

"You are naturally prejudiced against me, my dear," he said, "and you are not far out. You feel I am a morbid person; I think you sometimes felt I was probably a murderer. Well, I think you were right; not about the murder, but about the morbidity. I do live in the wrong atmosphere, as poor Mrs. Mowbray did, and for something of the same reason—because I have something of the artist who has taken the wrong turning. . . . I can't help being interested in the tragedies that are my trade; and you're quite wrong if you think my sentiment's all hypocritical. I've lost a good deal for my living; I can't hope to behave like a gentleman, but I do often feel like a man; only not like a healthy-minded man. The captain here has knocked about in all sorts of wild places; it is often an excellent way of remaining sane. I hope he'll take it as a compliment if I call it an excellent way of remaining commonplace. But we quiet people might really go mad, by digging away at one intellectual pleasure, as the poor lady did. My intellectual pleasure is criminology, which, I sometimes think, is itself a crime. Especially as I specialize in this department of it that concerns drugs. But I often think that in looking for dope I get almost as diseased as the dopers."

Catharine was conscious that he was talking with easy egotism to make her more at home in that unnatural room; and she did not doubt or depreciate his good nature. But the unanswered riddle still rode her imagination; and his last phrase about dope brought them all back to it.

"But I thought you said," she protested, "that Mrs. Mowbray was not killed by the drug."

"True," said Mr. Traill, "but this is a tragedy of dope for all that. She did not die of it, and yet it was the cause of her death."

He was silent again, looking at her wan and wondering face, and then added:

"She was not killed by the drug. She was killed for the drug. Did you notice anything odd about Dr. Mowbray when you were last in this room?"

"He was naturally agitated," said the girl doubtfully.

"No, unnaturally agitated," replied Traill; "more

The Man Who Knew Too Much

agitated than a man so sturdy would have been even by the revelation of another's weakness. It was his own weakness that rattled him like a storm that morning. He was indeed angry that the drug was stolen by his wife, for the simple reason that he wanted all that was left for himself. I have rather an ear for distant conversation, Miss Crawford, and I once heard you talking at the window about a pirate and a treasure. Can't you picture two pirates stealing the same treasure bit by bit, till one of them killed the other in rage at seeing it vanish? That is what happened in this house; and perhaps we had better call it madness, and then pity it. The drug had become the unhappy man's life, and that a horribly happy life. All his health and high spirits and humanitarianism flowered from that foul root. Can you fancy what it was to him when the last supply was shrinking, like the wild ass's skin in the story? It was like death to him; indeed, it was literally death. He had long resolved that when he had really emptied this bottle," and Traill touched the receptacle of opium, "he would at once turn to this"; and he laid his large lean hand on the green bottle of poison. "And now the end has come at last. All the opium is gone. Very little of the stuff in the green bottle is gone. But it is a more effective opiate."

Catharine did not doubt that a desolate dawn of truth was gradually invading the dark house; but her pale face was still puzzled. "You mean her husband killed her, and then killed himself," she said, in her simple way. "But how did he kill her, if not with the drug? Indeed how did he kill her at all? I left him in this room evidently amazed that the stuff was gone, and then I found her as if just struck down by a thunderbolt at the other end of the garden. How did he manage to kill her?"

"He stabbed her," replied Traill. "He stabbed her in a rather strange fashion, when she was far away at the other end of the garden."

"But he was not there!" cried Catharine. "He was up in this room."

"He was not there when he stabbed her," answered the detective.

The Garden of Smoke

"I told Miss Crawford," said the captain, in a low voice, "that the garden was full of daggers."

"Yes, of green daggers that grow on trees," continued Traill. "You may say if you like that she was killed by a wild creature, tied to the earth but armed."

His somewhat morbid fancy in putting things moved in her again her vague feeling of a garden of green mythological monsters; but the daylight was penetrating that thicket, and the daylight was white and terrible.

"He was committing the crime at the moment when you first came into that garden," said Traill. "The crime that he committed with his own hands. You stood in the sunshine and watched him commit it. But few crimes done in darkness have been so secret or so strange."

After a pause he began again, like a man trying different approaches to the same explanation.

"I have told you the deed was done for the drug, but not by the drug. I tell you now it was done with a syringe, but not a hypodermic syringe. It was being done with that ordinary garden implement he was holding in his hand when you saw him first. But the stuff with which he drenched the green rose-trees came out of this green bottle."

"He poisoned the roses," repeated Catharine almost mechanically.

"Yes," said the captain. "He poisoned the roses. And the thorns."

He had not spoken for some time, but the girl was gazing at him rather distractedly, and her next question had the same direction. She only said in a broken phrase: "And the knife. . . ."

"That is soon said," answered Traill. "The presence of the knife had nothing to do with it. The absence of the knife had a great deal. The murderer stole it and hid it, partly, perhaps, with some idea that its loss would look black against the captain; whom I did in fact suspect, as you did, I think. But there was a much more practical reason: the same that had made him steal and hide his wife's scissors. You heard his wife say she always wanted to tear off the roses with her fingers. If there

The Man Who Knew Too Much

was no instrument to hand, he knew that one fine morning she would do it. And one fine morning she did."

Catharine left the room without looking again at what lay in the light of the window under the sheet. She had no desire but to leave the room, and leave the house, and above all leave the garden behind her. And when she went out into the road she automatically turned her back on the fringe of fanciful cottages, and set her face towards the open fields and the distant woods of England. And she was already snapping bracken and startling birds with her step, before she became conscious of anything incongruous in the fact that Fonblanque was still strolling in her company. But they had fallen into a final companionship, and crossed a borderline together. It was the borderline she had faintly seen on that first evening, and which she had thought was like the end of the world. And, as the tales go, it was like the end of the world in one other respect : that it was the beginning of a better one.

THE FIVE OF SWORDS

It was doubtless a strange coincidence that the two friends, the Frenchman and the Englishman, should have argued about that particular subject on that particular morning. The coincidence may perhaps appear less incredible to a philosophic mind, if I add that they had argued about that subject every morning through the whole month of the walking tour that they took in the country south of Fontainebleau. Indeed, it was this repetition and variety of aspect that gave the more logical and patient mind of the Frenchman the occasion of his final criticism.

"My friend," he said, "you have told me many times that you can make no sense of the French duel. Permit me the observation that I can make no sense of the English criticism of the French duel. When we discussed it yesterday, for instance, you twitted me with the affair of old Le Mouton with that Jew journalist who calls himself Vallon. Because the poor old Senator got off with a scratch on the wrist, you called it a farce."

"And you can't deny it was a farce," replied the other stolidly.

"But now," proceeded his friend, "because we happen to pass the Château d'Orage, you dig up the corpse of the old count who was killed there, God knows when, by a vagabond Austrian soldier of fortune, and tell me with a burst of British righteousness that it was a hideous tragedy."

"Well, and you can't deny it was a tragedy," repeated the Englishman. "They say the poor young countess couldn't live there in the shadow of it, and has sold the château and gone to Paris."

"Paris has its religious consolations," said the Frenchman, smiling somewhat austerely. "But I think you are unreasonable. A thing cannot be bad because it is too

The Man Who Knew Too Much

dangerous and too safe. If the duel is bloodless you call our poor French swordsman a fool. If it end in bloodshed, what do you call him?"

"I call him a bloody fool," replied the Englishman.

The two national figures might have served to show how real is nationality, and how independent it is of race; or at least of the physical types commonly associated with race. For Paul Forain was tall, thin and fair, but French to the finger-tips, to the point of his imperial or the points of his long, narrow shoes, and in nothing more French than in a certain seriousness of curiosity that lifted his brow in a permanent furrow; you could see him thinking. And Harry Monk was short, sturdy and dark, and yet exuberantly English—English in his grey tweeds and in his short brown moustache; and in nothing so English as in a complete absence of curiosity, so far as was consistent with courtesy. He carried the humour, and especially the good humour, of the English social compromise with him like a costume; just as one might fancy his grey tweeds carried the grey English weather with him everywhere through those sunny lands. They were both young, and both professors at a famous French college—the one of jurisprudence, the other of English; but the former, Forain, had specialized so much in certain aspects of criminal law that he was often consulted on particular criminal problems. It was certain views of his about murder and manslaughter that had led to the recurrent disagreement about the duel. They commonly took their holidays together, and had just breakfasted at the inn of the Seven Stars half a mile along the road behind them.

Dawn had broken over the opposite side of the valley and shone full on the side on which their road ran. The ground fell towards the river in a series of tablelands like a terraced garden, and on the one just above them were the neglected grounds and sombre façade of the old château, flanked to left and right by an equally sombre façade of firs and pines, deployed interminably like the lost lances of any army long fallen into dust. The first shafts of the sun, still tinged with red, gleamed on a row of glass frames for cucumbers or some such vegetables,

The Five of Swords

suggesting that the place was at least lately inhabited, and warmed the dark diamonded casements of the house itself, here and there turning a diamond into a ruby. But the garden was overgrown with clumps of wood almost as accidental as giant mosses, and somewhere in its melancholy maze, they knew, the sinister Colonel Tarnow, an Austrian soldier, since not unsuspected of being an Austrian spy, had thrust his blade into the throat of Maurice d'Orage, the last lord of that place. The path descended, and the view over the hedge was soon shut out by a great garden wall so loaded with ivies and ancient vines and creepers that it looked itself more like a hedge than a wall.

"I know you've been out yourself, and I know you're far from being a brute yourself," conceded Monk, continuing the conversation. "For my own part, however much I hated a man, I don't fancy I should ever want to kill him."

"I don't know that I did want to kill him," answered the other. "It would be truer to say I wanted him to kill me. You see, I wanted him to be *able* to kill me. That is what is not understood. To show how much I would stake on my side of the quarrel—hallo! What on earth is this?"

On the ivied wall above had appeared a figure, almost black against the morning sky, so that they could see nothing of its face, but only its one frenzied gesture. The next moment it had leapt from the wall and stood in their path, with hands spread out as if for succour.

"Are you doctors, either of you?" cried the unknown. "Anyhow, you must come and help—a man's been killed."

They could see now that the figure was that of a slim young man whose dark hair and dark clothes showed the abrupt disorder only seen in what is commonly orderly. One curl of his burnished black hair had been plucked across his eye by an intercepting branch, and he wore pale yellow gloves, one of which was burst across the knuckles.

"A man killed?" repeated Monk. "How was he killed?"

The yellow-gloved hand made a despairing movement.

The Man Who Knew Too Much

"Oh, the wretched old tale!" he cried. "Too much wine, too many words, and the end next morning. But God knows we never meant it to go so far as this!"

With one of the lightning movements that lay hidden behind his rather dry dignity, Forain had already scaled the low wall and was standing on it, and his English friend followed with equal activity and more unconcern. As soon as they stood there they saw on the lawn below the sight that explained everything, and made so wild and yet apt a commentary on their own controversy.

The group on the lawn included three other men in black frockcoats and top hats, excluding the messenger of misfortune, whose own silk hat lay rolled at random by the wall over which he had leapt. He seemed to have leapt it, by the way, with an impetuosity that spoke of a swift reaction of horror or repentance, for Forain noticed, only a yard or two along the garden wall, a garden door, which, though doubtless disused, rustily barred and blotched with lichen, would have been the natural exit of a more normal moment. But the eye was very reasonably riveted on the two figures, clad only in white shirts and trousers, round whom the rest revolved, and who must have crossed swords a moment before. One of these stood with the rapier still poised in his hand, a mere streak of white, which a keen eye might have seen to end in a spot of red. The other white-shirted figure lay like a white rag on the green turf, and a sword of the same pattern, a somewhat antiquated one, lay gleaming in the grass where it had fallen from his hand. One of his black-coated seconds was bending over him, and as the strangers approached lifted a livid face, a face with spectacles and a black triangular beard.

"It's too late," he said. "He's gone."

The man still holding the sword cast it down with a wordless sound more shocking than a curse. He was a tall, elegant man, with an air of fashion even in his duelling undress; his face, with a rather fine aquiline profile, looked whiter against red hair and a red pointed beard. The man beside him put a hand upon his shoulder and seemed to push him a little, perhaps urging him to fly. This witness, in the French phrase, was a tall, portly

The Five of Swords

man with a long black beard cut as if in the square pattern of his long black frockcoat, and having, somewhat incongruously, a monocle screwed into one eye. The last of the group, the second of the slayer's formal backers, stood motionless and somewhat apart from the rest—a big man, much younger than his comrades, and with a classical face like a statue's and almost as impassive as a statue's. By a movement common to the whole tragic company, he had removed his top hat at the final announcement, as if at a funeral, and the effect gave to English eyes a slight shock; for the young man's hair was cropped so close and so colourless that he might almost have been bald. The fashion was common enough in France, yet it seemed incongruous to the man's youth and good looks. It was as if Apollo were shaved as an Eastern hermit.

"Gentlemen," said Forain at last, "since you have brought me into this terrible business, I must be plain. I am in no position to be pharisaic. I have all but killed a man myself, and I know that the riposte can be almost past control. I am not," he added, with a faint touch of acidity, "a humanitarian, who would have three men butchered with the axe of the guillotine because one has fallen by the sword. I am not an official, but I have some official influence; and I have, if I may say so, a reputation to lose. You must at least convince me that this affair was clean and inevitable like my own, otherwise I must go back to my friend the innkeeper of the Seven Stars, who will put me in communication with another friend of mine, the chief of police."

And without further apology, he walked across the lawn and looked down at the fallen figure, a figure peculiarly pathetic because plainly younger than any of the survivors, even his second who had run for help. There was no hair on the pale face; the hair on the head was very fair and brushed in a way which Monk, with a new shock of sympathy, recognized as English. There was no doubt of the death; a brief examination showed that the sword had been sent straight through the heart.

The big man with the big black beard broke the silence in reply:

"I will thank you, sir, for your candour, since I am,

The Man Who Knew Too Much

in some melancholy sense, your host on this occasion. I am Baron Bruno, owner of this house and grounds, and it was here at my table that the mortal insult was given. I owe it to my unfortunate friend Le Caron "—and he made a gesture of introduction towards the red-bearded swordsman, "to say it was a mortal insult, and followed by a direct challenge. It was a charge of cheating at cards, and it was clinched by one of cowardice. I mean no harshness to the dead, but something is due to the living."

Monk turned to the dead man's seconds. "Do you support this?" he demanded.

"I suppose it's all right," said the young man with the yellow gloves. "There were faults on both sides."

Then he added abruptly: "My name is Waldo Lorraine, and I'm ashamed to say I am the fool who brought my poor friend here to play. He was an Englishman, Hubert Crane, whom I met in Paris, and meant, heaven knows, only to give a good time! And the only service I've done him is to be his second in this bloody ending. Dr. Vandam here, being also a stranger in the house, kindly acted as my colleague. The duel was regular enough, I must fairly say, but the quarrel was——" He paused, a shadow of shame darkening his dark face. "I have to confess I was no judge of it, and have no memory but a sort of nightmare. In plain words, I had drunk too much to know or care."

Dr. Vandam, the pale man in the spectacles, shook his head mournfully, still staring at the corpse.

"I can't help you," he said. "I was at the Seven Stars, and only came in time to arrange for the fight."

"My own fellow-witness, M. Valence," observed the baron, indicating the man with the cropped hair, "will ratify my version of the dispute."

"Had he any papers?" asked Forain after a pause. "May I examine the body?"

There was no opposition, and, after searching the dead man and his waistcoat and coat that lay on the lawn, the investigator at last found a single letter, short but confirmatory, so far as it went, of the story told him. It was signed "Abraham Crane," and was plainly from

The Five of Swords

the dead man's father in Huddersfield; indeed, Monk was able to recognize the name as that of a noted manufacturing magnate in the north. It merely concerned business on which the young man had been sent to Paris, apparently to confirm some contract with the Paris branch of the firm of Miller, Moss & Hartman; but the rather sharp adjuration to avoid the vanities of the French capital suggested that perhaps the father had some hint of the dissipations that had brought the son to his death. One thing only in this very commonplace letter puzzled the inquirer not a little. It ended by saying that the writer might himself be coming to France to hear the upshot of the Miller, Moss & Hartman affair, and that if so he would put up at the Seven Stars and call for his son at the Château d'Orage. It seemed odd that the son should have given the address of the very place where he was living the riotous life his father so strongly condemned. The only other object in the pockets besides the common necessaries was an old locket enclosing the faded portrait of a dark lady.

Forain stood frowning a moment, the paper twisted in his fingers; then he said abruptly: "May I go up to your house, Monsieur le Baron?"

The baron bowed silently; they left the dead man's seconds to mount guard over his body, and the rest mounted slowly up the slope. They went the slower for two reasons—first, because the steep and straggling path was made more irregular by straggling roots of pine like the tails of dying dragons, and slippery with green slime that might have been their own green and unnatural gore; and second, because Forain stopped every now and then to take what seemed needless note of certain details of the general decay. Either the baron had not long been in possession of the place, or he cared very little for appearances.

What had once been a garden was eaten by giant weeds, and when they passed the cucumber frames on the slope Forain saw they were empty and the glass of one of them had a careless crack, like a star in the ice. Forain stood staring at the hole for nearly a minute.

Entering the house by the long french windows, they

The Man Who Knew Too Much

came first on a round outer room with a round card-table. It might by the shape have been a turret-room, but seemed somehow as light and sunny as a summer-house, being white and gold in the ornate eighteenth-century style. But it was as faded as it was florid, and the white had grown yellow and the gold brown. At the moment this decay was but the background of the silent yet speaking drama of a more recent disorder. Cards were scattered across the floor and table, as if flung or struck flying from a hand that held them; champagne bottles stood or lay at random everywhere, half of them broken, nearly all of them empty; a chair was overturned. It was easy to believe all that Lorraine had said of the orgy that now seemed to him a nightmare.

"Not an edifying scene," said the baron, with a sigh, "and yet I suppose it has a moral."

"It may appear singular," replied Forain, "but in my own moral problem it is even reassuring. Given the death, I am even glad of the drink."

As he spoke he stooped swiftly and picked up a handful of cards from the carpet.

"The five of spades," he said to Monk musingly in English, "the five of swords, as the old Spaniards would say, I suppose. You know 'spade' is 'espada,' a sword? The four of swords—spades, I mean. The three of spades. The—have you got a telephone here?"

"Yes—in another room, round by the other door of the house," answered the baron, rather taken aback.

"I'll use it, if I may," said Forain, and stepped swiftly out of the card-room. He strode across a larger and darker *salon* within, which for some reason had remained in a sterner and more antiquated style of decoration. There were antlers above him; a glimmer of armour showed on the gloom of oak and tapestry, and he saw one thing that arrested his eye as he strode towards the farther door. A trophy of two swords crossed was on one side of the fireplace, and on the corresponding place opposite the empty hooks of another. He understood why the two rapiers had seemed to be antiquated. Under the ominous empty hooks stood an ebony cabinet carved with cherubs as grotesque as goblins.

The Five of Swords

Forain felt as if the black cherubim were peering at him with a curiosity quite unangelic. He gazed a moment at the drawers of the cabinet, and passed on.

He shut the door behind him, and they heard another door close in a more distant part of the building, away towards the road that ran on the remoter side of the house. There was a silence; they could hear neither the bell nor the talk at the telephone.

Baron Bruno had dropped the glass from his eye, and was plucking a little nervously at his long dark beard.

"I suppose, sir," he said, addressing Monk, "we can count on your friend's feeling of honour?"

"I am certain of his honour," said the Englishman, with the faintest accent on the possessive pronoun.

The surviving duellist, Le Caron, spoke for the first time, and roughly.

"Let the man telephone," he said. "No French jury would call this miserable thing murder. It was almost an accident."

"One to be avoided, I think," said Monk coldly.

Forain had reappeared, and his brow was cleared of its wrinkle of reflection. "Baron," he said, "I have resolved my little problem. I will treat this tragedy as a private misfortune on one condition—that you all meet me and give me an account that satisfies me within this week, and in Paris. Say outside the Café Roncesvaux on Thursday night. Does that suit you? Is that understood? Very well, let us return to the garden."

When they went out again through the french windows the sun was already high in heaven, and every detail of the slope and lawn below glittered with a new clarity. As they turned the corner of a clump of trees and came out above the duelling-ground, Forain stopped dead and put on the Baron's arm a hand that caught like a hook.

"My God!" he said. "This will never do. You must get away at once."

"What?" cried the other.

"It's been quick work," said the investigator. "The father's here already."

They followed his glance down to the garden by the wall, and the first thing they saw was that the rusty

The Man Who Knew Too Much

old garden door was standing open, letting in the white light of the road. Then they realized that a few yards within it was a tall, lean, grey-bearded man, clad completely in black and looking like some Puritanic minister. He was standing on the turf and looking down at the dead. A girl in grey, with a black hat, was kneeling by the body, and the two seconds, as by an instinct of decency, had withdrawn to some distance and stood gazing gloomily at the ground. In the clear sunlight the whole group looked like a lighted scene on a green stage.

"Go back at once—all three of you," said Forain almost fiercely. "Get away by the other door. You must not meet *him*, at least."

The Baron, after an instant's hesitation, seemed to assent, and Le Caron had already turned away. The slayer and his two seconds moved towards the house and vanished into it once more, the tall young man with the shaven head going last with a leisure that made even his long legs look cynical. He was the only one of them who scarcely seemed affected at all.

"Mr. Crane, I think," said Forain to the bereaved father. "I fear you know all that we can tell you."

The grey-bearded man nodded; there was a certain frost-bitten fierceness about his face and something wild in the eye contrasting with the control in the features, something that seemed natural enough at such a time, but which they found afterwards to be more normal to him even in ordinary times.

"Sir," he said, "I have seen the end of cards and wine and the Lord's judgments for everything I feared." Then he added, with an incongruous simplicity somehow rather tragic than comic: "And fencing, sir. I was always against all that French fad of getting prizes for fencing. Football is bad enough, with betting and every sort of brutality, but it doesn't lead to this. You are English, I think?" he said abruptly to Monk. "Have you anything to say of this abominable murder?"

"I say it is an abominable murder," said Monk firmly. "I was saying so to my friend hardly half an hour ago."

"Ah, and you?" cried the old man, looking sus-

The Five of Swords

piciously at Forain. "Were you defending duels, perhaps?"

"Sir," replied Forain gently, "it is no time for defending anything. If your son had fallen from a horse, I would not defend horses; you should say your worst of them. If he had been drowned in a boat, I would join you in wishing every boat at the bottom of the sea."

The girl was looking at Forain with an innocent intensity of gaze which was curious and painful, but the father turned impatiently away, saying to Monk: "As you are English at least, I should like to consult you." And he drew the Englishman aside.

But the daughter still looked across at Forain without speech or motion, and he looked back at her with a rather indescribable interest. She was fair, like her brother, with yellow hair and a white face, but her features were irregular with that fairy luck that falls right once in fifty times, and then is more beautiful than beauty. Her eyes seemed as colourless as water, and yet as bright as diamonds, and when he met them the Frenchman realized, with a mounting and unmanageable emotion, that he was facing something far more positive than the laxity of the son or the limitations of the father.

"May I ask you, sir," she said steadily, "who were those three men with you just now? Were they the men who murdered him?"

"Mademoiselle," he said, feeling somehow that all disguises had dropped, "you use a harsh word, and heaven knows it is natural. But I must not stand before you on false pretences. I myself have held such a weapon and nearly done such a murder."

"I don't think you look like a murderer," she said calmly. "But they did. That man with the red beard, he was like a wolf—a well-dressed wolf, which is the worst part of it. And that big, pompous man—what could he be but horrible, with his big black beard and a glass in one eye?"

"Surely," said Forain respectfully, "it is not wicked to be well dressed, and a man might be more sinned against than sinning and still have a beard and an eyeglass."

The Man Who Knew Too Much

"Not all that big beard and that one little eyeglass," she replied positively. "Oh, I only saw them in the distance, but I know quite well I'm right."

"I know you must think any duellist is a criminal and ought to be punished," said Forain rather huskily. "Only, having been one myself——"

"I don't," she said. "I think those duellists ought to be punished. And, just to prove what I mean and don't mean"—and her pale face was changed with a puzzling and yet dazzling smile—"I want you to punish them."

There was a strange silence, and she added quietly:

"You have seen something yourself. You have some guess, I am sure, about how they came to fight, and what was really behind it all. You know there is really something wrong, much more wrong than the quarrel about cards."

He bowed to her, and seemed to yield like a man rebuked by an old friend.

"Mademoiselle," he said, "I am honoured by your confidence. And your commission."

He straightened himself equally abruptly, and turned to face the father, who had drawn near again in conversation with Monk.

"Mr. Crane," he said gravely, "I must ask you for the moment to trust me. This gentleman, as well as other countrymen of yours to whom I can refer you, will, I think, tell you that I can be trusted. I have already communicated with the authorities, and you may even regard me in a sense as their representative. I can answer for the fact that those responsible in this dreadful affair are under observation, and that justice can effect whatever may be found to be just. If you will honour me with an appointment in Paris after Tuesday next, I can tell you more of many things that you ought to know. Meanwhile, I will make any arrangements you desire touching the—formalities of respect for the dead."

The eye of old Crane was still choleric, but he bowed, and Forain and Monk, returning the salutation, retraced their way up the path to the château. As they did so

The Five of Swords

the Frenchman paused again by the cucumber frame and pointed to the broken glass.

"That's the biggest hole in the story so far," he said; "it gapes at me like the mouth of hell."

"That!" exclaimed his friend. "That might have happened any time."

"It happened this morning," said Forain, "or else—anyhow, the broken bits are fresh; nothing has grown round them. And there is the mark of a heel on the soil inside. One of these men stepped straight on to the glass going down to the duelling ground. Why?"

"Oh, well," observed Monk, "that fellow Lorraine said he was blind drunk last night."

"But not this morning," replied Forain. "And though a man blind drunk, even in broad daylight, might conceivably put his foot into a big glass frame right in front of him, I doubt if he could take it out again so neatly. If he were as drunk as that, I think the man-trap would trip and throw him, and there would be more broken glass. This does not look to me like a man who was blind drunk. It is more like a man who was blind."

"Blind!" repeated Monk, with a quite irrational creeping of the flesh. "But none of these men are blind. Is there any other explanation?"

"Yes," replied Forain. "They did it in the dark. And that is the darkest part of the business."

Anyone who had tracked the course of the two friends on the ensuing Thursday evening, when dusk had already kindled around them the many-coloured lights of Paris, might have imagined that they had no purpose but the visiting of a variety of cafés. Yet their course, though crooked and erratic, was designed according to the consistent strategy of the amateur detective. Forain went first to see the countess, the still surviving widow of the nobleman who fell fifteen years before, in a duel on the same spot. He went in a literal sense to see her, and not to call on her. For he contented himself with sitting outside the café opposite her house and playing with an *apéritif* until she came out to her carriage—a dark-browed lady, with a beauty rather fixed like a picture than still

The Man Who Knew Too Much

living like a flower : a portrait from a mummy-case. Then he merely glanced at the portrait in the old locket he had taken from the dead man's pocket, nodded almost approvingly, and made his way across the river to a less aristocratic and more purely commercial part of the town. Passing rapidly along a solid street of banks and public buildings, he reached a large hotel built on the same ponderous pattern, but having the usual litter of little tables on the pavement outside.' They were intercepted with ornamental shrubs and covered with an awning striped with white and purple, and at a table at the extreme corner, against the last green afterglow of evening, he saw the black bulk of Baron Bruno sitting between his two friends. The awning that shaded them just cut off the upper part of his tall black hat, and Monk had the fancy that he resembled some black Babylonian caryatid supporting the whole building; perhaps there was something Assyrian about his large square beard. The Englishman felt a subconscious temptation to share his countrywoman's prejudice, but it was evident that Forain did not share it. For he sat down with the three men, and began to exhibit a very unexpected camaraderie and even conviviality. He ordered wine and pressed it upon them, passing afterwards into animated conversation, and it was not until about half an hour afterwards that our imaginary spectator, hovering on his trail, would have seen him start up with a slight return to stiffness, salute the company and resume his singular journey.

His zigzag course through the lighted city carried him first to a public telephone and then to a public office, which Monk was able to identify as the place where the dead body was awaiting medical examination. From this place he came out looking very grim, like one who has faced an ugly fact, but he said nothing and pursued his course to the police headquarters, where he was closeted for some time with the authorities. Then he crossed the river once more, walking swiftly and still in silence, and in a quiet corner of Paris struck the worn white gateway of a building that had once been an hotel in the ancient and aristocratic sense, and was now an hotel in a more commercial, but particularly quiet fashion. Passing through the porch

The Five of Swords

and passages, he came out on a garden so secluded that the very sunset sky seemed a private awning of gold and green like the awning of purple and silver under which the sombre baron had sat. A few guests in evening dress were scattered at tables under the trees, but Forain went swiftly past them to one table near a flight of garden steps, at which he could see a girl in grey with golden hair. It was Margaret Crane; she looked up as he approached, but she only said, as if breathlessly: "Do you know any more about the murder?"

Before he could reply her father had appeared at the top of the steps, and Forain felt vaguely that while the girl's grey dress seemed to harmonize with everything, the rigid and rusty black of the old man's clothes remained like the protest of a Puritan in a garden of Cavaliers.

"The murder," he repeated in a loud and harsh voice, heard everywhere: "That's what we want to know about. This murder, sir!"

"Mr. Crane," said Forain, "I hope you know how I feel your position, but it is only fair to warn you that in these criminal matters one must speak carefully. If it comes to a trial, your case will be none the better if you have abused these men at random, even in private. And I am bound to say, not only that the duel as a duel seems to have been regular, but that the duellists seem to be men of marked regularity."

"What do you mean?" demanded the old man.

"I will be frank with you and own I have seen them since," said Forain. "Nay, I have passed a sort of festive evening with them—or what I meant to be a festive evening. But I am forced to say they are as little festive as your own conscience could desire. Indeed, they seem to have business habits very much like your own. Frankly, I tried to make them drink and to draw them into a game of cards, but the baron and his friends coldly declined, said they had appointments, and we parted after black coffee and a brief and rather curious conversation."

"I hate them the more for that," said the girl.

"You are quick, Mademoiselle," observed Forain, with

The Man Who Knew Too Much

a growing admiration. "I also took the matter in that spirit, if only for experiment. I said bluntly to our baronial friend: 'So long as I thought you were a drinking and a dicing company, I took this for a drunken accident. But let me tell you it does not look well when elderly men, themselves sober, themselves indifferent to play, get a mere boy among them and play cards with him. You know what is thought of that; it is thought that the old man takes a hand—well, rather too like an old hand. And it is worse when he silences his opponent by fencing like an old hand also.'"

"And what did they say to that?" asked the girl.

"It is painful to me to repeat it," said Forain, "but it was quite as uncomfortable a surprise to me. Just as I seemed to have cornered them finally, that red-bearded man, Le Caron, whose sword made the mortal thrust, himself broke in like one abandoning disguise, with impatience and passion. 'I respect the dead,' he said, 'but you force me from any reticence. I can only tell you it was not we, the elder men, who dragged the boy into drink; it was he who dragged us. He arrived at the château half drunk already, and insisted on the baron ordering champagne from the Seven Stars down the road, for we were a temperate party and the cellar was not even stocked. It was he who insisted on play; it was he who taunted us with being afraid to play; it was he who at last added, quite wantonly and in wild falsehood, the intolerable taunt that we cheated at play.'"

"I will not believe it," said Crane, but his daughter remained silent, with her pale and penetrating face turned towards the amateur detective, who continued his report of the conversation.

"'Oh, I don't ask you to take my word,' Le Caron went on. 'Ask Lorraine himself, ask Dr. Vandam himself, who was sent to the inn for the wine, so that he was away when the row occurred. He stopped behind there to settle, and wasn't sorry, I think, to be out of it. He also, like myself, is glad to be *bourgeois* in these matters. Ask the innkeeper himself; he will tell you the wine was bought well on in the evening, after the young man arrived. Ask the people at the railway station; they

The Five of Swords

will tell you when the young man arrived. You can easily test my story.'"

"I can see by your face," said the girl in a low voice, "that you have tested it. And you have found it true."

"You see the heart of things," said Forain.

"I cannot see the hearts of these men," she answered. "But I can see the hollows where their hearts should be."

"You still find them horrible," he said. "Who can blame you?"

"Horrible!" cried the old man. "Didn't they murder my son?"

"I speak only as an adviser," observed the Frenchman. "I know you cannot believe a duellist could be a respectable man. I only say that, as a fact, these seem to be respectable men. I have not only verified their tale, but traced back something of their past. They seem to have been concerned with commercial things, but solidly and on a considerable scale; I am in touch with the police dossiers, and should know of any other such scandals about them. Forgive me; I fear I do think that a duel is sometimes justifiable. I will not horrify you by saying that this one was justifiable; I only warn you that, in French opinion, they may be able to justify it."

"Yes," said the girl. "They grow more horrible as you speak of them. Oh! that is the really horrible man—the man who can always be justified. Honest men leave more holes gaping, like my poor brother, but the wicked are always in armour. Is there anything so blasphemous as the bad man's case when his case is complete, as the lawyers say; when the judge gravely sums up, and the jury agree and the police obey, and everything goes on oiled wheels? Is there anything so oily as the smell of that oil? It is then I feel I cannot wait for the Day of Judgment to crack their whited sepulchres."

"And it is then," said Forain quietly, "that I fight a duel."

The girl started a little. "Then?" she repeated.

"Then," repeated the Frenchman, lifting his head. "You, mademoiselle, have uttered the defence of the good duellist. You have proved the right of the private gentleman to draw a private sword. Yes, it is then that I do

The Man Who Knew Too Much

this criminal and bloody thing that so much horrifies you and your father. Yes, it is then that I become a murderer. When there is no crack in the whitewash and I cannot wait for the wrath of God. And permit me the reminder that you have not yet heard the end of my interview with the men who have left you in mourning."

Crane still stared in frosty suspicion, but the girl, as Forain suggested, had great intuitions. Her face and eyes kindled as she gazed.

"You don't mean——" she began, and then stopped.

Forain rose to his feet. "Yes," he said. "Being such a bloodthirsty character, I must no longer remain in company so respectable. Yes, mademoiselle, I have challenged the man who killed your brother."

"Challenged!" repeated the bristling Crane. "Challenged—more of this—of this butchery!" and he choked. But the girl had risen also and stretched out her hand like a queen.

"No, father," she said. "This gentleman is our friend, and he caught me out fairly. But I see now that there is more in French wit than we have understood; yes, and more in French duelling."

With a heightened colour and a lowered voice, Forain answered: "Mademoiselle, my inspiration is English." And, with a rather abrupt bow, he strode away, accompanied by Harry Monk, who regarded him with a contained amusement.

"I cannot affect to hope," said Monk airily, "that I myself constitute the English inspiration of your life."

"Nonsense," said the other rather testily, "let us get back to business. As I imagined your views on duelling were so similar to old Crane's that you could not consistently represent me, I've asked his unfortunate son's seconds to act as mine. I believe that young Lorraine will be of great use in helping us to probe this mystery. I have talked to him, and I am convinced of his great ability."

"And you have talked to me for years," said Monk, laughing, "and you are convinced of my great stupidity."

"Of your great sincerity," said Forain. "That is why I do not ask you to help me here."

The Five of Swords

Monk's scruples, however, did not prevent his being present at the new encounter that had been so rapidly and even irregularly arranged. And his travels with his eccentric friend, which had already begun to remind him of the overturns and recurrences of a nightmare, brought him a few days later back to the old duelling ground of the Château d'Orage. The garden of Baron Bruno had apparently been selected for a second time as a sort of concession to the baron's party, but it was a rather grim privilege, and they evidently felt it as such. So little disposed were they, indeed, to linger about the place where they had once feasted and fought, that the baron's motor was waiting in the road without to take them back immediately to Paris. Forain had always vaguely felt that the baron was very tenuously attached to his house and property, and in this case his party seemed to revisit it like ghosts. The prejudice of Margaret Crane would have said that a shadow of doom was visibly closing in on them. But it was more reasonable, and consonant with the more quiet and *bourgeois* character to which they seemed entitled, to suppose that they were naturally distressed at returning to the scene of their one reluctant deed of blood. Whatever the reason, the baron's brown face was heavy and sombre, and Le Caron, when he again found himself standing sword in hand on that fatal grass, was so white that his beard looked scarlet, like false hair or fiery paint. Monk almost fancied that the bright point of the poised rapier was faintly vibrant, as in a hand that shook.

The pine-shadowed park, with its careless and almost colourless decay, seemed a place where centuries might pass unnoticed. The white morning light served only to accentuate the grey details, and Monk caught himself fancying that it was truly the ashen vegetation of primeval æons. This may have been an effect of his nerves, which were not unnaturally strained. After all, this was the third duel in those grounds, and two had ended in death; he could not but wonder if his friend was to be the last victim. Anyhow, it seemed to him that the preliminaries were intolerably lengthy. Le Caron had long and low-voiced consultations with the lowering baron; and even

The Man Who Knew Too Much

Forain's own seconds, Lorraine and the doctor, seemed more inclined to wait and whisper than to come to the mortal business. And all this was the more strange because the fight, when it did come at last, seemed to be over in a flash, like a conjuring trick.

The swords had barely touched twice or thrice when Le Caron found himself swordless. His weapon had twitched itself like a live thing out of his hand, and went spinning and sparkling over the garden wall; they could hear the steel tinkle on the stones of the road. Forain had disarmed him with a turn of the wrist.

Forain straightened himself and made a salute with his sword.

"Gentlemen," he said, "I am quite satisfied, if you are. After all, it was a slight cause of quarrel, and the honour of both parties is, so far, secure. Also, I understand, you gentlemen are anxious to get back to town."

Monk had long felt that his friend was more and more disposed to let the opposite group off lightly; he had long been speaking of them soberly as sober merchants. But whether or no it was the anti-climax of safety, he had a sense that the figures opposite had shrunk, and were more commonplace and ugly. The eagle nose of Le Caron looked more like a common hook; his fine clothes seemed to sit more uneasily on him, as on a hastily dressed doll; and even the solid and solemn baron somehow looked more like a large dummy outside a tailor's shop. But the strangest thing of all was that the baron's other colleague, Valence, of the shaven head, was standing astraddle in the background, wearing a broad though a bitter grin. As the baron and the defeated duellist made their way rather sullenly through the garden door to the car beyond, Forain went up to this last member of the strange group, and (much to Monk's surprise) talked quickly and quietly for several minutes. It was only when Bruno's great voice was heard calling his name from without that this last figure also turned and left the garden.

"*Exeunt* brigands!" said Forain, with a cheerful change in his voice, "and now the four detectives will go up and examine the brigands' den."

The Five of Swords

And he turned and began once again to mount the slope to the château, the rest following in single file. Monk, who was just behind him, remarked abruptly when they were halfway up the ascent:

"So you didn't kill him, after all?"

"I didn't want to kill him," replied his French friend.

"What did you want?"

"I wanted to see whether he could fence," said Forain. "He can't."

Monk eyed in a puzzled manner the tall, straight, grey-clad back of the figure mounting ahead of him, but was silent till Forain spoke again.

"You remember," continued that gentleman, "that old Crane said his unfortunate son had actually got prizes for fencing. But that carroty-whiskered Mr. Le Caron hardly knows how to hold a foil. Of course, it's very natural; after all, he is but a quiet business man, as I told you, and deals more in gold than steel."

"But, my good man," cried Monk, addressing the back in exasperation, "what the devil does it all mean? Why was Crane killed in the duel?"

"There never was any duel," said Forain, without turning round.

Dr. Vandam behind uttered an abrupt sound as of astonishment, or perhaps enlightenment; but, though it was followed by many questions, Forain said no more till they stood in the long inner room of the château, with the weapons on the wall and the ebony cabinet, on which the black cherubs looked blacker than ever. Forain felt more darkly a certain contradiction between their colour and shape, that was like a blasphemy. Black cherubs were like the Black Mass—they were symbols of some idea that hell is an inverted copy of heaven, like a landscape hanging downwards in a lake.

He shook off his momentary dreams and stooped over the drawers of the cabinet, and when he spoke again it was lightly enough.

"You know the château, Monsieur Lorraine," he said, "and I expect you know the cabinet, and even the drawer. I see it's been opened lately." The drawer, indeed, was not completely closed, and, giving it a sudden jerk, he

The Man Who Knew Too Much

pulled it completely out of the cabinet. Without further words he bore it, with its contents, back into the cardroom and put it on the round table; and at his invitation his three colleagues or co-detectives drew up their chairs and sat round it. The drawer seemed to contain the contents of an old curiosity shop, such as Balzac loved to describe—a tumbled heap of brown coins, dim jewels and trinkets, of which tales, true and false, are told.

"Well, what about it?" asked Monk. "Do you want to get something out of it?"

"Not exactly," replied the investigator. "I rather fancy I want to put something into it."

He pulled from his pocket the locket with the dark portrait, and poised it thoughtfully in his hand.

"We have now to ask ourselves," went on the detective to his colleagues, "why young Crane was carrying this, which is a portrait of the countess?"

"He went about Paris a good deal," said Dr. Vandam rather grimly.

"If she knew him well," proceeded Forain, "it seems strange she has taken no notice of his sad end."

"Perhaps she knew him a little too well," cried Lorraine, with a little laugh. "Or, perhaps, though it's an ugly thing to say, she was glad to be rid of him. There were uglier stories when her husband, the old count——"

"You know the château, Monsieur Lorraine?" repeated Forain, looking at him steadily and even sternly. "I think that's where the locket came from." And he tossed it on to the many-coloured heap in the drawer.

Lorraine's eyes were literally like black diamonds as he gazed fascinated at the heap; he seemed really too excited to reply. Forain continued his exposition.

"Poor Crane, I fancy, must have found it here. Or else somebody found it here and gave it to him. Or else somebody—by the way, surely that's a real Renascence chain there—Italian and fifteenth century, unless I'm wrong. There are valuable things here, Monsieur Lorraine, and I believe you're a judge of them."

"I know a little about the Renascence," answered

The Five of Swords

Lorraine, and the pale Dr. Vandam flashed a queer look at him through his spectacles.

"There was a ring, too, I suspect," said Forain. "I have put back the locket. Would you, Monsieur Lorraine, kindly put back the ring?"

Lorraine rose, the smile still on his lips; he put two fingers in his waistcoat pocket and drew out a small circlet of wrought gold with a green stone.

The next moment Forain's arm shot across the table trying to catch his wrist; but his motion, though swift as his sword-thrust, was yet too late. Young Mr. Waldo Lorraine stood with the smile on his lips and the Renascence ring on his finger while one could count five. Then his feet slipped on the smooth floor and he fell dead across the table, with his black ringlets among the rich refuse of the drawer. Almost simultaneously with the shock of his fall, Dr. Vandam had taken one bound, burst out of the french windows and disappeared down the garden like a cat.

"Don't move," said Forain with a steely steadiness. "The police are on the watch. I laid them on the other day in Paris when I saw poor Crane's body."

"But surely," cried his bewildered friend, "it was not only then that you saw the wound on his body."

"I mean the wound on his finger," said Forain.

He stood a minute or two in silence, looking down at the fallen figure across the table with pity and something almost like admiration.

"Strange," he said at last, "that he should die just here, with his head in all that dustbin of curiosities that he was born among and had such a taste for. You saw he was a Jew, of course, but, my God, what a genius! Like your young Disraeli—and he might have succeeded too and filled the world with his fame. Just a mistake or two, breaking a cucumber frame in the dark, and he lies dead in all that dead bric-à-brac, as if in the pawnshop where he was born."

The next appointment Forain made with his friends was at the office of the *Sûreté*, in a private room. Monk was a little late for the appointment; the party was already assembled round a table, and it gave him a final shock.

The Man Who Knew Too Much

He was not, indeed, surprised to see Crane and his daughter sitting opposite Forain, and he guessed that the man presiding, with the white beard and the red rosette, was the chief of police himself. But his head turned when he found the fifth place filled with the broad shoulders, cropped hair and ghastly handsome face of Valence, the younger second of Le Caron.

Old Crane was in the middle of a speech when he entered, and was speaking with his usual smouldering and self-righteous indignation.

"I send my son to execute a deed of partnership in a good business with Miller, Moss and Hartman, one of the first firms in the civilized world, sir, with branches in America and all the colonies, as big as the Bank of England. What happens? No sooner does he set foot in your country than he gets in a dicing, drinking, duelling gang, and is butchered in a barbarous brawl with drawn swords."

"Mr. Crane," said Forain gently, "you will forgive me if I both contradict you and congratulate you. Given so sad a story, I give you the gladdest news a father could hear. You have wronged your son. He did not drink, he did not dice, he did not duel. He obeyed you in every particular. He devoted himself wholly to Messrs. Miller, Moss and Hartman; he died in your service, and he died rather than fail you."

The girl leaned swiftly forward, and she was pale but radiant.

"What do you mean?" she cried. "Then who were these men with swords and hateful faces? What were they doing? Who are they?"

"I will tell you," answered the Frenchman calmly. "They are Messrs. Miller, Moss and Hartman, one of the first firms in the civilized world, as big as the Bank of England."

There was a silence of stupefaction on the other side of the table, and it was Forain who went on, but with a change and challenge in his voice.

"Oh, how little you rich masters of the modern world know about the modern world! What do you know about Miller, Moss and Hartman, *except* that they have

The Five of Swords

branches all over the world and are as big as the Bank of England? You know they go to the ends of the earth, but where do they come from? Is there any check on businesses changing hands or men changing names? Miller may be twenty years dead, if he was ever alive. Miller may stand for Muller, or Muller for Moses. The back-doors of every business to-day are open to such new-comers, and do you ever ask from what gutters they come? And then you think your son lost if he goes into a music-hall, and you want to shut up all the taverns to keep him from bad company. Believe me, you had better shut up the banks."

Margaret Crane was still staring with electric eyes. "But what in the name of mercy happened?" she cried.

The investigator turned slightly in his chair and made a movement, as of somewhat sombre introduction, towards Valence, who sat looking at the table with a face like coloured stone.

"We have with us," said Forain, "one who knows from within the whole of this strange story. We need not trouble much about his own story. Of the five men who have played this horrible farce, he is certainly the most honest, and therefore the only one who has been in prison. It was for a crime of passion long ago, which turned him from being at worst a Lothario to being at worst an Apache. Hence these more respectable ruffians had a rope round his neck, and to-day he is not so much a traitor as a runaway. If on that hideous night he held a candle to the devil, he is no devil-worshipper; at least he has little worship for these devils."

There was a long silence, and the stony lips of the shaven Apollo curled and moved at last. "Well," he said, "I won't trouble you with much about these men I had to serve. Their real names were not Lorraine, Le Caron, etc., any more than they were Miller, Moss, etc., though they went by the first in society and the second in business. Just now we need not trouble about their real names; I'm sure they never did. They were cosmopolitan moneylenders mostly; I was in their power, and they kept me as a big bully and bodyguard to save them from what they richly deserved at the hands of many

The Man Who Knew Too Much

ruined men. They would no more have thought of fighting a duel than of going on a crusade. I knew something of the countess, who has nothing to do with the story, except that I got them a short lease of her house. One evening Lorraine, who was the leader and the cleverest rascal in Europe, young as he was, happened to be turning over the drawer of curios, which he had taken out of the black cabinet and put on the round card-table. He found the old Italian ring, and told us it was poisoned; he knew a lot about such toys. Suddenly he made a momentary gesture covering the drawer, like a fence when he hears the police. He recovered his calm; there was no danger, but the gesture told of old times. What had produced it was a man who had appeared silently, and was standing outside the french windows, having entered up the garden slope. He was a slim, fair young man, carefully dressed and wearing a silk hat, which he took off as he entered. 'My name is Crane,' he said a little stiffly and nervously, and plucked off his glove to offer his hand, which Lorraine shook with great warmth. The others joined in the greeting, and it gradually became apparent that this was the representative of some firm with whom they were to make an important amalgamation. In the entrance-room all was welcome and gaiety, but when young Crane had followed old Bruno into the big inner room, leaving his hat and gloves on the card-table by the curios, I fancy things did not go so smoothly. I did not understand the business fully, but I was watching the three others who did, and I came to the conclusion that Bruno, in their name, was making some proposition to the new junior partner which they regarded as a very handsome proposition for him, but which he did not regard as altogether handsome in other respects. They seemed quite confident at first, but as the talk went on in the inner room Vandam and Le Caron exchanged gloomy glances; and suddenly a full, indignant voice came from within: 'Do you mean, sir, that my father is to suffer?' and then, after an inaudible reply, 'Confidential, sir! The confidence, I imagine, is placed by my father in me. I shall instantly report this astounding proposal. . . . No, sir, I am not to be bribed,' I was

The Five of Swords

watching Lorraine's face, that seemed to have grown old as a yellow parchment, and his eyes glittered like the old stones on the table. He was leaning across it, his mouth close to the ear of Vandam, and he was saying: 'He must not leave the house. Our work all over the world is lost if he leaves this house.' 'But we can't stop him,' whispered the doctor, and his teeth chattered. 'Can't!' repeated Lorraine, with a ghastly smile, yet somehow like a man in a trance: 'Oh, one *can* do anything. I never did it before, though.' He picked the poison ring out of the heap. Then he swiftly drew the young man's glove out of his hat on the table. There came a burst of speech from the inner room: 'I shall tell him you are a pack of thieves!' and Lorraine quietly slipped the ring inside a finger of the glove, a moment before its owner swung into the room. He clapped on his hat, furiously pulled on his gloves, and strode to the French windows. Then he flung them open wide upon the sunset, stepped out and fell dead on the garden turf beyond. I remember his tall hat rolling down the slope, and how horrible it seemed that it should still be moving among the bushes, when he lay so still."

"He died like a soldier for a flag," said Forain.

"Perhaps you have already guessed," went on Valence, "the rest of the story. Hell itself must have inspired Lorraine that night, for the whole drama was his and worked out to the last detail. The difficulty in every murder is how to hide the corpse. He decided not to hide it, but to show it; I might say to advertise it. He had been striding up and down the inner hall, his flexible face working with thought, when his eye caught the crossed swords on the trophy. 'This man died in a duel,' he said. 'In England he'd have died out duck-shooting, and in Russia of dynamite. In France he died in a duel. If we all take the lighter blame, they will never look for heavier; it's a good rule with confessions,' and again he wore that awful smile He not only staged the duel, but the drunken quarrel that was to explain it. They were quite right when they said the champagne was not sent for till after the boy's arrival. It was not sent for till after the boy's arrival. It was not

The Man Who Knew Too Much

sent for till after his death. They carefully scattered cards, carefully threw furniture about and so on. By the way, they didn't shuffle the packs enough to deceive Monsieur Forain. Then they put Le Caron—the showiest —in his shirt-sleeves, did the same with the dead man, and then Lorraine deliberately passed the sword through the heart that had already ceased to beat. It seemed like a second murder, and a worse one. Then they carried him down in the dark, just before the dawn, so that no one could possibly see him save on the fighting ground. Lorraine thought of twenty little things; he took an old miniature of the countess from the cabinet and put it in the dead man's pocket, to put people off the scent—as it did. He left Mr. Crane's letter, because its warning against dissipation actually supported the story. It was all well fitted together, and if Le Caron hadn't put his foot on a cucumber-frame in the dark I doubt if even Monsieur Forain would ever have found a hole in the business."

Margaret Crane walked firmly out of the offices of the *Sûreté*, but at the top of the steps outside she wavered and might almost have fallen. Forain caught her by the elbow, and they looked at each other for a space; then they went down the steps and down the street together. She had lost a brother in that black adventure, and what else she gained is no part of the tale of the five strange men, or, as she came to call it afterwards, the five of swords. Margaret asked one more question about it, and their talk afterwards was of deeply different matters. She only said: "Was it the wound you discovered on his finger that made you certain?"

"Partly his finger," he assented gravely, "and partly his face. There was something still fresh on his face that made me fancy already that he was no waster, but had died more than worthily. It was something young and yet nobler than youth, and more beautiful than beauty. It was something I had seen somewhere else. In fact, it was the converse, so to speak, of the case in Rostand's play, '*Monsieur de Bergerac, je suis ta cousine.*'"

"I don't understand you," she said.

"It was a family likeness," replied her companion.

THE TOWER OF TREASON

At a certain moment, just before sunset, a young man was walking in a rather extraordinary fashion across a wild country bearded with grey and wintry forests. In the solitude of that silent and wooded wilderness he was walking backwards. There was nobody to notice the eccentricity; it could not arrest the rush of the eagles over those endless forests where Hungarian frontiers fade into the Balkans; it could not be expected to arouse criticism in the squirrel or the hare. Even the peasants of those parts might possibly have been content to explain it as the vow of a pilgrim, or some other wild religious exercise; for it was a land of wild religious exercises. Only a little way in front of him (or rather, at that instant, behind him) the goal of his journey and many previous journeys, was a strange half-military monastery, like some old chapel of the Templars where vigilant ascetics watched night and day over a hoard of sacred jewels, guarded at once like the crown of a king and the relic of a saint. Barely a league beyond, where the hills began to lift themselves clear of the forest, was a yet more solitary outpost of such devotional seclusion; a hermitage which held captive a man once famous through half Europe, a dazzling diplomatist and ambitious statesman, now solitary and only rarely visited by the religious, for whom he was supposed to have more invisible jewels of a new wisdom. All that land, that seemed so silent and empty, was alive with such miracles.

Nevertheless the young man was not performing a religious vow, or going on a religious pilgrimage. He had himself known personally the renowned recluse of the hermitage on the hill, when they were both equally in the world and worldly; but he had not the faintest intention of following his holy example. He was himself a guest at the monastery that was the consecrated casket

The Man Who Knew Too Much

of the strange jewels; but his errand was purely political and not in the least consecrated. He was a diplomatist by profession; but it must not be lightly inferred that he was walking backwards out of excessive deference to the etiquette of courts. He was an Englishman by nationality; but he was not, with somewhat distant reverence, still walking backwards before the King of England. Nor was he paying so polite a duty to any other king, though he might himself have said that he was paying it to a queen. In short the explanation of his antic, as of not a few antics, was that he was in love; a condition common in romances and not unknown in real life. He was looking backwards at the house he had just left, in an abstracted or distracted fashion, half hoping to see a last signal from it or merely to catch a last glimpse of it among the trees. And his look was the more longing and lingering on this particular evening, for an atmospheric reason he would have found it hard to explain; a sense of pathos and distance and division hardly explained by his practical difficulties. As the sunset clouds were heavy with a purple which typifies the rich tragedy of Lent, so on this evening passion seemed to weigh on him with something of the power of doom. And a pagan of the mystical sort would certainly have called what happened next an omen; though a practical man of the modern sort might rather have hinted that it was the highly calculable effect of walking backwards and being a fool. A noise of distant firing was heard in the forest; and the slight start he gave, combined with a loop of grass that caught his foot, threw him sprawling all his length; as if that distant shot had brought him down.

But the omens were not all ended; nor could they all be counted pagan. For as he gazed upwards for an instant, from the place where he had fallen, he saw above the black forest and against the vivid violet clouds, something strangely suitable to that tragic purple recalling the traditions of Lent. It was a great face between outstretched gigantic arms; the face upon a large wooden crucifix The figure was carved in the round but very much in the rough, in a rude archaic style, and was probably a old outpost of Latin Christianity in that laby-

The Tower of Treason

rinth of religious frontiers. He must have seen it before, for it stood on a little hill in a clearing of the woods, just opposite the one straight path leading to the sanctuary of the jewels, the tower of which could already be seen rising out of the sea of leaves. But somehow the size of the head above the trees, seen suddenly from below after the shock of the fall, had the look of a judgment in the sky. It seemed a strange fate to have fallen at the foot of it.

The young man, whose name was Bertram Drake, came from Cambridge and was heir to all the comforts and conventions of scepticism, further enlivened by a certain impatience in his own intellectual temper, which made him more mutinous than was good for his professional career; an active, restless man with a dark but open and audacious face. But for an instant something had stirred in him which is Christendom buried in Europe; something which is a memory even where it is a myth. Rising, he turned a troubled gaze to the great circle of dark grey forests, out of which rose in the distance the lonely tower of his destination; and even as he did so he saw something else. A few feet from where he had just fallen, and risen again to his feet, lay another fallen figure. And the figure did not rise.

He strode across, bent down over the body and touched it, and was soon grimly satisfied about why it was lying still. Nor was it without a further shock; for he even realized that he had seen the man before, though in a sufficiently casual and commonplace fashion; as a rustic bringing timber to the house he had just left. He recognized the spectacles on the square and stolid face; they were horn spectacles of the plainest pattern, yet they did not somehow suit his figure, which was clothed loosely like an ordinary peasant. And in the tragedy of the moment they were almost grotesque. The very fixity of the spectacles on the face was one of those details of daily habit that suddenly make death incredible. He had looked down at him for several seconds, before he became conscious that the deathly silence around was in truth a living silence; he was not alone.

A yard or two away an armed man was standing like

The Man Who Knew Too Much

a statue. He was a stalwart but rather stooping figure, with a long antiquated musket slung aslant on his shoulders; and in his hand a drawn sabre shone like a silver crescent. For the rest, he was a long-coated, long-bearded figure with a faint suggestion, to be felt in some figures from Russia and Eastern Europe generally, that the coats were like skirts and that the big beard had some of the terrors of a hairy mask; a faint touch of the true East. Thus accoutred, it had the look of a rude uniform; but the Englishman knew it was not that of the small Slav state in which he stood; which may be called, for the purpose of this tale, the kingdom of Transylvania. But when Drake addressed him in the language of that country, with which he himself was already fairly familiar, it was clear enough that the stranger understood. And there was a final touch of something strange in the fact that the brown eyes of this bearded and barbaric figure seemed not only sad but even soft, as with a sort of mystification of their own.

"Have you murdered this man?" asked the Englishman sternly.

The other shook his head; and then answered an incredulous stare by the simple but sufficient gesture of holding out his bare sabre immediately under the inquirer's eyes. It was an unanswerable fact that the blade was quite clean and without a spot of blood.

"But you were going to murder him," said Drake. "Why did you draw your sword?"

"I was going to——" and with that the stranger stopped in his speech, hesitated, and then suddenly slapping his sabre back into the sheath, dived into the bushes and disappeared, before Drake could make a movement in pursuit of him.

The echoes of the original volley that had waked the woods had not long died away on the distant heights beyond the tower; and Drake could now only suppose that the shot thus fired had been the real cause of death. He was convinced, for many causes, that the shot had come from the tower; and he had other reasons for rapidly repairing thither besides the necessity of giving the fatal news to the nearest human habitation. He hurried along

The Tower of Treason

the very straight and strictly embanked road that was like a bridge between the tower and the little hill in front of the crucifix; and soon came under the shadow of the strange monastic building, now enormous in scale though still simple in outline. For though it was as wide in its circle as a great camp, and even bore on its flat top a sort of roof garden large enough to allow a little exercise to its permanent guards and captives, it rose sheer from the ground in a single round and windowless wall; so high that it stood up in the landscape almost like a pillar rather than a tower. The straight road to it ended in one narrow bridge across a deep but dry moat, outside which ran a ring of thorny hedges, but inside which rose great grisly iron spikes; giant thorns such as are made by man. The completeness of its enclosure and isolation was part of an ancient national policy for the protection of an ancient national prize. For the building, and the men in it were devoted to the defence of the treasure known as the Coat of the Hundred Stones, though there were now rather less than that number to be defended. According to the legend, the great King Hector, the almost prehistoric hero of those hills, had a corslet or breastplate which was a cluster of countless small diamonds, as a substitute for chain mail; and in old dim pictures and tapestries he was always shown riding into battle as if in a vesture of stars. The legend had ramifications in neighbouring and rival realms; and therefore the possession of this relic was a point of national and international importance in that land of legends. The legend may have been false; but the little loose jewels, or what were left of them, were real enough.

Drake stood looking at that sombre stronghold in an equally sombre spirit. It was the end of winter, and the grey woods were already just faintly empurpled with that suppressed and nameless bloom which is a foreshadowing rather than a beginning of the spring, but his own mood at the moment, though romantic, was also tragic. The string of strange events he had left in his track, if they had not arrested him as omens, must still have arrested him as enigmas. The man killed for no reason, the sword drawn for no reason, the speech broken

The Man Who Knew Too Much

short also for no reason, all these incidents affected him like the images in a warning dream. He felt that a cloud was on his destiny; nor was he wrong, so far at least as that evening's journey carried him. For when he re-entered that militant monastery of which he was the guest, a new catastrophe befell him. And when next day he again retraced his steps on the woodland path along which he had been looking when he fell, and when he came again to the house towards which he had looked so longingly, he found its door shut against him.

On the day following he was striding desperately along a new path, winding upwards through the woods to the hills beyond, with his back both to the house and the tower. For something, as has been hinted, had befallen him in the last few days which was not only a tragedy but a riddle; and it was only when he reviewed the whole in the light, or darkness, of his last disaster, that he remembered that he had one old friend in that land, and one who was a reader of such riddles. He was making his way to the hermitage that was the home—some might almost say the grave—of a great man now known only as Father Stephen, though his real name had once been scrawled on the historic treaties and sprawled in the newspaper headlines of many nations. There is no space here to tell all the activities of his once famous acumen. In the world of what has come to be called secret diplomacy he was something more than a secret diplomatist. He was one from whom no diplomacy could be kept secret. Something of his later mysticism, an appreciation of moods and of the subconscious mind, had even then helped him; he not only saw small things, but he saw them as large things, and largely. It was he who had anticipated the suicide of a cosmopolitan millionaire judging from an atmosphere and the fact that he did not wind up his watch. It was he also who had frustrated a great German conspiracy in America, detecting the Teutonic spy by his unembarrassed posture in a chair when a Boston lady was handing him tea. Now, at long and rare intervals, he would become conscious of such external problems; and, in cases of great injustice,

The Tower of Treason

use the same powers to track a lost sheep, or recover the little hoard stolen from the stocking of a peasant.

A long terrace of low cliffs or rocks hollowed here and there ran along the top of a desolate slope that swept down and vanished amid the highest horns and crests of the winter trees. When this wall faced the rising of the sun, the stone shone pale like marble; and in one place especially had the squared look of a human building, pierced by an unquestionably human entrance. In the white wall was a black doorway, hollow and almost horrible like a ghost; for it was shaped in the rude outline of a man, with head and shoulders, like a mummy case. There was no other mark about this coffin-like cavity, except just beside it a flat coloured ikon of the Holy Family, drawn in that extreme decorative style of Eastern Christianity, which make a gaily painted diagram rather than a picture. But its gold and scarlet and green and sky-blue glittered on the rock by the black hole like some fabled butterfly from the mouth of the grave. But Bertram Drake strode to the gate of that grave and called aloud, as if upon the name of the dead.

To put the truth in a paradox, he had expected the resurrection to surprise him, and yet he was surprised unexpectedly. When he had last met his famous friend, in evening dress in the stalls of a great theatre in Vienna, he had found that friend pale and prematurely old, and his wit dreary and cynical. He even vaguely remembered the matter of their momentary conversation, some disenchanted criticism about the drop-scene or curtain, in which the great diplomatist had seemed a shade more interested than in the play. But when the same man came out of that black hole in the bleak mountains he seemed to have recovered an almost unnatural youth and even childhood. The colours had come back into his strong face; and his eyes shone as he came out of the shadow, almost as an animal's will shine in the dark. The tonsure had left him a ring of chestnut hair, and his tall bony figure seemed less loose and more erect than of old. All this might be very rationally explained by the strong air and simple life of the hills; but his visitor, pursued and tormented by fancies, felt for the moment

The Man Who Knew Too Much

as if the man had a secret sun or fountain of life in that black chamber, or drew nourishment from the roots of the mountains.

He commented on the change in the first few greetings that passed between them; and the hermit seemed willing, though hardly able, to describe the nature of his acceptance of his strange estate.

"This is the last I shall see of this earth," he said quietly, "and I am more than contented in letting it pass. Yet I do not value it less, but rather I think more, as it simplifies itself to a single hold on life. What I know, with assurance, is that it is well for me to remain here, and to stray nowhere else."

After a silence he added, gazing with his burning blue eyes across the wooded valley: "Do you remember when we last met at that theatre and I told you that I always liked the picture on the curtain as much as the scenes of the play. It was some village landscape, I remember, with a bridge, and I felt perversely that I should like to lean on the bridge or look into the little houses. And then I remembered that from almost any other angle I should see it was only a thin painted rag. That is how I feel about this world, as I see it from this mountain. Not that it is not beautiful, for after all a curtain can be beautiful Not even that it is unreal, for after all a curtain is real. But only that it is thin, and that the things behind it are the real drama. And I feel that when I shift my place, it will be the end. I shall hear the three thuds of the mallet in the French theatres; and the curtain will rise. I shall be dead."

The Englishman made an effort to shake off the clouds of mystery that had always been so uncongenial to him. "Frankly," he said, "I can't profess to understand how a man of your intellect can brood in that superstitious way. You look healthy enough, but your mind is surely the more morbid for it. Do you really mean to tell me it would be a sin to leave this rat-hole?"

"No," answered the other, "I do not say it would be sin. I only say it would be death. It might conceivably be my duty to go down into the world again; in that case it would be my duty to die. It would have

The Tower of Treason

been my duty at any time when I was a soldier; but I never should have done it so cheerfully. Now, if ever I see my signal in the distance, I shall rise and leave this cavern, and leave this world."

"How can you possibly tell?" cried Drake in his impatient way. "Living alone in this wilderness you think you know everything, like a lunatic. Does nobody ever come to see you?"

"Oh, yes," replied Father Stephen with a smile. "The people from round here sometimes come up and ask me questions; they seem to have a notion that I can help them out of their difficulties."

The dark vivacity of Drake's face took on a shade of something like shame, as he laughed uneasily and answered.

"And I ought to apologize for what I said just now about the lunatic. For I've come up here on the same errand myself. The truth is I have a notion that you can help me out of *my* difficulties."

"I will do my best," replied Father Stephen. "I am afraid they have troubled you a good deal, by the look of you."

They sat down side by side on a flat rock near the edge of the slope, and Bertram Drake began to tell the whole of his story, or all of it that he needed to tell.

"I needn't tell you," he began, "why I am in this country, or why I have been so long a guest in that place where they keep the Coat of the Hundred Stones. You know better than anybody, for it was you who originally wanted an English representative here to write a report on their preservation, for the old propaganda purpose we know of. You probably also know that the rules of that strange institution put even a friendly, and I may say an honoured, guest under very severe restrictions. They are so horribly afraid of any traffic with the outside world that I have had to be practically a prisoner. But the arrangements are stricter even than they were in your visiting days; ever since Paul the new Abbot came from across the hills. I don't think you've seen him; nobody's seen him outside the monastery; and I couldn't describe him any more than I could describe you. But while you,

The Man Who Knew Too Much

somehow, still seem to include all kinds of things, like the circle of the world, he seems to be only one thing, like the point that is the pivot of a circle. He is as still as the centre of a whirlpool. I mean there seems to be direction and a driving speed in his very immobility; but all pointed and simplified to a single thing: the guarding of the diamonds. He has repaired and made rigid the scheme of defence till I really do not think that loss or leakage from that treasure would be physically possible. Suffice it to say for the moment that it is kept in a casket of steel, in the centre of the roof garden, watched by the brethren who sleep only in rotation, and especially by the old abbot himself who hardly sleeps at all, except for a few hours just before and after sunset. And even then he sleeps sitting beside the casket, with which no man may meddle but himself, and with his hand on his heavy old gun, an antiquated blunderbuss enough, but with which he can shoot very straight for all that. Then sometimes he will wake quite softly and suddenly; and sit looking up that straight road to where the crucifix stands, like an hoary old white eagle. His watch is his world; though in every other way he is mild and benevolent, though he gave orders for the feeding of the poor for miles around, yet if he hears a footstep or faint movement anywhere in the woods around, except on the road that is the recognized approach, he will shoot without mercy as at a wolf. I have reason to know this, as you shall hear.

"Anyhow, as I said, you know that the rules were always strict, and now they're stricter than ever. I was only able to enter the place by being hoisted up by a sort of crane or open-air lift, which it takes several of the monks together to work from the top; and I wasn't supposed to leave the place at all. It is possible that you also know, for you read people so rapidly like pictures rather than books, that I am a most unfortunate sort of brute to be chained by the leg in that way. My faults are all impatience and irreverence; and you may guess that, in a week or two, I might have felt inclined to burn the place down. But you cannot know the real and special reason that made my slavery intolerable."

The Tower of Treason

"I am sorry," said Father Stephen; and the sincerity of the note again brought Drake's impatience to a standstill with abrupt self-reproach.

"Heaven knows it is I who should be sorry; I have been greatly to blame," he said. "But even if you call what I did a sin, you will see that it had a punishment. In one word, you are speaking to a man to whom no one in this country will speak. A monstrous accusation rests upon me, which I cannot refute, and have only some faint hope that you may refute for me. Hundreds in that valley below us are probably cursing my name, and even crying out for my death. And yet, I think, of all those scores of souls looking at me with suspicion, there is only one from whom I cannot endure it."

"Does he live near here?" inquired the hermit.

"She does," replied the Englishman.

An irony shining in the eyes of the anchorite suggested that the answer was not quite unexpected; but he said nothing till the other resumed his tale.

"You know that sort of château that some French nobleman, an exiled prince I believe, built upon the wooded ridge over there beyond the crucifix—you can just see its turrets from here. I'm not sure who owns it now; but it's been rented for some years by Dr. Amiel, a famous physician, a Frenchman, or, rather, a French Jew. He is supposed to have high humanitarian ideals, including the idealization of this small nationality here, which, of course, suits our Foreign Office very well. Perhaps it's unfair to say he's only 'supposed' to be this; and the plain truth is I'm not a fair judge of the man, for a reason you may soon guess. But apart from sentiment, I think somehow I am in two minds about him. It sounds absurd to say that like or dislike of a man could depend on his wearing a red smoking-cap. But that's the nearest I can get to it; bare-headed and just a little bald-headed, he seems only a dark, rather distinguished-looking French man of science, with a pointed beard. When he puts that red fez on he is suddenly something much lower than a Turk; and I see all Asia sneering and leering at me across the Levant. Well, perhaps it's a fancy of the fit I'm in; and it's only just

The Man Who Knew Too Much

to say that people believe in him, who are really devoted to this people or to our policy here. The people staying with him now, and during the few weeks I was there, are English and very keen on the cause, and they say his work has been splendid. A young fellow named Woodville, from my own college, who has travelled a lot, and written some books about yachting, I think. And his sister."

"Your story is very clear so far," observed Father Stephen with restraint.

Drake seemed suddenly moved to impetuosity. "I know I'm in a mad state and had no right to call you morbid; and it's a state in which it's awfully difficult to judge of people. How is it that two people, just a brother and sister, can be so alike and so different? They're both what is called good-looking; and even good-looking in the same way. Why on earth should her high colour look as clear as if it were pale, while his offends me as if it were painted? Why should I think of her hair as gold and look at his as if it were gilt? Honestly, I can't help feeling something artificial about him; but I didn't come to trouble you with these prejudices. There is little or nothing to be said against Woodville; he has something of a name for betting on horses, but not enough to disturb any man of the world. I think the reputation has rather dogged his footsteps in the shape of his servant, Grimes, who is much more horsy than his master, and much in evidence. You see there were few servants at the château, even the gardening being done by a peasant from outside; an unfortunate fellow in horn spectacles who comes into this story later. Anyhow, Woodville was, or professed to be, quite sound in his politics about this place; and I really think him sincere about it. And as for his sister, she has an enthusiasm that is as beautiful as Joan of Arc's."

There was a short silence, and then Father Stephen said dreamily:

"In short, you somehow escaped from your prison, and paid her a visit."

"Three visits," replied Drake, with an embarrassed laugh, "and nearly broke my neck at the end of a rope,

The Tower of Treason

besides being repeatedly shot at with a gun. I'll tell you later on, if you want them, all the details of how I managed to slip out and in again during those sunset hours of Abbot Paul's slumbers. They really resolved themselves into two; the accidental discovery of a disused iron chain, that had been used for the crane or lift, and the character of the old monk who happened to be watching while the Abbot slept. How indescribable is a man, and how huge are the things that turn on his unique self as on a hinge! All those monks were utterly incorruptible, and I owed it to a sympathy that was almost mockery. In an English romance, I suppose, my confederate would have been a young mutinous monk, dreaming of the loves he had lost; whereas my friend was one of the oldest, utterly loyal to the religious life, and helping me from a sort of whim that was little more than a lark. Can you imagine a sort of innocent Pandarus, or even a Christian Pan? He would have died rather than betray the holy stones; but when he was convinced that my love affair was honourable in itself, he let me down by the chain in fits of silent laughter, like a grinning old goblin. It was a pretty wild experience, I can tell you, swinging on that loose iron ladder, like dropping off the earth on a falling star. But I swung myself somehow clear of the spikes below, and crept along under the thick wood by the side of the road. Even as I did so came the crack and rolling echoes of the musket on the tower; and a tuft, from a fir tree spreading above me, dropped detached upon the road at my right. A terrible old man, the Abbot. A light sleeper."

Both men were gazing at the strange tower that rose out of the distant woods as Drake, after a pause, renewed his narrative.

"There is a high hedge of juniper and laurel at the bottom of the garden of Dr. Amiel's château. At least it is high on the outer side, rising above a sort of ledge of earth on the slope, but comparatively low when seen from the level garden above. I used to climb up to this ledge in that late afternoon twilight, and she used to come down the garden, with the lights of the house almost

The Man Who Knew Too Much

clinging about her dress, and we used to talk. It's no good talking to you about what she looked like, with her hair all as yellow light behind the leaves; though those are the sort of things that make my present position a hell. You are a monk and not—I fear I was going to say not a man; but at any rate not a lover."

"I am not a juniper bush, if the argument be conclusive," remarked Father Stephen. "But I can admire it in its place; and I know that many good things grow wild in the garden of God. But, if I may say so, seeing that so honourable a lady receives such rather eccentric attentions from you, I cannot see that you have much reason to be jealous of the poor Jewish gentleman, as you seem to be, even if he is so base and perfidious as to wear a smoking-cap."

"What you say was true until yesterday," said Drake. "I know now that until yesterday I was in paradise. But I had gone there once too often; and on my third return journey a thunderbolt struck me down, worse than any bullet from the tower. The old Abbot had never discovered my own evasion; but he must have had miraculous hearing when he woke, for every time I crept through the thicket, as softly as I could, he must have heard something moving, and fired again and again. Well, the last time I found the spectacled peasant who worked for Dr. Amiel, he was lying dead, a little way in front of the cross, and a foreign-looking fellow with a drawn sabre standing near him. But the strange thing was that the sabre was unstained and unused, and I was eventually convinced that one of the Abbot's shot must have killed the poor peasant in the goggles. Revolving all these things in growing doubt, I returned to the tower, and saw an ominous thing. The regular mechanical lift was lowered for me; and when I re-entered the place, I found that all my escapade had been discovered. But I found something far worse.

"When all those faces were turned upon me, faces I shall never forget, I knew I was being judged for something more than a love-affair. My poor old friend, who had connived at my escape, would not have been so much prostrated for the lesser matter; and as for the Abbot,

The Tower of Treason

the form of his countenance was changed, as it says in the Bible, by something nearer to his own lonely soul than all such lesser matters. Well, the truth of this tragedy is soon told. For the last week, as it appeared, the hoard of the little diamonds had dwindled, no man could imagine how. They were counted by the Abbot and two monks at certain regular intervals; and it was found that the losses had occurred at definite intervals also. Finally, there was found another fact; a fact of which I can make no sense; yet a fact to which I can find no answer. After each of my secret visits to the château, and then only, some of the diamonds had disappeared.

"I have not even the right to ask you to believe in my innocence. No man alive in the whole great landscape we are looking at believes in my innocence. I do not know what would have happened to me, or whether I should have been killed by the monks or the peasants, if I had not appealed to your great authority in this country; and if the Abbot had not been persuaded at last to allow the appeal. Dr. Amiel thinks I am guilty. Woodville thinks I am guilty. His sister I have not even been able to see."

There was another silence, and then Father Stephen remarked rather absently:

"Does he wear slippers as well as a smoking-cap?"

"Do you mean the doctor? No. What on earth do you mean?"

"Nothing at all, if he doesn't. There's no more to be said about that. Well, it's pretty obvious, I suppose, what are the next three questions. First, I suppose the woodman carried an axe. Did he ever carry a pickaxe? Did he ever carry any other tool in particular? Second, did you ever happen to hear anything like a bell? About the time you heard the shot, for instance? But that will probably have occurred to you already. And third, amid such plain preliminaries in the matter, is Dr. Amiel fond of birds?"

There was again a shadow of irony in the simplicity of the recluse; and Drake turned his dark face towards him with a doubtful frown.

The Man Who Knew Too Much

"Are you making fun of me?" he asked. "I should prefer to know."

"I believe in your innocence, if that is what you mean," replied Father Stephen, "and, believe me, I am beginning at the right end in order to establish it."

"But who could it be?" cried Drake in his rather irritable fashion. "I'll tell the plain truth, even against myself, and I'd swear all those monks were really startled out of their wits. And even the peasants near here, supposing they could get into the tower, which they can't —why, I'd be as much surprised to hear of them desecrating the Hundred Stones as if I heard they'd all suddenly become Plymouth Brethren this morning. No; suspicion is sure to fall on the foreigners, like myself; and none of the others round here have a case against them, as I have. Woodville may have a few racing debts; but I'd never believe this about *her* brother, little as I happened to like him. And as for Dr. Amiel——" And he stopped, his face darkening with thought.

"Yes, but that's beginning at the wrong end," observed Father Stephen, "because it's beginning with all the millions of mankind, and every man a mystery. I am trying to find out who stole the stones; you seem to be trying to find out who wanted to steal them. Believe me, the smaller and more practical question is also the larger and more philosophical. To the shades of possible wanting there is hardly any limit. It is the root of all religion that anybody may be almost anything if he chooses. The cynics are wrong, not because they say that the heroes may be cowards, but because they do not see that the cowards may be heroes. Now you may think my remark about keeping birds very wild and your remark about betting on horses very relevant, but I assure you it is the other way round; for yours dealt with what might be thought, but mine with what could be done. Do you remember that German Prime Minister who was assassinated because he had reduced Russia to starvation? Millions of peasants might have wanted to murder him; but how could a moujik in Muscovy murder him in a theatre in Munich? He was murdered by a man who came there because he was a trained Russian dancer, and

The Tower of Treason

escaped from there because he was a trained Russian acrobat. That is, the highly offensive statesman in question was not killed by all the Russians who may have wanted to kill him; but the one Russian who *could* kill him. Well, you are the only approximate acrobat in this performance, and, apart from what I know about you, I don't see how you could have burgled a safe inside the tower merely by dangling at the end of a string outside it. For the real enigma and obstacle in this story is not the stone tower, but the steel casket. I do not see how *you* could have stolen the jewels. I don't see how *anybody* could have stolen them. That is the hopeful part of it."

"You are pretty paradoxical to-day," growled his English friend.

"I am quite practical," answered Stephen serenely. "That is the starting-point, and it makes a good start. We have only to deal with a narrow number of conjectures about how it could just conceivably have been done. You scoffed at my three questions just now which I threw off when I was thinking rather about the preliminary approach to the tower. Well, I admit they were very long shots—indeed, very wild shots; I did not myself take them very seriously, or think they would lead to much. But they had this value: that they were not random guesses about the spiritual possibilities of everybody for a hundred miles round. They were the beginnings of an effort to bridge the real difficulties."

"I am afraid," observed Drake, "that I did not realize that they were even that."

"Well," the hermit went on patiently, "for the first problem of reaching the tower it was reasonable to think first, however hazily, of some sort of secret tunnel or subterranean entrance, and it was natural to ask if the strange workman at the château, who afterwards died so mysteriously, was seen carrying any excavating tools."

"Well, I did think of that," assented Drake, "and I came to the conclusion that it was physically impossible. The inside of the tower is as plain and bare as a dry cistern and the floor is really solid concrete everywhere.

The Man Who Knew Too Much

But what did you mean by that second question about the bell?"

"What I confess still puzzles me," said Father Stephen, "even in your own story, is how the Abbot always heard a man threading his way through a thick forest so far below, so that he invariably fired after him, if only at a venture. Now, nothing would be more natural to such a scheme of defence than to set traps in the wood, in the way of burglar alarms, to warn the watchers in the tower. But anything like that would mean some system of wires or tubes passing through the wall into the woods, and anything of that sort I felt in a shadowy way, a very shadowy way indeed, might mean a passage for other things as well. It would destroy the argument of the sheer wall and the dead drop, which is at present an argument against you, since you alone dared to drop over it. And, of course, my third random question was of the same kind. Nothing could fly about the top of that high tower except birds. For I infer that the vigilant Paul was not too absent-minded to notice any large number of aeroplanes. Now, it is not in the least probable—it is, indeed, almost wildly improbable—but it is not *impossible*, that birds should be trained either to take messages or to commit thefts. Carrier pigeons do the former, and parrots and magpies have often done the latter. Dr. Amiel, being both a scientist and a humanitarian, I thought he might very well be a naturalist and an animal-lover. So if I had found his biological studies specializing wholly on the breeding of carrier pigeons, or if I had found all the love of his life lavished on a particular magpie, I should have thought the question worth following up, formidable as would have been the difficulties still threatening it as a solution."

"I wish the love of his life *were* lavished on a magpie," observed Bertram Drake bitterly. "As it is, it's lavished on something else, and will be expected, I suppose, to flourish in the blight of mine. But, much as I hate him, I shouldn't like to say of him what he is probably saying of me."

"There again is the mistaken method," observed the other. "Probably he is not morally incapable of a really

The Tower of Treason

bad action; very few people are. That is why I stick to the point of whether he is materially capable. It would be quite easy to draw a dark suspicious picture both of him and Mr. Woodville. It is quite true that racing can be a raging gamble and that ruined gamblers are capable of almost anything. It is also true that nobody can be so much of a cad as a gentleman when he is afraid of losing that title. In the same way, it is perfectly true that the Jews have woven over these nations a net that is not only international, but anti-national; and it is quite true that inhuman as is their usury and inhuman as is often their oppression of the poor, some of them are never so inhuman as when they are idealistic, never so inhuman as when they are humane. If we were talking about Amiel or about Woodville, instead of about you and about the diamonds, I could trace a thousand mystery stories in the matter. I could take your hint about the scarlet smoking-cap, and say it was a signal and the symbol of a secret society; that a hundred Jews in a hundred smoking-caps were plotting everywhere, as many of them really are; I could show a conspiracy ramifying from the red cap of Amiel as it did from the *Bonnet Rouge* of Almereyda; or I could catch at your idle phrase about Woodville's hair looking gilded, and describe him as a monstrous decadent in a golden wig, a thing worthy of Nero. Very soon his horse-racing would have all the imperial insanity of charioteering in the amphitheatre, while his friend in the fez would be capable of carrying off Miss Woodville to a whole harem full of Miss Woodvilles, if you will pardon the image. But what corrects all this is the concrete difficulty I defined at the beginning. I still do not see how wearing either a red fez or a gilded wig could conjure very small gems out of a steel box at the top of a tower. But of course I did not mean to abandon all inquiry about the suspicious movements of anybody. I asked if the doctor wore slippers, on a remote chance in connexion with your steps having been heard in the wood, and I should like to know if you ever met anybody else prowling about in the forest."

"Why, yes," said Drake, with a slight start. "I once met the man Grimes, now I remember it."

The Man Who Knew Too Much

"Mr. Woodville's servant," remarked Father Stephen.

"Yes. A rat of a fellow with red hair," Drake said, frowning. "He seemed a bit startled to see me too."

"Well, never mind," answered the hermit. "My own hair may be called red, but I assure you I didn't steal the diamonds."

"I never met anybody else," went on Drake, "except, of course, the mysterious man with the sabre and the dead man he was staring at. I think that is the queerest puzzle of all."

"It is best to apply the same principle even to that," replied his friend. "It may be hard to imagine what a man could be doing with a drawn sword still unused. But, after all, there are a thousand things he might have been doing, from teaching the poor woodman to cut timber without an axe to cutting off the dead man's head for a trophy and a talisman, as some savages do. The question is whether felling the whole forest or filling the whole country with howling head-hunters would necessarily have got the stones out of the box."

"He was certainly going to do something," said Drake in a low voice. "He said himself, ' I was going to,' and then broke off and vanished. I was very profoundly persuaded, I hardly knew why, that there was something to be done to the dead man which could not be done till he was dead."

"What?" asked the hermit, after an abrupt silence; and it sounded somehow like a new voice from a third person suddenly joining in the conversation.

"Which could not be done till he was dead," repeated Drake, staring at him.

"Dead," repeated Father Stephen.

And Drake, still staring at him, saw that his face, under its fringe of red hair, was as pale as his linen robe, and the eyes in it were blazing like the lost stones.

"So many things die," he said. "The birds I spoke about, flying and flashing about the great tower. Did you ever find a dead bird? Not one sparrow, it is written, falls to the ground without God. Even a dead bird would be precious. But a yet smaller thing will serve as a sign here."

The Tower of Treason

Drake, still gazing at his companion, felt a growing conviction that the man had suddenly gone mad. He said helplessly, "What is the matter with you?" But Father Stephen had risen from his seat and was gazing calmly across the valley towards the west, which was all swimming with a golden sunlight that here and there turned the tops of the grey trees to silver.

"It is the thud of the mallet," he said, "and the curtain must rise."

Something had certainly happened which the mind of Bertram Drake found it impossible at the moment to measure, but he remembered enough of the strange words with which their interview had opened to know that in some way the hermit was saying farewell to the hermitage and to many more human things. He asked some groping question, the very words of which he could not afterwards recall.

"I see my signal at last," said Father Stephen. "Treason stands up in my own land as that tower stands in the landscape. A great sin against the people and against the glory of the dead is raging in that valley like a lost battle. And I must go down and do my last office, as King Hector came down from these mountains to his last battle long ago, to that Battle of the Stones where he was slain and his sacred coat of mail so nearly captured. For the enemy has come again over the hills, though in a shape in which we never looked for him."

The voice that had lately lingered with irony and shrewdness over the details of detection had the simplicity which makes poetry and primitive rhetoric still possible among such peoples. He was already marching down the slope, leaving Drake wavering in doubt, being uncertain to tell the truth, whether his own problem had not been rather lost in this last transition.

"Oh, do not fear for your own story," said Father Stephen. "The Battle of the Stones was a victory."

As they went down the mountain-side Drake followed with a strange sense of travelling with some immobile thing liberated by a miracle, as if the earth were shaken by a stone statue walking. The statue led him a strange and rather erratic dance, however, covering considerable

The Man Who Knew Too Much

time and distance, and the great cloud in the west was a sunset cloud before they came to their final halt. Rather to Drake's surprise, they passed the tower of the monastery, and already seemed to be passing under the shadow of the great wooden cross in the woods.

"We shall return this way to-night," said Stephen, speaking for the first time on their march. "The sin upon this land to-night lies so heavy that there is no other way. *Via Crucis.*"

"Why do you talk in this terrible way?" broke out Drake abruptly. "Don't you realize that it's enough to make a man like me hate the cross? Indeed, I think by this time I really do. Remember what my story is, and what once made these woodlands wonderful to me. Would you blame me if the god I saw among the trees was a pagan god, and at any rate a happy one? This is a wild garden that was full, for me, of love and laughter; and I look up and see that image blackening the sun and saying that the world is utterly evil "

"You do not understand," replied Father Stephen quite quietly. "If there are any who stand apart merely because the world is utterly evil, they are not old monks like me; they are much more likely to be young Byronic disappointed lovers like you. No, it is the optimist much more than the pessimist who finally finds the cross waiting for him at the end of his own road. It is the thing that remains when all is said, like the payment after the feast. Christendom is full of feasts, but they bear the names of martyrs who won them in torments. And if such things horrify you, go and ask what torments your English soldiers endure for the land which your English poets praise. Go and see your English children playing with fireworks, and you will find one of their toys is named after the torture of St. Catherine No, it is not that the world is rubbish and that we throw it away. It is exactly when the whole world of stars is a jewel, like the jewels we have lost, that we remember the price. And we look up, as you say, in this dim thicket and see the price, which was the death of God."

After a silence he added, like one in a dream: "And the death of man. We shall return by this way to-night."

The Tower of Treason

Drake had the best reasons for being aware of the direction in which their way was now taking them. The familiar path scrambled up the hill to a familiar hedge of juniper, behind which rose the steep roof of a dark mansion. He could even hear voices talking on the lawn behind the hedge, and a note or two of one which changed the current of his blood. He stopped and said in a voice heavy as stone:

"I cannot go in here now. Not for the world."

"Very well," replied Father Stephen calmly. "I think you have waited outside before now."

And he composedly entered the garden by a gate in the hedge, leaving Drake gloomily kicking his heels on the ledge or natural terrace outside, where he had often waited in happier times. As he did so he could not help hearing fragments of the distant conversation in the garden; and they filled him with confusion and conjecture, not, however, unmingled with hope. It seemed probable that Father Stephen was stating Drake's case and probably offering to prove his innocence. But he must also have been making a sort of appointment, for Drake heard Woodville say: "I can't make head or tail of this, but we will follow later if you insist " And Stephen replied with something ending with "the cross in half an hour."

Then Drake heard the voice of the girl, saying: "I shall pray to God that you may yet tell us better news."

"You will be told," said Father Stephen.

As they redescended towards the little hill just in front of the crucifix, Drake was in a less mutinous mood; whether this was due to the hermit's speech or the words about prayer that had fallen from the woman in the garden. The sky was at once clearer and cloudier than in the previous sunset, for the light and darkness seemed divided by deeper abysses; grey and purple cloudlands as large as landscapes now overcasting the whole earth and now falling again before fresh chasms of light; vast changes that gave to a few hours of evening something of the enormous revolutions of the nights and days. The wall of cloud was then rising higher on the heights behind them and spreading over the château; but the western half of heaven was a clear gold, where the lonely cross

The Man Who Knew Too Much

stood dark against it. But as they drew nearer they saw that it was in truth less lonely, for a man was standing beneath it. Drake saw a long gun aslant on his back; it was the bearded man of the sabre.

The hermit strode towards him with a strange energy and struck him on the shoulder with the flat of his hand.

"Go home," he said, "and tell your masters that their plot will work no longer. If you are Christians, and ever had any part in a holy relic, or any right to it in your land beyond the hills, you will know you should not seek it by such tricks. Go in peace."

Drake hardly noticed how quickly the man vanished this time, for his eye was fixed on the hermit's finger which seemed idly tracing patterns on the wooden pedestal of the cross. It was really pointing to certain perforations, like holes made by worms in the wood.

"Some of the Abbot's stray shots, I think," he remarked. "And somebody has been picking them out of the wood strangely enough."

"It is unlucky," observed Drake, "that the Abbot should damage one of your own images; he is as much devoted to the relic as to the realm."

"More," said the hermit, sitting down on the knoll a few yards before the pedestal. "The Abbot, as you truly say, has only room for one idea in his mind. But there is no doubt of his concern about the stones."

A great canopy of cloud had again covered the valley, turning twilight almost to darkness; and Stephen spoke out of the dark.

"As for the realm, the Abbot comes from the country beyond the hills, which hundreds of years ago went to war about——"

His words were lost in a distant explosion. A volley had been fired from the tower.

With the first shock of sound Stephen sprang up and stood erect on the little hillock. The world had grown so dark that his attitude could hardly be seen, but as minute followed minute in the interval of silence, a low red light was again gradually released from the drifting cloud, faintly tracing his grey figure in silver and turning

The Tower of Treason

his tawny hair to a ring of dim crimson. He was standing quite rigid with his arms stretched out, like a shadow of the crucifix. Drake was striving with the words of a question that would not come. And then there came anew a noise of death from the tower; and the hermit fell all his length crashing among the undergrowth, and lay still as a stone.

Drake hardly knew how he lifted the head on to the wooden pedestal; but the face gave ghastly assurance, and the voice in the few words it could speak was like the voice of a new-born child, weak and small.

"I am dying," said Father Stephen. "I am dying with the truth in my heart."

He made another effort to speak, beginning "I wish——" and then his friend, looking at him steadily, saw that he was dead.

Bertram Drake stood up, and all his universe lay in ruins around him. The night of annihilation was more absolute because a match had flamed and gone out before it could light the lamp. He was certain now that Stephen had indeed discovered the truth that could deliver him. He was as clearly certain that no other man would ever discover it. He would go blasted to his grave because his friend had died only a moment too soon. And to put a final touch to the hideous irony, that had lifted him to heaven and cast him down, he heard the voices of his friends coming along the road from the château.

In a sort of tumbled dream he saw Dr. Amiel lift the body on to the pedestal, producing surgical instruments for the last hopeless surgical tests. The doctor had his back to Drake, who did not trouble to look over his shoulder, but stared at the ground until the doctor said:

"I fear he is quite dead. But I have extracted the bullet."

There was something odd about his quiet voice, and the group seemed suddenly, if silently, seething with new emotions. The girl gave an exclamation of wonder, and it seemed of joy, which Drake could not comprehend.

"I am glad I extracted the bullet," said Dr. Amiel. "I fancy that's what Drake's friend with the sabre was trying to extract."

The Man Who Knew Too Much

"We certainly owe Drake a complete apology," observed Woodville.

Drake thrust his head over the other's shoulder, and saw what they were all staring at. The shot that had struck Stephen in the heart lay a few inches from his body, and it not only glittered but sparkled. It sparkled as only one stone can sparkle in the world.

The girl was standing beside him and he appreciated, through the turmoil, the sense of an obstacle rolled away and of a growth and future, and even in all those growing woods the promise of the spring. It was only as the tail of a trailing and vanishing nightmare that he appreciated at last the wild tale of the treason of the foreign Abbot from beyond the hills, and in what strange fashion he loaded his large-mouthed gun. But he continued to gaze at the dazzling speck on the pedestal and saw in it as in a mirror all the past words of his friend.

For Stephen the hermit had died indeed with the truth in his heart; and the truth had been taken out of his heart by the forceps of a wondering Jew; and it lay there on the pedestal of the cross, like the soul drawn out of his body. Nor did it seem unnatural, to the man staring at it, that the soul looked like a star.